Sri Sarada Devi
The Holy Mother

"If you want peace, then do not look into anybody's faults. Look into your own faults. Learn to make the world your own. No one is a stranger; the whole world is your own."

—Holy Mother's last message

Sri Sarada Devi
The Holy Mother
Her Teachings
and Conversations

Translated with Notes by Swami Nikhilananda

A direct disciple of Holy Mother

Edited with an Introduction by Swami Adiswarananda

Minister and Spiritual Leader of the Ramakrishna-Vivekananda Center of New York;
author of *The Vedanta Way to Peace and Happiness* and *Meditation and Its Practices*

Walking Together, Finding the Way
SKYLIGHT PATHS® Publishing
Woodstock, Vermont

RAMAKRISHNA-VIVEKANANDA
CENTER OF NEW YORK
"As Many Faiths, So Many Paths"

Sri Sarada Devi, The Holy Mother:
Her Teachings and Conversations

2004 First Printing
© 2004 by Swami Adiswarananda

Page 257 constitutes a continuation of this copyright page.

For information regarding permission to reprint material from this book, please write or fax your request to SkyLight Paths Publishing, Permissions Department, at the address / fax number listed below, or e-mail your request to permissions@skylightpaths.com.

Library of Congress Cataloging-in-Publication Data

Sri Sarada Devi, the Holy Mother : her teachings and conversations / translated with notes by Swami Nikhilananda ; edited with an introduction by Swami Adiswarananda.
   p. cm.
In English; includes translations from Bengali.
ISBN 1-59473-070-9 (Hardcover)
1. Sarada Devi, 1853–1920. 2. Ramakrishna, 1836–1886—Disciples. 3. Ramakrishna Mission. 4. Spiritual life—Hinduism. I. Sarada Devi, 1853–1920. II. Nikhilananda, Swami. III. Adiswarananda, Swami, 1925–
BL1280.292.S27S73 2004
294.5'55—dc22

2004016210

10   9   8   7   6   5   4   3   2   1
Manufactured in Canada
Jacket Design: Bridgett Taylor
Jacket Photo: The lotus flower symbolizes spiritual awakening and devotion to God. The photograph on the cover was taken at Holy Mother Temple in the village of Jayrambati, West Bengal, India, the birthplace of Holy Mother Sri Sarada Devi.

SkyLight Paths Publishing is creating a place where people of different spiritual traditions come together for challenge and inspiration, a place where we can help each other understand the mystery that lies at the heart of our existence.

SkyLight Paths sees both believers and seekers as a community that increasingly transcends traditional boundaries of religion and denomination—people wanting to learn from each other, *walking together, finding the way.*

SkyLight Paths, "Walking Together, Finding the Way" and colophon are trademarks of LongHill Partners, Inc. registered in the U.S. Patent and Trademark Office.

Walking Together, Finding the Way
Published by SkyLight Paths Publishing
A Division of LongHill Partners, Inc.
Sunset Farm Offices, Route 4, P.O. Box 237
Woodstock, VT 05091
Tel: (802) 457-4000   Fax: (802) 457-4004
www.skylightpaths.com

Contents

Preface

The year 2003 marks the 150th anniversary of the birth of Sri Sarada Devi, known affectionately by her devotees in India and throughout the world as the Holy Mother. A rare combination of human and divine qualities, the Holy Mother continues to inspire millions of spiritual seekers. Her life and teachings touch our very souls and grant us peace and joy. Her words of assurance are a blessing for all humanity: "I am the mother of the wicked; I am the mother of the virtuous. Whenever you are in distress, just say to yourself, I have a mother."

The present volume is the first American edition of the conversations of Holy Mother Sarada Devi as recorded by her disciples, both lay and monastic. The book was originally published in Bengali by Swami Arupananda, who served the Holy Mother for many years as personal attendant, and was later translated into English by Swami Nikhilananda, who was a direct disciple of Holy Mother.

The translator, Swami Nikhilananda, a brilliant teacher with a special gift for speaking and writing, had the rare privilege of intimately associating with many of the direct disciples of Sri Ramakrishna and received their blessings. His translation of the Upanishads; his biographies of Sri Ramakrishna, Holy Mother, and Swami Vivekananda; his compilation of the works of Swami Vivekananda; and his other books are considered modern classics of spiritual literature. The swami's monumental work, for which he will ever be remembered, is *The Gospel of Sri Ramakrishna,* his English translation of the Bengali *Sri Sri Ramakrishna Kathamrita*, as recorded by M., a disciple of Sri Ramakrishna—a work that *Time* magazine called "one of the world's most extraordinary religious documents."

In chapter 1, "Holy Mother, Spiritual Teacher of Humanity," the reader will find an illuminating discussion of the role of the teacher in spiritual life and a description of Holy Mother's relationship with her disciples as the teacher par excellence. This chapter has been excerpted from Swami Nikhilananda's biography *Holy Mother: Being the Life of Sri Sarada Devi, Wife of Sri Ramakrishna, and Helpmate in His Mission* (published by Ramakrishna-Vivekananda Center of New York). It is our hope that in bringing out this new book about Holy Mother and her teachings on the occasion of the 150th anniversary of her birth, an ever greater number of sincere spiritual seekers will be introduced to the Holy Mother, become inspired by her words, and be strengthened in their spiritual quest.

The Ramakrishna-Vivekananda Center of New York is grateful to SkyLight Paths Publishing for bringing out this important new book.

Swami Adiswarananda
Ramakrishna-Vivekananda Center of New York

Introduction

Holy Mother, Embodiment of the Divine

The Marriage of Sri Ramakrishna and Holy Mother

It was 1858. Sri Ramakrishna, then twenty-two and an unknown priest at the Kali Temple of Dakshineswar, was engaged in the severest forms of spiritual practices and austerities. People around Sri Ramakrishna thought that the priest had become insane because of excessive thinking of God. News of his spiritual madness spread and eventually reached Kamarpukur, the small village in West Bengal where he had been born and where his mother, Chandramani Devi, lived. After persuading him to come to Kamarpukur, Chandramani consulted other family members and came to the conclusion that marriage would be the remedy for her son's condition. A search for a suitable girl began, but nowhere could such a girl be found. At last Sri Ramakrishna himself said that the one he was meant to marry could be found in the nearby village of Jayrambati. The marriage took place, but instead of removing his spiritual madness, marriage only intensified it a thousandfold. The little girl who set off this new storm of spirituality in Sri Ramakrishna was Sarada Devi, known later as the Holy Mother. Sarada Devi was born in 1853, married Sri Ramakrishna when she was five, came to Dakshineswar to stay with her God-intoxicated husband

Sri Ramakrishna

at eighteen, was nearly thirty-three when Sri Ramakrishna passed away, and lived for thirty-four years thereafter.

Mother Sarada, the Awakener of Souls

Holy Mother Sarada Devi is a rare spiritual personality who towers very high in the realm of spirituality. She is a powerful inspiration to many and is literally worshiped by millions in India and abroad. She did not write or preach. She just lived her life, setting an example for us to follow. By a mere look, touch, or wish she transformed sinners into saints. If Sri Ramakrishna was a leaping flame of spiritual realization, Holy Mother was a steady glowing fire of God-consciousness. To the Master, Sri Ramakrishna, she was the goddess of wisdom in human form. To her disciples she was the Divine Mother herself. To her devotees she was a more real mother than their own earthly mother. To the seekers of truth she was the final word, and to sinners she was the last refuge.

In the Company of the Master

Holy Mother was with the Master for fourteen years. The Master looked upon her not only as his disciple but as his spiritual companion and helper in his earthly mission. Deep inside he regarded her as Mother Kali herself. Far above the reach of carnal desires, the two lived the purest lives of free souls, one the counterpart of the other. Mother's spiritual eminence was manifested even when she was a little girl in the village. Her love and compassion were all-engulfing. By her love she conquered everybody. Her compassion flowed not only to humans but also to animals, be they cat, bird, or calf. Mother said, "He is unfortunate indeed who does not feel my compassion. I do not know anyone, not even an insect, for whom I do not feel compassion." She was the embodiment of the Master's message of the motherhood of

God. Motherhood represents grace, compassion, and love. Sri Ramakrishna brought his long years of austerity and spiritual practice to consummation by his worship of the Mother Divine in the body of Holy Mother.

Why Marriage for the Master?

It is a puzzle to many why Sri Ramakrishna, whose life-breath was renunciation, whose glory was the conquest of lust and gold, and who regarded all women as so many forms of the Divine Mother, ever married. No event in the life of a Godman is without significance. Through his marriage Sri Ramakrishna set the example of an ideal householder. He proved that married life is not antagonistic to God-realization. He sanctified the institution of marriage, which had been tarnished by sensuality. Through his marriage the Master gave the greatest honor to womanhood. Among the Godmen of history, some did not marry, some renounced their wives, and some shunned women. Holy Mother exemplified the state of *sthitaprajna* (steady in wisdom) of the Bhagavad Gita. A *sthitaprajna* is a knower of the Self but does not wear any outward mark of holiness, just as birds do not leave any footprints in the sky and fish do not leave any trail in the water. Holy Mother lived among people of a worldly nature—her relatives and others—yet her purity, compassion, and love overwhelmed all. Wherever she went she carried heavenly bliss and showered that bliss on everyone who came near her.

Holy Mother's Austerities

Sages and saints practice austerities in mountain caves, deserts, and other remote places. Sri Ramakrishna himself practiced unheard-of austerities. Holy Mother did not go to any mountain or desert for austerities, but what she practiced in everyday life is beyond the human imagination. Practices of the severest austerities pale into insignificance when compared with the privations and difficulties she underwent throughout her life. In Dakshineswar she lived twenty-four hours a day confined within a small octagonal room, the maximum distance between walls being less than eight feet, with no windows (there were only two ventilators), and a door just over four feet high and two feet wide. She remained there all the time or on the narrow verandah around the room that for privacy was screened off with bamboo mats, which cut off the sun and fresh air. On the east side of the verandah was a staircase leading upstairs. Under the stairs she had her kitchen. She never went outside for recreation. Serving the Master day and night was her worship. The same austerity continued in a house at Shyampukur, to which Sri Ramakrishna moved when he left Dakshineswar for medical treatment. Here, Holy Mother had a small room next to the Master's, but before three o'clock in the morning until all others had retired for the night, she stayed in a small covered space that was part of a stairwell on the way to the roof where she meditated and did everything for the Master. At the Cossipore garden house, where Sri Ramakrishna moved after living for about two months at Shyampukur, Mother lived in a small, almost windowless room, spending every moment in the service of Sri Ramakrishna.

After the Master's passing away, and following an extended pilgrimage to Vrindavan and other holy places, Mother came to live in Sri Ramakrishna's native village of Kamarpukur. The Master had told her to stay there by herself and not to stretch out her hand to others for anything. He said, "Grow some greens, eat boiled rice and greens, and repeat Hari's name [a name of God]." But now, with the Master gone, things took a different turn for the Mother. Sri Ramakrishna's monastic disciples were in their wandering days and had no idea of the difficulties she faced. Mother was almost forgotten by the devotees. Her relatives and neighbors were hostile to her. Her garment was a mere rag. On some days she did not even have money to buy salt for her plain rice. An allowance of seven rupees a month she had been receiving from the authorities of the Kali Temple at Dakshineswar was abruptly stopped when one of her relatives advised them that she did not need it. Only M. (Mahendranath Gupta), the chronicler of *The Gospel of Sri Ramakrishna,* used to send her a small sum of money each month. He was the only person to whom Mother would write for anything she needed. She had to contend with the merciless and restrictive social customs for a brahmin widow, the hostility of relatives, dire poverty, and the indifference of the devotees. She now and then had visions of Sri Ramakrishna, and these made her suffering somewhat bearable. Eventually word of Mother's plight reached her mother, Shyamasundari Devi, in Jayrambati, and she sent word to one of her sons who lived in Calcutta. He informed a devotee. Soon other disciples of the Master were informed, and some money was sent to Mother with the fervent request that she come to Calcutta. Holy Mother went to Calcutta in April 1888.

Later, circumstances improved for Holy Mother only when Swami Vivekananda, through his letters from America, reminded everyone of the Mother. In one letter he wrote, "Let Ramakrishna disappear; that does not frighten me. But it will be a calamity if people forget Mother.... Don't be angry with me. None of you has understood Mother. Her grace upon me is one hundred thousand times greater than that of the Master.... About Mother I am a little fanatic. I can do anything if she gives the order. I shall give a sigh of relief when you purchase a piece of land and install this living Durga there.... Brother, when I think of Mother, I say to myself: Who is this Ramakrishna? I say this because of my fanaticism. Whether Ramakrishna was God or man—you may say whatever you like. But, brother, shame upon him who is not devoted to Mother."

Swami Vivekananda founded the Ramakrishna Order in 1897. The land on which the present Ramakrishna Temple and Monastery (Belur Math) stands was purchased in Holy Mother's name. Once a disciple asked her, "If the Master is God, then what are you?" "Who else am I?" The Mother replied without any hesitation: "I am Bhagavati, the Divine Mother of the universe."

Holy Mother's Love for All

Mother became the power, scripture, inspiration, joy, and guiding spirit of the Order. She prayed to Sri Ramakrishna: "Master, those who renounce everything in your name, please give them shelter and protection." Up to her last moment she remained as the second form of Sri Ramakrishna, distributing the blessings and grace of the Master to all. She took the responsibility of countless souls who came to her for solace, assured them that their liberation was certain, and gave them fearlessness. "Those who are my children are already free," she said. "Even Providence cannot send them to hell." Overriding the injunctions of the scriptures, she stated: "In this Kali Yuga, mental sin is no sin. Free your mind from all worries on that score. You need not be afraid." Emphasizing *japa*, or chanting the name of God, she remarked: "Practice *japa*. Through that you will achieve everything." She consoled weak devotees and disciples with the words "Do as much as you can do, and the rest I will do." To the disciples she often said, "Whenever you are in danger or in trouble, remember that you have a mother." "Do not be afraid, the Master is behind you, and I am too as your mother." Assuring a disciple that he would always have her affection, she said, "Yes, my child, in my love there is no ebb tide or flood tide."

Yet, Holy Mother was human to the core; she shared the joys and sufferings of all and wept bitterly when Sister Nivedita died. With the innocence of a little girl she had a fear of ghosts, was perplexed by machines, and mingled with everybody. Even when not well she told rosaries for hours at a time for the welfare of her disciples. "If you want peace, make the whole world your own," she said. "In the fullness of spiritual realization, a person finds that the God who resides in his heart resides in the hearts of all—the oppressed, the persecuted, the lowly, and the untouchable. This realization makes one truly humble." "Behave according to the time, place, and person." "Forgiveness is a great religious austerity. There is no higher virtue than forbearance." "If you want to succeed, seek divine grace." "The goal of life is God-realization, and the way is self-surrender." "Whoever surrenders himself to God is saved." "One who has renounced everything for God is a living God." "Those who surrender to the Master, he always stands behind them." "Even the injunctions of destiny are canceled if one takes refuge in God. Destiny strikes off with its own hand what it has foreordained for such a person." Holy Mother tried to fulfill the requests of all her disciples, no matter how unusual or demanding these requests were. No one went away disappointed. "How will you understand the sufferings of the afflicted?" she said to a monk who poked fun at some of the unusual requests, "You are not a mother."

Holy Mother's love for the monastic disciples of Sri Ramakrishna was boundless. She looked upon them as her very own sons and regarded them as the bearers of the Master's message to the world. To the monastic disciples she was the embodiment of the Divine Mother. In her presence they would be overwhelmed with spiritual emotion.

She regarded renunciation as the foundation of spiritual life and would say, "With whom shall I live but with those who have renounced the world for the sake of God?" Mother's attendant, Golap-Ma, once found fault with a young novice monk and threatened to leave Mother's house unless he left. "Let her leave if she likes," said Holy Mother. "She is, after all, a householder. The novice has given up everything in order to serve me."

She was the nurturing mother to her disciples, tolerant and indulgent older sister to her much younger brothers, teacher of household arts to her sisters-in-law, and affectionate aunt to her nieces and nephews. She mediated disputes, looked to the needs of everyone, and constantly gave motherly love to all. Women devotees felt at home with her, seeing her as one of them. But through it all she remained unattached, and at will she would see the world around her as unreal and be brought back to her true divine nature.

The Uniqueness of Holy Mother

Holy Mother served her husband, Sri Ramakrishna, selflessly in every way up to his last days, and she never placed any physical demands on him. Again, though living in the world, she lived as a nun. She once said that even a bad thought had never crossed her mind. In reply to a question, "What is the aim of life?" Mother said, "To realize God and to be absorbed uninterruptedly in his consciousness is the aim." Holy Mother lived that literally. Above all she was Mother, tending to her disciples' needs—physical, mental, and spiritual—never expecting anything in return. She was the teacher who made their path clear and certain, the Divine Mother who granted them liberation, and at the same time their mother who looked after them, wept with them in sorrow, laughed with them in joy, and accepted them as they were. Those who came to her and wholeheartedly called her "mother" received her blessings in abundance—sometimes more than they deserved.

Up to the last moment of her life, Holy Mother granted sacred initiation to all the devotees who came to her and set them free. She unhesitatingly took the sins of all upon herself. This burden of sins eventually brought her intense physical suffering and illness. After a long illness, she passed away on July 21, 1920. Yet, her passing away is not the end of the story. In her invisible form she continues to give her blessings, even today, to anyone who accepts her as the real Mother and surrenders to her. Holy Mother Sarada is our *real Mother*, not an adopted mother or a vague mother. Our *real Mother*.

1

Holy Mother, Spiritual Teacher of Humanity

Holy Mother was the wife of Sri Ramakrishna (1836–1886), now regarded in India and abroad as a rare manifestation of divinity in modern times. She was his constant companion during the most eventful period of his life and a witness of his spiritual experiences. Sri Ramakrishna himself molded her life and assigned her place in the carrying out of his mission after his death.

Outwardly Holy Mother lived as an average Hindu woman, devoting herself to the faithful discharge of her household duties, which were often unpleasant and frustrating. Inwardly she practiced total nonattachment and remained undisturbed by what happened in the physical world. Never did her mind deviate from contact with God. Thus she has become, today, a model for both householders and world-renouncing monks.

I deem it necessary to point out here two important features of her teachings and personality that may help the general reader, especially anyone unfamiliar with the background of Hindu culture, to respond sympathetically to her life. First, Holy Mother, when instructing her disciples, often asked them to regard Sri Ramakrishna as God incarnate. She accepted other divine incarnations, too, but she looked upon Sri Ramakrishna—on account of his unceasing absorption in God, his total renunciation, and his acceptance of different faiths as valid ways to the realization of God—as the one suited to our present

1

age. In her own experience she realized her husband's divinity. Therefore, it was natural for her to speak of him as a visible symbol of the Godhead. But she was by no means dogmatic or exclusive. In teaching seekers who cherished other spiritual ideals, she always deepened their faith in those.

Second, Holy Mother is often described by such epithets as the Mother of the universe and the Divine Power. These are not mere sentimental expressions on the part of her devotees but have a philosophical significance. According to Vedanta philosophy, Brahman, or Ultimate Reality, is inactive. It is not, itself, involved in the activities of creation, preservation, and dissolution. These are carried on by its inscrutable energy, called maya or Shakti. Brahman and Shakti are inseparable, like fire and its power to burn, or a gem and its luster. The two names are given to one and the same Reality according to its two different functions. The whole universe of the living and nonliving is the projection of this divine energy, which, like an earthly mother, produces creatures from its womb and then nourishes them. This energy, again, finally withdraws the created beings into the Godhead, thus liberating them from the bondage of the world. The Hindus therefore regard it as the Mother and Savior of all. Though this energy is present in all creatures, to a Hindu it resembles a woman more than a man. Undoubtedly all women are channels of Shakti, but a woman totally undefiled by worldliness becomes its most potent channel. Holy Mother was such a woman. Thus, she too has been described as the Savior or the Divine Mother of the universe. She looked on all children born of a woman's womb as her own.

Holy Mother's life and teachings have a direct bearing on the present human situation. Physical scientists and professional philosophers influenced by the scientific method of reason and experimentation are preoccupied to discover the laws that explain and control life and nature. They are revealing various dimensions of reality that tell us about human beings and the world and also how to use this knowledge for the physical welfare of humanity. A growing number of thoughtful people regard intellectual knowledge, unillumined by spiritual insight, as inadequate to satisfy the deep yearning of the soul. They look to religion for inner peace. But unfortunately, most of the religions, as practiced today, are cluttered with dogmas and creeds that conceal the truth. People want a guide with direct experience of the true nature of the Godhead, the world, and the soul. Only thus can the guide's words and actions become imbued with love and compassion. Moreover, this experience, if it is to transform our lower nature and lead to the welfare of all, must be expressed in simple words. Perceptive readers may find in Holy Mother's life the fulfillment of these conditions. They will also find one who, instead of luxuriating in the enjoyment of inner peace, worked until the last moment of her life to transmit that peace to others.

Spiritual Ministry

Sri Ramakrishna, during his lifetime and afterwards, in assigning Holy Mother her place in the scheme of his mission on earth, made her his spiritual successor. On her part, she was born with unique spiritual tendencies. To her devotees and disciples she was the embodiment of the Divine Mother, or the Primordial Shakti. Sri Ramakrishna, from the beginning of his association with her, gradually prepared her for her future role, and he later instructed her in the various phases of spiritual discipline and experience. Her full divinity was awakened when he formally worshiped her in his room as the personification of the Divine Mother. Even before his death, Sri Ramakrishna told her that she would have to bring light to deluded people groping in darkness. After his death, when Holy Mother lost all interest in the world and even in her body, the Master reminded her, through many visions, of the tremendous task awaiting her. One day he appeared before her and said, "No, no. You must live. There are many things to be done." He certainly did not mean that Sarada Devi was to serve as an abbess or mother superior in a religious organization, which would not have been in keeping with her temperament or nature. All that he meant was that she should be the central guide and mentor of his devotees. At his bidding, she had already given her first formal initiation to Swami Yogananda in Vrindavan.

It will be useful here to discuss briefly the significance of spiritual initiation, according to Hindu tradition, and also the part a preceptor plays in unfolding a disciple's spiritual life.

Spirituality is awakened by the transmission of light from the living, through the living, to the living. The transmitter is called the guru, or teacher, the method of transmission is known as initiation, and the person to whom it is transmitted is called the *śishya*, or disciple. Spiritual truth is the living truth coexisting with and inherent in God. Initiation is the descent of God through a human channel and is bestowed upon a living disciple. This bestowal may be designated as grace. No doubt God transcends name and form and is present everywhere. But God must be attuned to our receptivity so that our minds can receive God. This is a law of the spiritual world demonstrated even by Godmen like Krishna, Christ, Chaitanya, and Ramakrishna, who in spite of their divine nature accepted human teachers, as it were, to set an example for the common person. The idea of apostolic succession or the laying on of hands in Christianity seems to be based upon this fact. God is the real guru but uses a human instrument to manifest power. The purer the channel, the clearer the manifestation of the power.

The human teacher must possess qualifications to discharge this task. The Upanishads emphasize that knowledge and realization of Brahman are the primary qualification. Knowledge, which belongs to the domain of intellect, is necessary to dispel the disciple's doubts. Furthermore, the guru must be sinless and free from worldly motive. The guru should act as a friend of those who, with humility, seek help.

An ocean of infinite compassion, the guru wants the welfare of the disciple and helps, unnoticed and unheralded, in unfolding the disciple's spirituality, as the spring unfolds leaves and blossoms after the cold and bleak months of winter. No wonder these qualifications of an ideal teacher are fully found only in Godmen, who visit earth from time to time. Holy Mother possessed them fully. But an aspirant can obtain help even from a lesser teacher. It would be folly for a beginner in science or art to refuse to begin to study without obtaining the guidance of an Einstein or a Leonardo. Even if such a teacher were available, would the beginner be able to understand the teacher? How many contemporaries of Christ and Ramakrishna availed themselves of the presence of these exalted teachers? The right teacher always appears in the proper time to help the qualified pupil.

Spirituality can be literally handed down like any physical object, if the teacher possesses it and the student is capable of receiving it. A thought can be as vivid and real as a tangible thing. An aspirant can be initiated by a look or a touch or by mystical words. Only the most exalted teacher can awaken spirituality by a look or by a touch, and then only in exceptional cases. The imparting of a mystical word, called the mantra, is the usual method of initiation. Real mantras are not created by the human intellect. They exist in the cosmic mind of God and are revealed to a qualified teacher. "In the beginning was the Word." Different mantras are adapted to the different aspects of the Godhead and the needs of the pupil. Through some mantras the pupil can commune with God's impersonal aspect; through some, with God's personal aspect. Some mantras stimulate a disciple's love of God, some knowledge of God, and so on. Holy Mother said, "The mantra purifies the body. One becomes pure by repeating the name of God given by the guru." The mantra is to be regularly repeated by the disciple with concentration and devotion. It has an intrinsic power of its own. It kindles the spark of spirituality in the disciple. A disciple asked the Mother if the mere repetition of the holy word taught by a qualified guru really helped the aspirant if he did not possess intense devotion. "Whether you jump into water or are pushed into it," she replied, "your cloth will be soaked, will it not?" The mantra is generally chosen by the guru, who sometimes in its selection takes into consideration the feelings of the *śishya*. Besides imparting the mantra, the guru teaches through instruction, personal example, and silent influence. The last method can be used only by highly qualified teachers.

An illumined teacher, endowed with direct knowledge of God, assumes responsibility for the disciple's sins and often suffers on the disciple's account, physically and mentally. The relationship between such a teacher and student is eternal and cannot be severed by death. The teacher stands by the pupil both here and hereafter and does not cease giving guidance until the pupil is liberated from the bondage, delusion, and suffering of the world. The guru is the pupil's father—more real than an earthly father, who gives birth only to the physical body—for it is the guru who gives the pupil spiritual birth. When, however, a blind teacher guides a blind student, both find themselves in the ditch. As Sri Ramakrishna said, when a bullfrog is seized by an ordinary water snake, there is no end of suffering for both. The frog can be neither easily swallowed nor ejected, and it goes on croaking. But when it is seized by a cobra, its agony stops after three croaks at the most. Holy Mother suffered intensely, as we shall presently see, when people with sinful minds touched her feet. When, on the other hand, an earnest seeker touched her, she felt soothed in both body and mind.

The knowledge of God that the teacher transmits is, according to the Upanishads, dearer than a son, dearer than wealth, and dearer than all precious things of the world. It should be imparted only to a qualified son or daughter or to a disciple. It cannot be bartered for any material consideration. Like the teacher, the student also must be qualified. According to Hinduism, besides acquiring a general knowledge of the scriptures, the student should perform the daily obligatory activities and other duties prescribed for special occasions, and refrain from sinful actions. An advanced student should be able to distinguish between the permanent and the transitory and renounce the transitory. The student should be endowed with control of the body and mind, forbearance, nonattachment to the world, faith, and concentration. These disciplines create the inner purity through which one experiences spiritual truths. Patience is important in spiritual progress. The time factor is involved in the elimination of past worldly tendencies and the creation of spiritual ones. Anyone who has a sincere longing for the higher life and is ready to work for it can approach a teacher. According to the Bhagavad Gita, the student should have unbounded faith in the teacher. Full of humility, the student should put intelligent questions to the teacher. Religious instruction, according to one of the Upanishads, becomes fruitful only when it is obtained from a teacher.

Spiritual experience involves, as already mentioned, the descent of God and the ascent of the soul—the grace of God and the right effort of the seeker. The meeting of a competent teacher and a qualified pupil is an unusual phenomenon. An Upanishad says: "Many there are who do not even hear of Atman [Self or soul]; though hearing of it, many do not comprehend. Wonderful is the expounder and rare the hearer; rare indeed is the experiencer of Atman taught by an able preceptor."

That Holy Mother was a teacher par excellence goes without saying. In her relationship with her disciples she acted as mother, teacher, and divinity incarnate. But for the most part she covered herself with a veil of humanity. Who can look straight at the blazing midday sun without the help of a colored glass?

Holy Mother lived for thirty-three years after her return from Vrindavan in 1887. During the first eleven of these years she lived a virtually retired life, visiting Calcutta only now and then. During the second eleven years the public began to learn about her, and she initiated a few disciples. During the third period (1909–1920), which she spent mostly at her own houses in Calcutta and Jayrambati, devotees thronged to receive her blessings. From the fullness of her heart she bestowed her grace upon all. Men and women of every station and stage of life came to her. Among them were high and low, young and old, students and lawyers, physicians and teachers, revolutionaries, spiritually evolved souls and people entangled in the world, and some eccentrics as well. With a very few exceptions, none went away empty-handed. A silent yearning constantly welled up from her heart: "Come, all of you, I am here for your sake. I shall soothe my heart by showing you the way to liberation." She did not publicly summon the devotees. She did not write books, issue statements, or mount a public platform. The disciples of Sri Ramakrishna were extremely reticent about her. Perhaps they were afraid that ordinary people would take her lightly or not show her proper respect. But drawn by her irresistible attraction, they all came. She seemed to be waiting for them. "Let them all come," her motherly heart said. "None will be rejected. Suppose they have lived sinful lives. Will they be deprived of my blessings on that account?" She initiated them in the shrine room and from her sickbed, on roads and railway platforms, in meadows and under trees. All felt, when with her, that they were in the presence of an affectionate mother and made all kinds of demands upon her— reasonable and unreasonable. To the best of her power she tried to satisfy them. She had hardly any respite even when she badly needed it. If no devotee came to her on a particular day, she would say: "No one has come. This day seems to be passing in vain." Very shortly a seeker would arrive. This went on till nearly the end of her life.

How did she give initiation? For the purpose of meditation, prayer, and worship, one requires an Ishta or Chosen Ideal, which may be a personal God or the impersonal Brahman. The average aspirant needs a concrete symbol of God. To Holy Mother, Sri Ramakrishna was the manifestation of the Supreme Spirit, the Incarnation for modern times. Most of her disciples accepted him as their Chosen Ideal.

But she was not dogmatic. She often asked the aspirant, as she did the present writer, whom he would accept as his Ishta. She also advised seekers to follow their family tradition. When they could not decide, she herself suggested the particular form and name of the Godhead. It is said that just before the initiation, she herself would meditate and thus discover the mantra suited to the aspirant. It would be revealed in her pure mind. Sri Ramakrishna said that whatever one hears in the pure mind is the word of God. Pure mind and pure Atman are one and the same.

To the devotees of Sri Ramakrishna she sometimes said, "For you there is the Ramakrishna-loka, the heaven where Sri Ramakrishna is eternally present with his intimate disciples." There, she told them, they would experience eternal communion with the Lord. But to seekers of the Impersonal, she taught that Sri Ramakrishna would provide a wide doorway. To them she would say that finally the Ishta, the guru, and the śishya all merge in the Supreme Spirit.

Some of Holy Mother's disciples were impressed by her motherly solicitude, some by her ability as a teacher to dispel their doubts, and some by her unshakable reassurance regarding their ultimate salvation, which can be given only by Divinity. But these features must not be compartmentalized. Whenever she appeared as mother, one saw behind her motherhood the power of a teacher, the transmitter of spiritual wisdom. Again, when she acted as teacher, she was not aloof or severe; she attracted her disciples by her motherly love. Finally, her divine nature supplied the foundation of the other two features.

While Sri Ramakrishna was alive, Holy Mother sometimes felt sad because she had no children of her own. The Master had spoken to her about the many disciples who would regard her as their mother. More importantly, Sri Ramakrishna wanted to present through Holy Mother the Motherhood of God, for this relationship hastens the aspirant's spiritual progress. Holy Mother's motherly longing was fulfilled not only through her giving initiation to hundreds of spiritual seekers but also through the extreme tenderness, compassion, patience, and sweetness with which she ministered to their various other needs. At the Udbodhan, her Calcutta residence, Golap-Ma, Yogin-Ma, Swami Saradananda, and the other inmates kept an eye on her physical comfort and tried to curtail her activities. But at Jayrambati, where she was her own mistress, things were somewhat different. There Holy Mother dedicated herself fully to the physical welfare of her disciples. One day a monastic disciple wanted to wash his own plate, but the Mother would not allow him to do this, remarking, "How little I am doing for you! You are a treasure highly cherished even by the gods." Sometimes her women companions complained, "You belong to the brahmin caste, besides being their guru. It will be inauspicious for them if you wait on them." The Mother replied in a natural way, "I am their mother. Who will look after the children, if not their mother?" She showed the same feeling toward low-caste disciples and even untouchables. She regarded the devotees as being above all caste distinctions. They belonged to Sri Ramakrishna's family. When a disciple arrived at her home after a long journey, many times she herself fanned him to cool him off. She often nursed disciples when they were sick. She knew how difficult it was to come to Jayrambati, especially for people accustomed to the comforts of the city. She once remarked that it was rather easier to visit Gaya, Benares, and other sacred places than Jayrambati. She always insisted that the disciples spend at least two or three days at her home. As good food was scarce in the village, she procured fish, fruit, or vegetables from distant villages. Girish Ghosh at one time spent several days at the Mother's home.[1] He was surprised to see clean linen on his bed every night, and on inquiry he found out that the Mother herself daily washed his sheets and pillowslips in the village tank. Even in her Calcutta house she would not allow any devotees who arrived at mealtime to go away without taking food. This often exasperated Golap-Ma, who was the housekeeper, because she had to provide meals for the unexpected guests. She would complain to Holy Mother, "You are a fine person, indeed! You entertain anybody and everybody who comes to you and addresses you as 'Mother.'" Holy Mother brushed off the complaint with a smile. When a disciple referred to all she did for the comfort of disciples and the gratification of her relatives, she remarked, "I have done more than is necessary so as to set up a model for others."

Once Swami Arupananda, a monastic disciple,[2] had to go to a neighboring village on business and did not return till late in the afternoon. When he came back he found that the Mother had not taken her midday meal. The disciple complained about her fasting when her own health was bad. But she replied, "You have not taken your meal; how could I?" One day she remarked to a disciple, "If a thorn hurts the sole of your foot, I feel as if a ploughshare had gone into my heart."

Whenever a devotee took leave of her at Jayrambati she would be distressed, like an earthly mother, at the thought of parting with her child. She would walk with the devotee some distance from her house and bid him farewell with tears in her eyes. A personal experience comes to the present writer's mind. He and Gauri-Ma were returning to Calcutta. As he was about to take leave of the Mother in her room, she gave him some rice pudding, of which she had touched a little to her tongue, thus making it *prasad*.[3] She caressed him affectionately, touching his chin. "Mother, I am going," he said. At once she corrected him and said, "Never say that. Say, 'Let me come again.' You come from East Bengal and do not know the custom."[4] The Mother shed tears of grief and fervently prayed to the Master for their safe trip. She said, "Master, please look after their welfare; they are undertaking a long journey."

Gauri-Ma was a dynamic woman, an organizer and lecturer. In her younger days she had traveled all over India as a wandering nun. Vehemently she assured the Mother that it was only a night journey by train and they would return safely to Calcutta. The more she roared, the more humble the Mother became. As the writer watched

Holy Mother seated on the porch
of her ancestral home in Jayrambati

the scene he said to himself, "Here is a woman who does not possess a millionth part of the Mother's power, and she is bubbling all over. And the Mother has suppressed all her power and is acting like an ordinary mother." Even after a lapse of forty-five years the scene remains vivid with him. On another occasion, in 1920, the writer took leave of Holy Mother at the Udbodhan, probably for the last time. He went out of the house and walked to the end of the street, and as he looked back he saw the Mother standing on the north porch of the house wistfully looking at him.

Often devotees made unreasonable demands upon Holy Mother. Some would ask for a forthright reply to such questions as whether she was the Divine Mother of the universe, and if so why he did not realize her as such. Some would want an immediate vision of God or of Sri Ramakrishna. She always succeeded in pacifying their restless minds. This happened at Jayrambati, Calcutta, and elsewhere. One day Holy Mother had just finished her daily worship when an unknown devotee appeared with some flowers, evidently to worship her feet. At the sight of the stranger, she sat on the bed wrapping herself with a shawl, as was her habit. The man made an elaborate genuflection, offered flowers, and began to perform breathing exercises and other rituals, as one does before an image. This went on for a long time, and the Mother began to perspire heavily under the shawl. Golap-Ma came to her rescue. She pulled the man up by the hand and said in her usual loud voice, "Do you think she is a wooden image, that you would awaken her spirit by breathing exercises and other rituals? Don't you see the Mother is getting hot and very uncomfortable?"

A monastic disciple, out of pique because he felt he was not making any spiritual progress, did not visit Holy Mother for two or three years, although he lived within a few blocks of the Udbodhan. Finally he wrote a long letter to her and asked her to take back the mantra with which she had initiated him. The Mother sent for him. When he came she said, "Look here, my child, the sun dwells high in the sky and water remains on the earth. Does the water have to shout at the sun and ask: 'O sun, please take me up'? It is the very nature of the sun to take up the water in the form of vapor. Let me assure you that you will not have to practice any discipline."

Another disciple made a similar complaint, and the Mother said to him, "Suppose you are asleep in Calcutta and someone is removing you with your couch to Benares. Will you at that time know that you are on your way to Benares? When you wake up you will be surprised to see where you have come."

One disciple found it impossible to control his mind and said to the Mother with great anguish, "Mother, either remove my inner restlessness or take back your mantra." Her eyes became filled with tears at the disciple's suffering, and she said fervently: "All right, you will not have to repeat the mantra anymore." These words frightened him, and he thought that his relationship with her was severed once and for all. He said: "You have taken away everything from me! What shall I do now? Does it mean that I am going to hell?" Holy Mother said in an animated voice, "What do you mean? You are my child; how can you go to hell? Those who are my children are already free."

Holy Mother often had to put up with eccentricity. One day a woman devotee while taking leave of the Mother bit her big toe. The Mother cried aloud: "Goodness gracious! What kind of devotion is this? If you want to touch my feet, why not do so? Why this biting of the toe?" The woman said, "I want you to remember me." "Indeed!" the Mother replied. "I never before saw such a novel way of making me remember a devotee." Another time a male devotee while saluting her struck her little toe with his forehead with such force that the Mother cried out in pain. Those present asked the devotee the reason for this strange conduct. He replied: "I purposely gave her pain while saluting her so that she will remember me as long as the pain lasts."

The Mother had to deal with many odd demands. One of her intimate disciples was Kanjilal, a physician. His wife one day prayed to her, "Mother, please give your blessings so that my husband's income may increase." The Mother looked at her and said firmly, "Do you want me to wish that people may be sick and that they may suffer? Certainly I can never do that. I pray that all may be well, all may be happy."

We shall conclude this rather bizarre section about the deranged devotees with one more incident. A young man, who later came to be known as Padmabinode, was a student in the school of M. He had visited Sri Ramakrishna and received his blessings. Afterwards he joined a theater and furthermore became addicted to alcohol. Padmabinode knew Swami Saradananda intimately and addressed him as "friend." While returning home late at night from the theater he used to talk incoherently, under the influence of drink. Often he called for his "friend" while passing by the Udbodhan. But the residents of the house were instructed not to respond for fear of disturbing Holy Mother's sleep. One night, finding no one paying attention to his call, he started to sing in a plaintive voice:

Waken, Mother! Throw open your door.
I cannot find my way through the dark;
My heart is afraid.
How often I have called out your name,
Yet, kindly Mother,
How strangely you are acting today!

Soundly you are sleeping in your room,
Leaving your poor child alone outside.
I am all skin and bones from crying,
"Mother, O Mother!"
With proper tone, pitch, and mode, using
All the three gamuts,
I call so loud, and still you sleep on.

Is it because I was lost in play
That you shun me now?
Look on me kindly, and I shall not
Go playing again.
To whom can I run, leaving your side?
Who but my Mother will bear the load
Of this wretched child?

As Padmabinode sang in the street with all his soul, the shutters of a window of the Mother's room opened. He saw this and said with great satisfaction, "Mother, so you have awakened. Have you heard your son's prayer? Since you are up, please accept my salutation." He began to roll on the ground and take its dust on his head. Again he sang:

Cherish my precious Mother Syama[5]
Tenderly within, O mind;
May you and I alone behold her,
Letting no one else intrude.

With emphasis, he improvised a new line: "And surely not my 'friend,'" referring to Swami Saradananda. The next day Holy Mother asked about him and was told his story. "Did you notice his firm conviction?" she remarked. At least once more he saw Holy Mother thus. When the devotees complained about the disturbance of her sleep, she replied, "I cannot contain myself when he calls on me in that way."

A few days later Padmabinode became seriously ill and was taken to the hospital. At the hour of death he wanted to hear something from *The Gospel of Sri Ramakrishna*. As he listened tears rolled from his eyes. Repeating the name of the Master, he breathed his last. When the Mother heard about this she said, "Why should it not be like that? Surely he was a child of the Master. No doubt he covered himself with mud. But now he has gone back to the Master's arms, where he belongs."

Holy Mother's love for her disciples was not just like the love an earthly mother feels for her children. It was much deeper. Once a monastic disciple asked her, "How do you regard us?"

Mother: As God himself.

Disciple: But we are your children. If you think of us as God,
*   you cannot regard us as children.*

Mother: I regard you as God and also as children.

God has implanted philoprogenitiveness in the hearts of ordinary mothers for the preservation of family and society. In Holy Mother's case, the same love showed her spiritual children the way to liberation from the bondage of the world.

Holy Mother's love was not confined to her disciples alone. It was showered upon all who went to her for succor, irrespective of caste and creed, merit or demerit. She helped them with food, clothes, or medicines, according to their need. One day while she was living at Koalpara, an untouchable woman came to her and sought her help with tearful eyes. She had suddenly been discarded by her paramour, for whose sake she had left her own home, and now she was completely helpless. Holy Mother sent for the man and said to him with gentle reproof, "Look here, she has renounced all for your sake. And you have accepted her service for a long time. It will be very sinful for you to reject her now; there will be no room for you even in hell." The couple was reconciled.

The story of Radhu's pet cat gives even more striking insight into Holy Mother's love. She had arranged for it to have a daily ration of milk. The cat used to lie peacefully near her. Sometimes she would pretend that she was going to punish it with a stick, but this only made the animal creep nearer her feet. Laughing, she would throw away the stick, and the inmates of the house would also laugh. The cat, following its own nature, often stole food, and the Mother would remark, "To steal is its *dharma*.[6] Who is there always to feed it lovingly?" One day a monastic attendant treated the cat roughly and dashed it against the earth. The Mother looked very sad. She said to the monk, "Scold the cat but do not beat it. Please feed it regularly and see that it does not go to any other house to steal food." She again reminded him solemnly, "Do not beat the cat. I dwell inside the cat too."

In the Role of Teacher

God is the real teacher. Spiritual light comes from God alone, generally through a human channel, called the guru or teacher. Like a magnet's attraction is the irresistible and silent attraction of the guru. Yearning souls, afflicted with the world and seeking release from the apparently interminable round of birth and death, feel the power of this attraction. The teacher takes on the burden of sin and iniquity of the disciples and suffers on their account. The teacher kindles in their hearts the light of spirit and finally takes them to the realm of bliss and immortality.

Holy Mother did not seek disciples. She once said, "Those who care to come to me will do so of themselves after severing the shackles of the world. I shall not send for them." She herself lived a secluded life unknown to the public. Very few knew of her existence. The present writer, in 1916, expressed the desire for initiation to Swami Premananda at the Belur Math and suggested the name of one of Sri Ramakrishna's foremost disciples. The swami asked him to go to the Mother. In his utter ignorance the writer asked who the Mother was and received a thorough scolding from the swami. Nothing was written about her except for a brief mention in *The Gospel of Sri Ramakrishna*. A life of the Master in Bengali that spoke of Holy Mother was read by only a very few. Her pictures were not shown in public. How, then, did people come to know about her?

Some were recommended, as was the present author, by the disciples of Sri Ramakrishna or other swamis of the Ramakrishna Mission.

Some heard about her from friends or relatives who had already been initiated. Some came to know of her through a dream or vision. And there were some who came to pay their respects to her as a holy person and received her grace unsolicited. She also initiated people at the request of her own disciples. Once when Holy Mother was going to Calcutta she had to wait for the train at the Vishnupur railroad station. A poor porter came running to her and said, "You are my Janaki.[7] How long I have been searching for you! Where have you been all this time?" With these words he began to weep profusely. Holy Mother consoled him, asked him to bring a flower to offer at her feet, and initiated him then and there. Some received initiation from her in a dream. When they told her about it, she explained the meaning of the mantra to them and asked them to continue to repeat it, and sometimes she gave an additional mantra. In the choice of her disciples, Holy Mother looked into their hearts and did not consider their race or social position. Thus, among them one finds not only Bengalis, who naturally form the majority, but also men and women of South India, Europeans, and a Parsi. It may be mentioned that she neither understood nor spoke any language except her mother tongue, Bengali.

One of the remarkable features of Holy Mother's spiritual ministry was her catholicity. She did not ask all her disciples to accept Sri Ramakrishna as their Ishta or Chosen Ideal, though she often emphasized the fact that one's spiritual life would be more easily unfolded through the Master, who was the greatest manifestation of divinity in the present age. She knew that the austerities practiced by Sri Ramakrishna were not for his own sake but for the welfare of the world. As the Master taught, while excavating an old city an archaeologist may find a rare coin of great value, a precious museum piece, but it cannot be used for everyday purposes, for one can transact business only with modern currency. Holy Mother often asked her future disciples about the deities worshiped in the family, and she initiated them in accordance with that tradition. Sometimes a seeker would not be sure about the choice of a spiritual ideal and would ask the Mother to select one. Before giving initiation she would become introspective and thus discover what would be best for the disciple. In these moments of introspection she would often come to know about the disciple's spiritual future. When the present writer went to Holy Mother for initiation he was a college student and lived with his family. After the ceremony, he placed a silver coin near her feet as the customary fee. The Mother said that she did not accept any money from her monastic disciples. The writer protested that he was not a monk. Still the Mother refused to accept the fee, giving the same reason. Thrice the disciple offered the money, and each time he received the same reply.

During the 1920s there was a great political ferment in the country. Many young men joined revolutionary societies organized to achieve India's freedom. They were under the constant surveillance of the police, who also kept watch on anyone who gave them shelter. One such revolutionary young man went for initiation to Koalpara, where Holy Mother was then living. For fear of incurring the displeasure of the government, the local devotees arranged for him to spend the night in a private house, being nervous about keeping him in the ashrama. Early next morning Holy Mother was going to visit Radhu when the young man met her on the road and received initiation.

Here we shall make a slight digression to narrate a few incidents about Holy Mother's attitude toward some religious-minded political suspects and also toward the oppressive measures of the British rule in India. Many revolutionaries were inspired by the patriotic fervor of Swami Vivekananda and read his books and *The Gospel of Sri Ramakrishna* for inspiration.[8] Some of them later joined the Ramakrishna Order. For a long time the police kept a close watch on the Ramakrishna Mission.

There were two young women, sisters-in-law, who bore the same name of Sindhubala, one of whom was a political suspect. They hailed from the district where Holy Mother was born. By mistake the police first arrested the innocent one and then the other. One of them was pregnant. They were made to walk on foot in public. The mistake of the police was pointed out, and a suitable conveyance was suggested for their transportation. But the police refused and insisted on their walking. In addition, the request for bail was refused. The women were subjected to various humiliations. When the matter was reported to Holy Mother, she shuddered and then said in an extremely angry voice: "What does all this mean? Has it been done by the order of the government, or is it an act of smartness of the police officers concerned? We never heard of such cruelty to innocent women during the reign of Queen Victoria. If the government is responsible for the matter, then it will not last long. Was there no young man near who could slap the police and snatch away the girls?" A little while after, her brother told her that the women had been released. Then she became somewhat pacified and said, "If I had not heard of their release, I could not have slept tonight."

A disciple of Holy Mother, a quiet and spiritual-minded young man, was harassed for nothing by the police. One day as he came out of the shrine room after meditation, the police arrested him and took him away without giving him time to take refreshment. Holy Mother was very sad to hear about it and said, "This was certainly an unjust action on the part of the English. He is one of my good children, and for nothing he is being harassed. He could not take even a little *prasad*. Will the British rule last long?"

Another disciple of the Mother was interned with the present writer. Unable to bear the rigors of internment, he committed suicide. After the writer's release he told the Mother about the young man's death. With a sigh she said, "O God, how long will you put up with the iniquity of this government?"

Holy Mother was patriotic in her own way, and she cherished the welfare of the country. During the First World War people suffered intensely, especially the women, from scarcity of clothes. Many of them could hardly go out in public. Newspapers often reported the news of their suicide. One day, after hearing several reports of these heartrending episodes, Holy Mother could not control herself. Weeping bitterly, she said: "When will the English go? When will they leave our country? Formerly we had spinning wheels in every house. People used to make yarn and weave their clothes. There was no scarcity of wearing apparel. The British have ruined the whole thing. They tricked us and said: 'You will get four pieces of English cloth for a rupee, and one piece extra.'[9] All our people took to an easy life, and the spinning wheel disappeared. Now, what has happened to these fops? There is no end to their misery." She asked a disciple to give her a spinning wheel.

But all this protest against injustice did not interfere in the slightest with her innate generosity. It was the time of the Durga Puja,[10] when new clothes are presented to both men and women. Holy Mother asked one of her *brahmachari* attendants to buy clothes for her nieces. The *brahmachari* was a patriot, and he purchased coarse native clothes. But the girls wanted fine English stuff and refused to wear what was bought. There was a heated argument. The Mother listened to the discussion and said with a smile, "The English people, too, are my children. I must live with all. I cannot be exclusive." She asked the attendant to buy the British goods.

To resume the narrative of Holy Mother's method of initiation: Generally the Mother needed only a few minutes to initiate a disciple. Someone later asked Swami Saradananda why he took half an hour to perform this task. The swami said that Holy Mother could tell by a glance or a touch whether the Master had accepted the aspirant, whereas he required long meditation to be assured of this acceptance.

It is recounted that in a very few cases she declined to give initiation. Perhaps the candidates were not ready, or perhaps such initiation would have drained too much of her spiritual strength. She herself once said, "Embodiment limits the power of the Spirit." Sometimes she would say: "This body will one day surely perish. Let it go now, if it must, but let me give initiation." The poignancy she felt for people's affliction can be realized from one of her remarks: "Now and then I think if this body, instead of being such a small frame of bone and flesh, were a big one, how many people I could help."

We have already mentioned Holy Mother's physical suffering. It is said that the price of sin is suffering. But the Mother was sinless. She herself said that she did not remember ever having committed a sinful act, and she explained the cause of her suffering as her taking on herself the iniquities of her disciples. It was vicarious atonement. Regarding initiation, Holy Mother said: "The power of the teacher enters into the disciple, and the power of the disciple enters into the teacher. That is why, when I initiate and accept the sins of the disciples, I fall sick. It is extremely difficult to be a teacher. On the other hand, by leading a virtuous life the disciple does good to the teacher." Initiation, the Mother said more than once, had made her rheumatism chronic.

In 1916, Holy Mother went to the Belur Math to attend the worship of Durga. On the second day of the worship, many devotees saluted her by touching her feet. Afterwards it was noticed that she was washing her feet time and again with Ganges water. "What are you doing?" warned Yogin-Ma. "You will catch cold." The Mother replied, "How shall I explain it to you? When some persons touch my feet I feel as if my body has been set on fire. Ganges water alone refreshes me." One day she suffered excruciating pain from the touch of the devotees and said to Swami Arupananda, "This is why I fall ill. Tell the devotees to salute me from a distance. But do not mention this to Sarat, otherwise he will not allow them to salute me at all."

A disciple has recorded a striking example of this phenomenon at Jayrambati. Holy Mother's attendant had gone out on some business. After his return he found her lying on a straw mat on the verandah.

At the sight of the attendant she said, "A rather elderly man came here. Seeing him from a distance, I entered my room and sat on my bed. He was very eager to touch my feet. Though I protested, he saluted me by touching my feet by force, as it were. Since then I have been almost at the point of death because of a pain in my feet and my stomach. I washed my feet three or four times; still I cannot get rid of the burning. Had you been here, you could have forbidden him to touch my feet." Many instances like this could be recounted.

Holy Mother did not really mind this excruciating physical pain. Her motherly love and the consciousness of her mission made her regard suffering as a privilege. At Koalpara a disciple hesitated to touch her feet, thinking this would cause her pain. The Mother said, "No, my child, we are born for this purpose. If we do not accept others' sins and sorrows and do not digest them, who else will? Who will bear the responsibilities of the wicked and the afflicted?"

When she felt the urge to give initiation, the Mother was heedless of all considerations of health and comfort. Once when she was suffering from malaria at Jayrambati, Swami Saradananda asked her attendants not to allow anyone to approach her for initiation. Then a devotee from a far-off part of the country arrived just for that purpose. The attendants refused to take him to the Mother. A heated argument ensued. The Mother came to the door and asked her attendants why they were not allowing the devotee to see her. When they told her of Swami Saradananda's order, she said, "Who is Sarat to prohibit my giving initiation? I am born for this purpose."

Holy Mother often said, "I initiate people purely out of compassion. They do not leave me alone. They weep. That moves my heart. Out of kindness I give initiation."

One morning three devotees arrived at Jayrambati with a letter from Swami Brahmananda in which he requested Holy Mother to initiate them. When informed of the content of the letter she said, "Alas, Rakhal has sent me this stuff. A son generally sends his mother good things." At first she did not agree to initiate them and told them to go back to the Belur Math. Afterwards she relented and said, addressing Sri Ramakrishna, "O Lord, yesterday I prayed to you that I might not spend a day in vain. And at last you have brought this to me. All right. As long as the body lasts I shall continue to do your work." The devotees received their initiation. When the matter was afterward reported to Swami Brahmananda and several other senior swamis, the former became very grave. Swami Premananda said with a deep sigh, "Grace! Grace! By this unique grace the Mother has been protecting us. I cannot describe in words the poison which she swallows. If we had done so, the very suffering would have burnt us to ashes." People came to Holy Mother after having committed all kinds of sin. "But," she said, "when they address me as 'Mother,' I forget everything, and they get more than they deserve."

At one time, some of her attending disciples thought that the Mother was too generous in the matter of initiation, and one of them said to her: "Mother, you give initiation to so many people; certainly you can't remember them all. You cannot always think what happens to them. A guru should constantly look after the welfare of the disciples. Wouldn't it be more prudent of you to initiate only as many as you can remember?" To which she replied: "But the Master never forbade me to do so. He instructed me about so many things; could he not have told me something about what you have said? I give the responsibility for my disciples to the Master. Every day I pray to him: 'Please look after the disciples, wherever they may be.' Further, I received these mantras from the Master himself. They are very potent. One is sure to attain liberation through them." But she did concern herself with her disciples in a more active sense. Daily she practiced *japa* for their spiritual welfare. This continued till the end of her life. She slept very little. One night she was up at two o'clock in the morning. Asked for the reason, she said: "What can I do, my child? All these children come to me with great longing for initiation, but most of them do not repeat the mantra regularly. Why regularly? Many do not repeat it at all. But since I have taken responsibility for them, should I not see to their welfare? Therefore I do *japa* for their sake. I constantly pray to the Master, saying: 'O Lord, awaken their spiritual consciousness. Give them liberation. There is a great deal of suffering in this world. May they not be born here again!'"

Another time Holy Mother said: "I am the mother of the virtuous; I am the mother of the sinful." No repentant sinner was ever deprived of her grace. She was incapable of seeing others' faults. To one disciple she said: "What should frighten you as long as I, your Mother, exist? The Master said to me: 'At the end, I will appear to those who come to you, and lift them up, holding them by the hand!' The Master must reveal himself to you at the hour of death, no matter what you do or how you live. God has given you hands, feet, and organs, and they will play their part."

One woman of a respectable family became morally delinquent. Coming to realize her mistake, she went to the Udbodhan, stood in front of the Mother's room, and said to her, "Mother, what will happen to me? I am not entitled even to enter this shrine room." Holy Mother came forward, encircled the woman's neck with her own arms, and said tenderly, "Come in, my child, come inside the room. You have realized that you have sinned and are repentant. Come in, I shall initiate you. Offer everything at the feet of the Master. What is there to fear?"

A young man, a householder, said to the Mother one day: "Mother, I have suffered a great deal from the world. You are my guru, you are my Ishta. I do not know anything else. Truly, I have done such vile things that I am ashamed to tell you about them. I am still here only on account of your grace." The Mother affectionately stroked his head and said, "To the Mother, a child is always a child." Deeply moved by her compassion, he said, "It is true, Mother. I have received so much of your kindness. But may I never feel that such kindness is easy to win."

All these incidents bear out what the Lord said in the Bhagavad Gita: "Even if the most sinful man worships Me with unswerving devotion, he must be regarded as virtuous; for he has made the right effort."

To her disciples Holy Mother showed love, forgiveness, and compassion in a transcendent degree and gave them her assurance of final liberation. She said: "Those who have been initiated by me need not practice spiritual austerities for their salvation. At the hour of death all will realize God; surely they will see him. But those who want immediate results will have to practice discipline. The more they practice, the quicker they will get them. Those, however, who idle away their time will have to wait. Even those who give up all spiritual effort will realize God at the hour of death; there is no doubt about it." She often spoke of her disciples' present birth as being their last one.

Holy Mother did not, however, promise all her disciples liberation in the present life.[11] "If I freed everyone immediately," she said, "my spiritual strength would be sapped, and my body would not be able to help many seekers. It would fall off after those few had attained freedom." To some disciples the Mother remarked: "Why do you worry so much? Fulfill all your worldly desires; afterwards you will enjoy abiding peace in communion with Sri Ramakrishna. For you he has created a new heaven." She assured the disciples that they were the heirs to the spiritual treasures earned by her and the Master.

Holy Mother knew the spiritual capacity of her disciples. One day Yogin-Ma said to the devotees, in front of the Mother: "Mother may show us very much love, but still it is not as intense as the Master's. What compassion and love he showed for his disciples! We saw that with our own eyes. Words cannot describe it." "What is there to wonder at?" the Mother replied. "He accepted only a few chosen disciples, and those too after much testing. And to me he pushed a whole row of ants." How true are the words of a great householder disciple of Sri Ramakrishna: "Mother is more kind than Father!"[12]

As to whether all people really want liberation, the Bhagavad Gita says, "Only a rare one, among thousands, seeks perfection." How can God liberate one who still wants to enjoy the fun of the world, or, as Sri Ramakrishna said, one who, "being infatuated with the red toys of physical pleasures, has forgotten the Divine Mother"? There was a worker at the Udbodhan, a householder, Chandra by name, who often ran errands for Holy Mother; he was one of her disciples. He was very fond of eating, and the Mother loved to feed him. Whenever he came to her he got something to eat. One day a senior swami said to Chandra, "You always go to the Mother for *prasad;* can you ask her for something I am going to suggest?"

Chandra: Surely.

Swami: Can you say to her, "Mother, I want liberation"?

Chandra: Surely I can. I shall do it right away.

Chandra went upstairs and found Holy Mother engaged in worship. Slowly he entered the shrine room, but his body began to tremble. A little later, Holy Mother looked at him and asked, "What do you want?" Chandra felt as if someone were choking his voice. "*Prasad,*" he blurted out. The Mother pointed out to him some food under the couch.

Here is another example of the Mother's compassion and thoughtfulness. It was the occasion of the Sivaratri, the Night of Siva, when devotees spend the night in meditation, religious singing, and the reading of various episodes from the life of Siva. The inmates of the Udbodhan, as was the custom, were fasting the whole day and night. In the morning someone had teased Chandra, asking him to observe the fast too. At first he raised objections, but at last he was prevailed upon to go without food along with the rest. In the evening he went to the Mother's room to offer his salutation to her. The Mother looked at his pale and hungry face and asked him what the matter was. In a sad voice Chandra said that he was compelled to go without food on account of the persuasion of the inmates of the Udbodhan. At once Holy Mother asked him to take food. When he objected that in that case he would not derive the merit of fasting, she said, "I will fast for you, and you will have the merit." Chandra beamed with pleasure and at once ate to his heart's content. And the Mother went without food.

We shall now briefly describe Holy Mother's attitude toward the life of monks and of householders, and toward marriage. In her one finds all these three elements present. She herself was married. Surrounded by relatives, she lived a householder's life. But at the same time she was a living demonstration of the monastic ideals of compassion, service, purity, nonattachment to the world, and constant communion with the Supreme Spirit.

Both monks and householders were among the Mother's disciples. She imparted the spirit of brahmacharya and sannyasa to the members of the Ramakrishna Order, sometimes giving them the appropriate robe, and asked them to perform the formal ceremonies under the guidance of Swami Brahmananda, who was then the president of the Ramakrishna Order.

Her advice to her disciples about whether they should remain householders or embrace the monastic life differed according to their temperaments and competency. Holy Mother cherished a soft corner in her heart for her lay disciples who, despite all their worries and difficulties in the world, sincerely practiced spiritual disciplines. When some of them spoke of envying the monastic life, she would say to them: "Is the ocher robe everything? You will realize God without it. What is the need of taking the ocher robe?" She also pointed out the dangers of the monastic life, especially the pique that a monk might feel if he was not shown proper respect by householders. She said, "It is much better," pointing to her own white cloth, "to dress like this. It is rather nice." When one day a young man, out of temporary dispassion, expressed unwillingness to marry, she said laughingly, "How is that? God has created things in pairs: two eyes, two ears, two legs— and likewise, man and woman." To another young man hesitant about marriage she said, "Why can't one lead a good life if one is married? The mind alone is everything. Did not the Master marry me?" One disciple said to her that he had tried to lead an unmarried life but now found it impossible to remain a celibate. The Mother gave him assurance and said, "Don't be afraid to marry. Sri Ramakrishna had many householder disciples. Go and marry. Don't worry." In some cases she strongly discouraged the attempt to lead a monastic life. One married disciple with children wanted to become a monk and urged his wife to live with her father's family. When the helpless woman wrote to the Mother about the matter, she said with annoyance, "See how unjust he is! Where will this poor girl find shelter for her tots? He wants to be a monk; why then did he marry at all? If he must renounce the world, let him first provide for his family." Sometimes she refused to give her opinion about marriage and would say, "I won't say anything about it. If after marriage a man is troubled by the worries of this world he will blame me for them."

But Holy Mother never had any doubt about the supreme value of the monastic life. How often she said to the monks, "Look at the suffering of the householders! You have renounced the world and can at least enjoy peaceful sleep!" She also said, "Will a man who has strong desires for worldly pleasures listen to me if I ask him to renounce them? But if a fortunate soul has realized the world to be the sport of maya and God alone to be real, shall I not help him a little? Is there an end to the suffering in the world?"

She held her monastic disciples in high respect. Once a householder devotee quarreled with a monk and used harsh words toward him. Holy Mother reprimanded him and asked him to show respect to the monks. "For," she said, "an unkind word or thought on the part of a monk may injure a householder." She scolded her niece Nalini severely for speaking slightingly of the monks. One of her disciples, a college student, wanted to renounce the world, and the Mother encouraged him. Nalini said: "Look at our aunt's strange conduct.

Here is a bright young man studying for his B.A. degree. His parents have worked hard to defray his expenses. Now he wants to join the monastery instead of earning money and supporting his parents in their old age." "How little you know of him!" said the Mother sharply to Nalini. "He is not a young crow but a cuckoo.[13] When the cuckoo fledgling grows up, it recognizes its mother and flies to her, leaving the adopted mother behind." This young man afterward became a monk.

On another occasion a young disciple received the ocher robe of a monk from Holy Mother's hand and was exceedingly happy. One of her sisters-in-law remarked, "There! She has made him a monk." A niece added: "With what high hopes his parents have brought him up! Now all this is shattered. Marriage is also a duty. If our aunt goes on making monks, Mahamaya will certainly be angry with her. If anyone wants to renounce the world, let him do so of his own accord. Why should Aunt be the instrument?" The Mother said in reply, "Look here, child, these are my godly children. They will live in the world, pure as flowers. Can anything be grander than this? When I see the suffering of the householders my very bones are scorched."

Holy Mother encouraged worthy disciples to become monks. A young man with an M.A. degree came to her at Jayrambati and presented his problem to her. He wanted to embrace the monastic life and had received encouragement from Swami Shivananda. But M., a lay disciple of the Master, asked him to wait a while to avoid giving a shock to his family. Holy Mother heard the story but did not at once say anything to the young man. Afterward she said to an attending disciple regarding him: "He lives near M.'s house and has his mother and brothers at home. That is why M. is hesitant about his becoming a monk. But Tarak[14] is urging him to be one. After all, M. is a householder and Tarak is a monk. One needs good fortune, indeed, to accept the ideal of renunciation taught by the Master. Tarak is right. How few can be rescued from the world once they are entangled in it! The boy has real strength of mind." The next day, when the disciple again spoke to the Mother about his sincere longing to join the monastery, she said, "My child, may your desire be fulfilled. Tarak has said the right thing."

A mother whose married son had renounced the world became bitter toward Holy Mother and complained to her about it. The Mother said, "He has not done anything wrong. Rather he has followed the right path. I have heard he has made provision for his family."

Holy Mother respected the high ideals of monastic life and rebuked the monks if they deviated from them. Once she said about one of them: "I understand he was ill. But why did he live with a householder? There are monasteries. A monk must not lower the ideal of renunciation. Even if a wooden image of a woman lies upside down in the road, he must not turn it the other way, even with his foot, to look at its face. It is dangerous for a monk to save money. Money can create all kinds of trouble, even endanger one's life." About another monastic disciple who had not seen the Mother for several months and felt sad about it, she said: "Why should he feel so? A monk must sever all the chains of maya. A chain of gold is also a chain. He must not be attached. This idea of the 'Mother's love'—this moaning that one has not obtained it—is pure nonsense. I do not like my male disciples to hang around me constantly. After all, I have a human body. To regard it as divine is not easy."

A monastic disciple had arranged to go to Benares with Girish Ghosh, who had agreed to pay his fare. Holy Mother said to him: "You are a monk. Won't you be able to procure your passage money? After all, Girish is a householder; why should you travel with him? As you both will occupy the same compartment in the train, he may ask you to do something or other for him. You are a monk; why should you take orders from him?"

The Mother fully approved of women's renouncing the world if they were ready. A young girl refused to marry, and her mother wrote to Holy Mother to persuade her to remain in the world. The Mother replied, "How much a woman suffers during her whole life as a slave of her husband, always catering to his whims."

Men and women of various temperaments and natures became the Mother's disciples. Some visited her many times, although they did not render her any personal service and made no demands on her kindness. Many of them practiced spiritual austerities. Holy Mother said of them: "I regard all the disciples as my children, but with these I have a special relationship. They visit me always and look on me as their own." Some householders—and their number was considerable—were satisfied to receive initiation from the Mother. They did not visit her frequently, nor did they particularly devote themselves to meditation and prayer. But they had the firm belief that they need not worry about liberation, which surely would be attained after death if not earlier. They surrendered themselves to her and performed their ordinary duties in the world. Two statements of Holy Mother's may apply to them. First: "Even if my disciples do not practice any disciplines, they will surely realize God at the hour of death." Second: "To surrender oneself to God and cherish sincere faith in God is in itself a spiritual discipline." A third group of disciples, few in number, suffered terribly if they did not see the Mother or had to live away from her. For many years they frequented her place and rendered her personal services. Some of them attended her with unbelievable devotion. This service was their spiritual austerity. Certainly they were needed to help the Mother in her work and for the very preservation of her body. Referring to them, she said, "Those who are my own are born with me in every cycle." Last, there were monks who were quiet and serious and who led an austere life. Although they believed that Holy Mother was the Divine Mother of the universe, they seldom bothered her, once having been initiated by her. They felt that the contact of the soul was the real contact, the outer contact being only a means to it. They further felt that the Mother's blessings and grace became fruitful when this inner contact was made. That is why they seldom visited her after initiation, and when they visited her they were satisfied with mere prostration. They did not want to bother her with many questions. One such disciple, Swami Madhavananda, who was a former general secretary of the Ramakrishna Mission, remarked that though he had lived at the Udbodhan for over three years, he seldom talked to her. He was satisfied to take the dust of her feet daily along with the others. It was enough for him to feel that she was there in the house. Holy Mother was exceedingly pleased to see such disciples and said, "May I obtain children like them in every birth."

It had been much the same with Sri Ramakrishna's devotees. Broadly speaking, those who visited him may be divided into three groups. All regarded him as a great yogi, an illumined saint who could fulfill their desires. One group sought the Master's blessings for success in their worldly life and for relief from suffering. A second group prayed to him to guide them in their spiritual practices. No devotee ever went away empty-handed. There was a small number of devotees whom the Master designated as his inner circle: these did not care for spiritual visions or even liberation. They felt an eternal relationship with the Master and were attracted by his irresistible love. They surrendered themselves to him completely: body, mind, and soul. Sri Ramakrishna often treated them as his playmates and companions from birth to birth. One of them, Swami Brahmananda, asked Sri Ramakrishna one day, at the request of another devotee, to teach him meditation and other spiritual disciplines. The Master at once burst into tears and reprimanded him for acting as if he were a beggar, adding that he would naturally inherit, like a prince, all that the Master had earned. He exhorted these intimate disciples to never forget who he was, who they were, and what was the nature of their unique relationship with him. The devotees afterward became potent interpreters and bearers of his message.

Translator's Note

The translation of Holy Mother's conversations that follows was begun at the request of an American student who wanted to know of the daily activities of a Hindu woman who has had a tremendous influence over the spiritual lives of hundreds of *sannyasins* of the Ramakrishna Order. Other students, after reading the manuscripts, also gradually began to evince a keen interest in the unique and exalted life of Sri Sarada Devi. They, too, were impressed by the simple and artless life of a woman who transformed her worldly actions into devotional worship, who saw the divine in the drudgery of uninteresting duties, who showed a mother's solicitude for the welfare of all who sought her unfailing help in their inner development, and who drew all close to her by the magnet of her unsullied purity and by her love that never sought reward.

The Holy Mother was created by Sri Ramakrishna as the last word in the perfection of Hindu womanhood. Born in the quiet atmosphere of a peaceful village of Bengal, and brought up among simple country folk who did not know any of the arts of modern civilization, she was recognized during her lifetime as the great woman saint of India. People from all strata of society visited her and felt blessed. She traveled widely and met men and women with whom the exchange of ideas through spoken words was an impossibility; yet they accepted her as the guru, who teaches more by silent influence than by word. And she was a guru of no ordinary type. Her daily life was an unceasing performance of duties not only toward her numerous disciples but toward her relatives as well, who tried their utmost to make her life unpleasant. One such relative, for example, was Radhu, a niece with an undeveloped mind, whom, with all her failings, the Holy Mother humbly accepted as a beneficent gift of God. In the midst of all these trials and tribulations, and even while being subjected to the discomforts of physical maladies, she was unfailingly established in a state of serenity and cheerfulness, which demonstrated a constant communion with an inner bliss.

During the years of her spiritual ministration, the Holy Mother could show so much naturalness, ease, strength, and wisdom because these years were preceded by years of austere spiritual disciplines, both in the lifetime of Sri Ramakrishna and after his passing. The Master was, to her, God incarnate.

The conversations of the Holy Mother are bound to be a revelation to readers in India and in the West alike. India has always respected woman as the manifestation of the Divine Shakti, and the secret of her power lies in her looking upon all men born of women as her own children, whose highest homage to her is to recognize her divinity.

Swami Nikhilananda
Ramakrishna-Vivekananda Center of New York

2

Conversations from the Diary of a Disciple, Sarajubala Devi

Udbodhan Office, Calcutta
January 1911

One Friday morning Shokaharan came to our home at Pataldanga in Calcutta and said, "We shall go to Baghbazar tomorrow afternoon to pay our respects to the Holy Mother. Please be ready at that time." Well, after all I shall now have the good fortune to prostrate myself at the feet of the Holy Mother! Such was my exuberance of joy that I could hardly sleep during the night. I had been living in Calcutta for the last fourteen or fifteen years. And after such a length of time the Mother was gracious enough to afford me this opportunity to pay my respects to her.

Next day in the afternoon we hired a carriage, fetched Sumati from the Brahmo Girls School, and set out to the Holy Mother's house at Baghbazar. I can hardly describe the eagerness and fervor I felt at the time of this pilgrimage. I reached her house at Baghbazar and found her standing at the door of the shrine room. She was standing with one foot at the doorsill and the other on the doormat. There was no veil on her head. Her left arm was raised high and placed on the door; her right arm was hanging by the side. The upper part of her body was bare. She had been looking wistfully as if expecting somebody. As soon as I prostrated myself at her feet, she asked Sumati about me. Sumati introduced me as her elder sister. She had been visiting the Holy

Holy Mother at age 45

Mother for some time past. Then the Mother looked at me and said, "Look here, my child, how much I am troubled by these people here. My sister-in-law and her daughter Radhu are all down with fever. I do not know who will look after them and nurse them. Will you wait for a minute?—Let me wash my cloth and come back." We waited, and she returned after a few minutes. Then she offered us two handfuls of some sweets and asked me to share those with my sister. Sumati had to go back to her school. Therefore we could not stay for a longer time. We saluted her and took leave of her. The Mother said, "Come again." This interview of five minutes could not satiate the inordinate hankering of my soul. I returned home all the more thirsty.

February 12, 1911

When I went to the Udbodhan Office on this day, I found that the Holy Mother had gone to the house of Balaram Bose. I had not to wait long before she returned. As soon as I saluted her, she asked me with a smile, "Who has accompanied you today?" "One of my nephews," I replied.

> Mother: How are you today? How is your sister? You did not come for a long time. I was anxious about you and thought you might not be doing well.

I was surprised, because I had met her only once—and that just for five minutes. But she had not forgotten us. My eyes were filled with tears of joy.

The Mother said with great tenderness, "You have come here, and I was feeling restive at the house of Balaram."

I was completely taken aback. My sister Sumati had sent two woolen caps through me for Khude, the baby nephew of the Holy Mother. I handed them over to her. She expressed such joy at these trifles. She sat on the bed and said, "Sit by me here." I sat by her side. The Mother said with great tenderness, "It seems, my child, as if I have met you many a time before, as if we had known each other for a long time." "I do not know," said I. "I was here one day only for five minutes."

The Mother laughed and began to speak highly of my and my sister's devotion and sincerity. But I do not know how far I deserve those compliments. Gradually many women devotees assembled. All of them looked wistfully and with great love at the smiling and compassionate face of the Mother. I had never seen such a sight before. My mind was feasting upon the spiritual joy when someone reminded me that the carriage was ready for my return. The Mother at once left her seat and offered me some *prasad*. She held these before me and said, "Eat these." I felt shy of eating in the presence of others without sharing. The Mother said, "Why do you hesitate? Take these sweets." I accepted the offerings in my hand. I bowed down before her and took my leave. She said, "Come again. Can you go down the steps alone, or shall I go with you?" She came with me as far as the staircase. I said, "I can go alone. You need not take the trouble." The Mother said in parting, "Come another day in the morning." I returned with a sense of fulfillment and thought, "What a wonderful love!"

May 14, 1911

No sooner had I prostrated myself before the Holy Mother today than she said, "It is so nice that you have come. I was thinking all the time about you. Why did you not come all these days?"

Devotee: *I was not in Calcutta. I was at my father's house.*

Mother: *What is the matter with Sumati? She has not come here for a long time. Is she very busy with her studies?*

Devotee: *Her husband was not here.*

Mother: *Well, she goes to school. Do they follow the duties of the world?*

Devotee: *We do not know, Mother, what the world is and what our duty is. You alone know that.*

The Mother smiled. "What a warm day," she said and gave me a fan. "Ah dear, you took a hurried meal and ran up here. Now lie down by my side."

A mat was spread on the floor. I hesitated to lie on her bed. But she said, "Why do you hesitate? Lie down. Listen to my words." I could not help lying down. The Mother became drowsy and I lay silent. A few women devotees and two nuns arrived. One of the nuns was middle-aged, and the other was young. The Mother said, with her eyes closed, "Who is there? Is it Gaurdasi?" The young nun said, "How did you know it, Mother?" The Mother said that she felt so. After a few moments she sat up. The young nun then said: "We have been to the Belur Math. Swami Premananda fed us sumptuously. When he is there, one cannot return from the Math without being thus fed." The Mother gently reprimanded someone of the party for not having put the vermilion mark on her forehead, such a mark being obligatory on every married woman if her husband is alive.[1]

Gauri-Ma learned about me from the Holy Mother and invited me to her girls' school. About sixty girls attended the school. She asked me if I knew how to sew. I said that I could sew a little, and she asked me to teach that much to the students of the ashrama. With the permission of the Holy Mother, I visited the school of Gauri-Ma one day. Gauri-Ma was very loving to me and asked me to go there every day for an hour or two and give the girls some lessons. I said, "It is absurd for me to be a teacher with my little training. If you insist, I can just teach them the simple alphabet." But Gauri-Ma was inexorable. I had to yield.

One day, after leaving the school of Gauri-Ma, I went to see the Holy Mother. It was then summer, and I was quite tired. The Mother was seated in her room surrounded by a group of women devotees. As soon as I prostrated myself before her, she looked at me and at once took a small fan from the top of the mosquito curtain. She began to fan me so that I might be refreshed. Then she said anxiously, "Take off

your blouse quickly so that the body may be cool." What an unprece-
dented love! She began to caress me before many devotees. I felt
ashamed. All eyes were fixed upon me. Seeing her eagerness, I had to
take off the blouse. The more I asked her to hand over the fan to me,
the more she insisted with great tenderness, "That is all right. Be a little refreshed." She brought a tumbler of water and some sweets. Seeing
me partake of them, she became happy. The carriage from the school
had been waiting for me, so I had to take leave soon.

August 3, 1911

This morning I went early to Baghbazar. I had the desire to be initiated
by the Holy Mother today, so I took a few articles with me for the purpose. Gauri-Ma gave me the list of articles, and she also accompanied
me to the Holy Mother's place. When I arrived there, I found her
absorbed in worship. She asked me by signs to take a seat. After the
worship was over, Gauri-Ma broached the subject of my initiation. I
had also spoken about it to her one day. I had taken some good
bananas with me. She was very pleased to see the fruits and said, "Ah,
I see you have brought many bananas." One of the monks present
expressed his desire for them. Then she added, "Take that carpet and
sit on my left." I replied, "I have not yet finished my bath in the
Ganges."

Mother: *That does not matter. It is enough if you have changed
your clothes.*

I sat by her side. I felt my heart palpitating. The Mother asked the
others to leave the room and then said to me, "Now tell me what
mantra was revealed to you in your dream."

Devotee: *Shall I utter those words or write them down?*

Mother: *You may tell them to me.*

At the time of initiation the Holy Mother explained to me the meaning of the mantra that I had received in the dream. She at first asked

me to repeat that mantra and then communicated to me a new one. I was instructed to repeat the first mantra a few times every day, and then repeat the second and meditate.

I saw the Mother absorbed in meditation for a few minutes before she explained the meaning of the mantra to me. At the time of initiation my whole body began to tremble. I began to weep, for which I could not divine any cause. The Mother put a big mark of red sandal paste on my forehead. I gave her a few rupees for offering at the shrine. She handed over the money to Golap-Ma.

I noticed the Mother to be severely grave at the time of initiation. Then she left the seat of worship. She asked me to repeat the mantra for some time and to meditate and pray. I did as I was asked to do. As I bowed at her feet she blessed me with these words, "May you attain devotion to God!" Even now I remember those words and pray to her, "Please remember your blessing. May I not be deprived of its effect."

The Holy Mother was going to the Ganges for her bath. Golap-Ma accompanied her. I also joined the party, taking with me the towel and the cloth of the Mother. It was drizzling. After finishing her bath, the Mother gave the priest on the ghat a coin and a mango. As she made these offerings she said, "I am giving you the fruit, but it is the fruit of the gift that belongs to you." Ah, the priest could hardly realize who had made this gift. He could hardly understand the significance of those words. Nor can we, puny creatures, torn as we are by millions of petty selfish desires!

The Holy Mother changed her dress and gave me the wet cloth to carry. Golap-Ma headed the party while I walked behind. The Mother was between us. She carried some water of the Ganges in a small vessel and offered a little of it at every sacred banyan tree that stood along the way. There was a water jar near the cistern close to the tap on the ground floor. The Mother washed her feet with that water and said to me, "There is mud on your feet. Wash it off." As I was looking for some water she said, "There is water in the jar. Why do you not wash your feet with that?" "You have touched that water. How can I use it?" said I with some reluctance.[2] "Sprinkle a little over your head," replied the Mother. But I hesitated and said, "I cannot use that water." I took some water from the cistern in another jar and washed my hands and feet. She waited for me all the time. Then we went upstairs. She took some offered sweets and fruits in two leaf plates and asked me to sit by her. With great tenderness she fed me with the *prasad* and also partook of it herself.

Gradually many women devotees arrived. I did not know them. They would take their meal at noontime at the Mother's place. After the worship was over, we all sat to eat. The Mother also occupied her seat. She took three morsels of food and then gave me some *prasad,* which was also distributed among all others. The Mother now became her former self. She became jolly again. Since the time of initiation she had been altogether in a different mood, grave and introspective— a veritable goddess ready to grant favor and punish iniquity. I had been trembling with awe. I have seen her, later on, giving initiation to many devotees, but I have never again seen her in such a grave mood. Laughing and joking, she initiated many persons. They were also happy and satisfied. Goaded by curiosity, I sometimes asked the devotees how they found her at the time of initiation. One middle-aged widow once said in reply, "Just as we see her always. Nothing very particular. I had been initiated before by my family guru. Afterwards I heard of the Mother and came to her for initiation. She at first asked me to repeat ten times the mantra I had received from my family preceptor. Then she gave me initiation. She pointed out Sri Ramakrishna as my guru and another deity as my Ishta. She instructed me to pray thus to Sri Ramakrishna: 'O Lord, please relieve me of all sins committed in this and in previous lives,' and so on. I am greatly troubled nowadays. Can you explain it? I cannot repeat the mantra for more than half an hour. Someone, as it were, pushes me out of the seat. Do you also feel like that? I often think of asking the Holy Mother about it, but I cannot do so. You are so free with her. Has the Mother deceived me, then?" I never wanted to know all these details. But the woman spoke out all this very frankly. I said, "Please open your heart to the Mother. At first you may feel a little constraint. But it will be easy by and by. We also could not be so free with her at first. Even now she, at times, becomes so serious that we cannot approach her."

In the evening, the women devotees took their leave of the Mother one by one. She asked her nieces to meditate and pray. They were late, and she said in a tone of displeasure, "It is evening. Instead of meditating, they are gossiping!" Golap-Ma, Yogin-Ma, and other devotees prostrated themselves at her feet. She blessed them all, laying her hand on their heads or kissing them by touching the chin. She bowed before the image of Sri Ramakrishna and then took her seat for meditation. After she finished her meditation, I took leave of her and returned home.

I was not able to visit the Holy Mother for some days on account of the pressure of my school duties. No sooner had I saluted her today than she began to show her love for me in countless ways. Bhudev[3] was reading the *Mahabharata*. He was a mere boy and therefore could not read fluently. The Mother also had her other duties to attend to. It was almost evening. She said to Bhudev, pointing to me, "Give her the book. She will read it quite easily. The reading cannot be stopped without finishing this chapter." It was her order, so I began to read the *Mahabharata*. Never before had I read a book in her presence. At first I felt a sort of shyness, but somehow I finished the chapter. The Mother saluted the book with folded hands. We went to the shrine to witness the evening worship. The Mother took her wonted seat and soon became absorbed in meditation.

The Mother completed her *japa*, uttering the name of God in a loud voice, and bowed down before the image of Sri Ramakrishna. The *prasad* was then distributed to all. After this, the conversation drifted to our daily duties. The Mother, referring to her own busy days at Jayrambati, advised us to be always engaged in some work or other, as it was conducive to the health of both body and mind.

In the open square in front of the Holy Mother's house, there lived some people belonging to some parts of India outside Bengal. They earned their livelihood by hard manual labor. One of them had a mistress. They lived together. Once the mistress was seriously ill. Referring to her illness, the Holy Mother said, "He nursed her with such great devotion. I have never before seen anything like it. He has shown a real spirit of service." She began to speak highly of the devotion of this man.

The idea of a mistress would certainly have made us turn up our noses in disgust. Ah, how often we fail to recognize goodness when veiled in an evil garb!

A poor upcountry woman from the house across the street came to the Holy Mother, carrying a sick child in her arms. She solicited her blessings. The Mother was gracious to that child. She said that the child would soon recover and gave her blessings. Two big pomegranates and some grapes had been offered in the shrine. She handed over all these fruits to the poor woman, saying, "Give these to your sick child." The woman was overjoyed at this generosity of the Mother and repeatedly bowed down before her.

February 11, 1912

The moment I met the Holy Mother today and sat down after saluting her, she began to say with great sorrow, "Alas! Girish Babu[4] is dead. Today is the fourth day. His relatives came here to invite me to go to their house. Is it possible for me to go there anymore?"

Mother: *What devotion for and faith in Sri Ramakrishna Girish had! Have you heard this incident? He begged Sri Ramakrishna to be born as his son. Sri Ramakrishna said in reply, "Why should I care to be born as your son?" But who knows, my child, the inscrutable ways of the Lord. A son was born to Girish some time after the passing away of Sri Ramakrishna— a strange boy indeed. Even when he was four years old, he would not exchange a word with anybody. People could know his mind only from his gestures. His parents looked upon him as Sri Ramakrishna himself. They kept apart everything belonging to him—his dress, plate, cup, glass, etc. Nobody else would use those things.*

One day the boy became extremely restive to see me. My picture was in the upper floor of the house. He dragged the whole household there and, uttering a cry, pointed out the picture to them. At first they did not understand him. Then they brought him to me. Though he was but a little child of four, he pros- trated himself before me. Then he went to the first floor and began to pull his father by his cloth. He wanted that his father also should see me. Girish wept bitterly and said, "I cannot, my darling, see the Holy Mother. I am a great sinner!" But the boy was inexorable. So Girish had to yield. He took the boy in his arms. With his whole body trembling and tears trickling down his cheeks, he came up and prostrated on the ground before me. He said, "Mother, this boy has made me see your holy feet!" But the boy passed away when he was four years old.

Once Girish and his wife were airing themselves on the roof of their house. I had been staying then at the house of Balaram. The houses were near each other. I also went to the roof that day. I did not notice that Girish could see me from the roof of his house. His wife said to him, "Look there, the Holy

Holy Mother in the company of her relatives and devotees

Mother is pacing on the roof of that house." Girish at once turned his back on me and said to his wife, "No, no, I cannot thus stealthily look at the Holy Mother. My eyes are vicious!" He at once came down from the roof. I heard this from his wife.

June 15, 1912

The Holy Mother was seated with a number of women devotees. I was acquainted with some of them. The Mother was very cheerful in their company. She welcomed me with a smile. I requested Gauri-Ma to bring from the library two books: the life of Sister Nivedita and the Indian lectures of Swami Vivekananda. I wished to read something from the life of Sister Nivedita. The Mother agreed and said, "Please read Nivedita's life. I also received a copy of the book the other day. But I have not yet looked into it." I felt a little shy to read the book in the presence of so many people. At the same time, I was eager to read to the Mother the beautiful biography of the sister written by Saralabala. So I obeyed her order. The Mother as well as the other devotees began to listen with rapt attention. Their eyes became moist on hearing of the wonderful devotion of Nivedita. Tears trickled down the cheeks of the Mother. Referring to Nivedita, she said, "What sincere devotion Nivedita had. She never considered anything too much that she might do for me. She would often come to see me at night. Once, seeing that light struck my eyes, she put a shade of paper around the lamp. She would prostrate herself before me and with great tenderness take the dust of my feet with her handkerchief. I felt that she even hesitated to touch my feet." The thought of Nivedita opened the floodgate of her mind, and she suddenly became grave.

Those present began to give their reminiscences of Sister Nivedita. Durgadidi said, "It is the misfortune of India that she passed away at such an early age." Another woman said, "She looked upon India as her motherland. She herself said so many a time. On the day of the Sarasvati Puja she would walk barefoot, putting on her forehead the mark of the sacred ash of the sacrificial fire." I finished reading. The Mother now and then expressed her feelings toward the sister. She said at last, "The inner soul feels for a sincere devotee."

It was the hour for afternoon worship. The Mother changed her clothes and sat on the carpet before the image of Sri Ramakrishna. She had made some flower garlands with her own hands to decorate the image. Rashbehari, a young *brahmacharin*, had kept near the garland some sweets for offering. Ants gathered around the sweets. Some ants were seen also in the garlands. Mother said with a laugh, "See what Rashbehari has done! Sri Ramakrishna will be bitten by these ants." She removed the ants and tenderly decorated the image with the garlands. Seeing her thus decorate the picture of her husband with flowers before others, Surabala, her sister-in-law, laughed.[5] Later the *prasad* was distributed to all.

> *A woman devotee: Mother, I have five daughters. I cannot find*
> *suitable bridegrooms for them. I am so anxious about it.*
>
> *Mother: Why do you worry about their marriage? If you cannot*
> *find suitable husbands for them, please send them to the Sister*
> *Nivedita Girls' School. They will be educated there. They will*
> *be very happy in the school.*
>
> *Another woman devotee: If you have faith in the Holy Mother,*
> *then do as she asks you to do. That will be for your good. If*
> *you listen to her, you will have no worry.*

Needless to say, the mother of the five girls could hardly appreciate the advice.

> *Third devotee: It is very difficult to find suitable bridegrooms*
> *nowadays. Many boys refuse to marry.*
>
> *Mother: Yes, the boys have learned how to discriminate. They are*
> *gradually realizing that the happiness of the world is transitory.*

The less you become attached to the world, the more you enjoy peace of mind.

It was quite late before I took leave of her that night.

Another day I went to Baghbazar and found the Holy Mother resting after her lunch. She was gracious enough to request me to fan her. Suddenly I heard her speaking to herself, "Well, you all have come here. But where is Sri Ramakrishna?" I said in reply, "We could not meet him in this life. Who knows in which future birth we shall be able to see him? But this is our greatest good fortune: that we have been able to touch your feet." "That is true, indeed," was the brief remark of the Holy Mother. I was rather amazed at this confession. Very seldom would she speak of herself in such a way.

I could hardly realize at the time that people might possibly have their secrets to confide to the Holy Mother. I was a foolish girl, so I could not comprehend that. Therefore, if I happened to miss her on entering her room, I would search the house for her; I could hardly wait for her to come. One evening, two pretty young women had been taking the Holy Mother into their confidence in the northern porch of her room when I suddenly presented myself there, not finding her anywhere else. I heard the Mother saying to them, "Lay the burden of your mind before Sri Ramakrishna. Tell him your sorrows with your tears. You will find that he will fill up your arms with the desired object." I could at once understand that the women were praying to be blessed with children. They were abashed at the sight of me. My state of mind was even worse. But I was taught a great lesson that day. I took a vow that I would never again go to the presence of the Holy Mother without previously intimating my arrival. A few months later, I again met those women in the house of the

Holy Mother. I was glad to find that their cherished desire was going to be fulfilled soon.

Gauri-Ma was present there. In reply to our request, she shared some of her reminiscences of Sri Ramakrishna. She said, "I had visited Sri Ramakrishna long before many devotees began to go to him. I saw Naren and Kali [Swami Abhedananda] while they were quite young."

It was evening. The conversation had to be cut short. Gauri-Ma took leave of the Holy Mother. I also had to go. As I was about to take leave of her, she called me to the porch and gave me some *prasad*. She said, "Come again. You do not stay here long at a time. Come one morning at seven o'clock and have your noonday meal with us."

September 8, 1912

I was a little busy with some work in Gauri-Ma's Girls' School. Therefore I was not free to go to the Holy Mother according to my desire. It was an auspicious day when one morning I arrived at her place. She was getting ready to go to the Ganges for her bath. At the very sight of me she said with evident pleasure, "I am very glad you have come today. It is an auspicious day, being the birthday of Radhika. Wait here till I return from the Ganges." I expressed my desire to accompany her, and at first she agreed. It was drizzling, and Golap-Ma sternly objected to my going, as I would be exposed to the rain. The Mother supported Golap-Ma and said, "Please wait here. I shall return presently." We often noticed her behaving like a gentle young girl. She would never press her views over those of others. As soon as she came to the street, the rain stopped. She returned home after finishing the bath and said, "Well, the rain stopped as soon as I came out into the street. You also wanted to accompany me. I thought it would have been nice if you had come with me. You could have had a sight of the holy Ganges." To tell the truth, I was not so eager for the Ganges as for her holy company, for as we are involved in a thousand

and one duties of the world, we can hardly find time to visit her. On those few days when we can fortunately go to her, we do not like to leave her presence even for a minute. Golap-Ma, however, heard the words of the Holy Mother and remarked, "What does it matter if she has not seen the Ganges? All desires will be fulfilled by touching your holy feet." I also nodded assent to these words. But the Mother said at once, "Do not say so! Ah, it is the Mother Ganges after all."

The Mother would seldom reveal her divine greatness through any word or deed. She would always act in such a way that people might take her to be an ordinary human being like themselves. Only on rare occasions would she, out of grace to some fortunate devotee, reveal her divine aspect. She entered the room, sat on the bed, and said, "Look here. I have finished my bath in the Ganges." I understood that she had come to know of my innermost desire of worshiping her lotus feet. I said to myself, "Thou art ever pure. It is not necessary for thee to bathe in the Ganges to purify thyself." When I sat at her feet with flowers and sandal paste, she said, "Don't put any tulasi leaves." I worshiped her feet with flowers and sandal paste. I bowed down to her. Afterward she began to take her breakfast. She made me sit near and began to give me, with infinite love, half of every article of food she ate. I ate the *prasad* with great joy. As I was eating from the leaf plate I was reminded of Saint Durgacharan Nag.[6]

> Devotee: *This leaf plate often reminds me of Nag Mahasaya.*
>
> Mother: *What wonderful devotion he had! Look at this dry leaf plate. Who can eat it? But he had an exuberance of devotion and would swallow the leaf that had touched the* prasad. *Ah, what loving eyes he had: bloodshot and always moist with tears. His body was emaciated by hard austerities. He would come to see me. He could hardly climb the steps. His emotion would well up at the very sight of me. He would tremble like a leaf. He would stagger while walking. I have never seen such devotion in anybody.*

Devotee: I have read in his biography that he gave up his medical practice and was absorbed day and night in his meditation on Sri Ramakrishna. One day, his father said in an angry mood, "You are so indifferent to the world. What will be your fate? You will not have a piece of cloth to cover your body with. And you will have to eat frogs to satisfy your hunger!" There was a dead frog in the courtyard. Nag Mahasaya threw away the cloth he had been wearing and ate the frog. Then he said to his father, "I have fulfilled your two prophecies. Please banish all your anxieties regarding my food and clothing and devote yourself to the thought of God."

Mother: What wonderful devotion to his father! He did not make any difference between purity and impurity. This speaks of his high spiritual realization.

Devotee: Once, on a very auspicious day, he came home from Calcutta. The father reprimanded him and said, "You were in Calcutta near the Ganges. How foolish of you to have come home away from the Ganges on such an auspicious day! You should have stayed in Calcutta and taken your bath in the holy river." But just at the auspicious moment of that day, all noticed water rising in a spout from the courtyard. Every place was flooded. Nag Mahasaya became mad with ecstasy and cried, "Come, Mother Ganges!" He sprinkled that water on his head. The people of his locality bathed in that water and felt as if they had bathed in the Ganges.

Mother: True, even the impossible becomes possible through devotion. Once I gave him a piece of cloth. He always tied it around his head. His wife is also very good and devoted. She came to see me the other day during the summer season. She is still alive.

At this time some devotees arrived, and the conversation was stopped. They prostrated themselves before the Holy Mother. She asked me to prepare some rolls of betel leaves. I prepared two and handed them over to her. She ate one herself and returned the other to me. I left her again to prepare the rest of the betel leaves. The Mother, after a while, came to our room with two devotees. They started to help me, and the work was over very quickly. The Mother separated a few leaves to make an offering to them. She was very happy and said, "Ah, my good girls have finished their job so quickly."

The Holy Mother retired to the room of Golap-Ma on the second floor. I went there a few minutes after and saw that she was lying on the floor, resting her head on the doorsill, so I could not step over the doorsill and enter the room. She looked at me and said, "Come in. It is all right." She was always so free and informal. She raised her head from the sill, and I entered the room. I sat by her side and began to fan her. She asked me various things regarding the school of Gauri-Ma. I gave her suitable replies. Just then the two women devotees came there. One of them began to dress the Mother's hair. She separated one or two gray hairs and tied them in the skirt of her cloth. She said, "I shall preserve them as a souvenir." The Holy Mother felt abashed and said with hesitation, "Why are you doing so? I have thrown away so much hair before." She went to the roof to bask in the sun. We also followed her. There were many clothes drying in the sun. She asked me to take them away to the room.

Later, when the worship was over, the Holy Mother asked me to make the necessary preparation for the noonday meal of the devotees. We all sat together for the meal. The Mother took a morsel or two. The *prasad* was then distributed among us. The two women devotees mentioned above were with us. One of them was old and had her husband. She had seen Sri Ramakrishna. The other one was her daughter-in-law.

The old lady said, "Sri Ramakrishna gave us many instructions, but we have carried out very few of them. Had we followed his advice, we would not have suffered so much in the world. We are attached to the world and are always running after this or that work."

The Mother replied, "One must do some work. Through work alone can one remove the bondage of work, not by avoiding work. Total detachment comes later on. One should not be without work even for a moment."

After the meal, the Mother rested for a while. She lay down on the bed. All the devotees were eager to do her some personal service. But she asked them all to take some rest. They all therefore went away to their respective places, as they had various things to attend to. I remained there with an old widow who was a contemporary of Sri Ramakrishna. I was massaging the Mother's body. The widow sat by her side and began to narrate the various incidents of her family life. "Mother," said she, "you always excuse my shortcomings, but my people are so exacting." I asked her if she had seen Sri Ramakrishna. "Yes, dear," she replied. "I have seen him. He often visited our place. The Holy Mother was quite young at that time."

Devotee: Please tell us something about Sri Ramakrishna.

Widow: Not I. Ask the Mother to tell us something about him.

The Mother was resting with her eyes closed, so I did not ask her. After a while, the Mother herself said, "He who will pray to God eagerly will see him."

Mother: The other day one of our devotees, Tej Chandra, passed away. What a sincere soul he was. Sri Ramakrishna used to frequent his house. Someone had deposited two hundred rupees with Tej Chandra. One day he was robbed of that amount by a pickpocket in the tramcar. He discovered the loss after some time and suffered a terrible mental agony. He came to the bank of the Ganges and prayed to Sri Ramakrishna with tears in his eyes: "O Lord, what have you done with me?" He was not rich enough to make up that amount from his own pocket. As he was thus weeping, he saw Sri Ramakrishna appear before him and say, "Why do you weep so bitterly? The money is there under a brick on the bank of the Ganges." He quickly removed the brick and found there a bundle of bank notes. He narrated the incident to Sarat [Swami Saradananda]. Sarat said, "You are lucky to get the vision of Sri Ramakrishna even now. But we do not see him." Why should Sarat and others like him see him anymore? They have had enough of him, and all their desires have been fulfilled. Those who have not seen him with their physical eyes are most anxious for his vision. When Sri Ramakrishna was staying at Dakshineswar, Rakhal [Swami Brahmananda] and other devotees were very young. One day Rakhal came to Sri Ramakrishna and said that he was very hungry. Sri Ramakrishna came to the Ganges and cried out, "O Gaurdasi, come here! My Rakhal is hungry." At that time there was no refreshment stall at Dakshineswar. A little later, a boat was seen coming up the Ganges. It anchored near the temple. Balaram Babu, Gaurdasi, and some other devotees came out of the boat with some sweets. Sri Ramakrishna was very happy and shouted for Rakhal. He said, "Come here. Here are sweets. You said that you were hungry." Rakhal became angry and remarked, "Why are you broadcasting my hunger?" Sri Ramakrishna said, "What is the harm? You are hungry. You want something to eat. What is wrong in speaking about it?" Sri Ramakrishna had a childlike nature.

Bhudev, the nephew of the Holy Mother, just then returned from school. He had an attack of fever. The Mother asked me to arrange a bed for him. She was preparing to go to Balaram Babu's house to see his son, who was suffering from an attack of dysentery. She finished the evening worship and offered me some *prasad*. I said that I would eat it later on. She agreed and asked Nalini, her niece, to give me the *prasad* later. A carriage was brought for her. She asked me to wait there till her return. Golap-Ma accompanied her.

They returned after an hour. The Holy Mother was glad to see me and said, "I have come back quickly for you. Have you eaten the *prasad?*" When I replied in the negative, she remarked, "Nalini why did you not give her the *prasad* as I had asked you?"

  Nalini: I forgot to do so. I shall bring it presently.

  Mother: You need not worry about it anymore. I shall give her that prasad *myself.* (to me) *Why did you not ask for it yourself? This is your own home.*

  Devotee: I was not very hungry. Had I been so, I would have asked for it.

The Mother, shortly after that, brought some sweets that had been offered in the shrine and gave them to me. I partook of them joyously. I prostrated myself before her and asked for her leave. She said, "Come again, dear child. Durga! Durga! Shall I come with you to the ground floor? Can you go alone? It is night." "I shall be able to go alone, Mother," said I. Still she began to repeat the name of God and accompanied me as far as the staircase. "You need not take any more trouble," said I. "It will be easy for me to find the way."

It was the Akshaya Tritiya, a very auspicious day with the Hindus. I came to see the Holy Mother. The old woman with her daughter-in-law, mentioned before, was also there. She was about to give the Mother, as is the practice on such holy occasions, some fruits and a piece of sacred thread. The Mother interrupted her and said, "Why do you give these to me? Give them to Bhudev." Then in the course of her conversation, she looked at us and said, "I bless you on this holy day that you may attain to liberation in this life. Birth and death are extremely painful. May you not suffer from them anymore."

Holy Mother in the shrine of the Udbodhan,
her house at Baghbazar, Calcutta

It was the day of the sacred Car Festival.[7] At seven o'clock in the morning I went to Gauri-Ma's ashrama. She had invited me there for lunch. I had a desire to go to the Holy Mother from the school as soon as possible. We finished our meal at two o'clock. When Gauri-Ma and I came to the place of the Holy Mother, it was four o'clock. The Mother had been performing the evening service at the shrine room. We prostrated ourselves before her. Gauri-Ma took her aside and whispered something into her ears. I was asked to join them later on. I had taken with me a piece of silk cloth for her. I placed it near her feet and said, "Mother, will you kindly use it?" "Oh yes, darling," she said with a laugh.

Just then some men devotees came to bow down before her. We retired to the porch. One devotee brought with him some hibiscus flowers and roses, a garland of jasmine, fruits, and sweets. He placed these offerings near her feet and began to worship her. The Mother was seated quietly with a sweet smile playing on her lips. The garland was hanging round her neck. The flowers adorned her feet. After the worship was over, the devotee took a little from every fruit and prayed to her to eat it. Gauri-Ma said with a laugh, "You are in the grip of a staunch devotee. You must eat a little of everything." The Mother also was laughing and said, "Not so much. I cannot eat so much!" She ate a little from every article of the offering. The devotee took the *prasad* in his hand and touched his forehead with it. He beamed with an indescribable joy. He prostrated himself before the Mother and then came away. The Mother took off the garland from her neck and gave it to Gauri-Ma. The offered flowers were distributed among the devotees.

As I have already stated, it was the sacred day of the Car Festival. Bhudev improvised a car for the occasion. Arrangements were made for taking the image of Sri Ramakrishna in this car. Gauri-Ma had an important engagement in the school, so she had to leave us. The conversation drifted to Gauri-Ma. The Mother said, "She devotes her energy to bring up the girls in the school. She nurses them when they are ill. She has no family of her own. Her motherly instinct has been finding expression through these girls. This is her last birth; therefore she has been passing through all these experiences."

The image of Sri Ramakrishna was taken in the car. The Mother from her bed looked at the image intently. She was very happy. The car with the image was taken down. The procession went along the streets and along the bank of the Ganges. The party returned after dusk. The women devotees pulled the car in the porch of the upper floor. The Mother, her two nieces, and I joined them. When the car was going along the street, the Mother remarked, "All cannot go to Puri to see the Car Festival.[8] Those who have seen Sri Ramakrishna in this car will realize God."

October 1912

One day, during the Durga Puja holidays, I went to visit the Holy Mother. I found her very busy. I sat near her. She sent for a devotee who had come from Ranchi. He had brought with him many flowers, fruits, a piece of cloth, and a garland of linen flowers. He requested the Mother to wear the garland on her neck. As she did so, Golap-Ma took him to task, for the iron wire of the garland might hurt her. The Mother said tenderly, "No, I have put on the garland over my cloth." I had taken with me some fruits and sweets. The Mother asked me to offer them to the Lord. She ate a grape and said that it was very sweet.

The Mother had on her person the cloth I had given her a few days ago. Pointing that out to me, she remarked, "See, I have used it, and now it is dirty." I was amazed to see this and thought what infinite tenderness Mother had for even such an unfit devotee as myself.

Nalini, the Mother's niece, was in an angry mood. The Mother reprimanded her and said, "Women should not get angry so easily. They must practice forbearance. In infancy and childhood their parents are their only protection, and in youth their husbands. Women are generally very sensitive. A mere word upsets them. And words also are so cheap nowadays. They should have patience and try to put up with parents or husbands in spite of difficulties."

Radhu sat near us with her cloth pulled above her knees. The Mother reproved her and said, "Dear me, why should a woman pull her cloth above her knees?" She cited a verse that says, "It is as good as being naked when the cloth is pulled above the knees."

Chandra Babu's sister came to see us. She asked me in the course of conversation, "Is the husband of the Holy Mother still alive? Are these his children and daughters-in-law?" "Goodness gracious," said I, "have you not read the teachings of Sri Ramakrishna? He always exhorted people to renounce lust and gold." The lady was nonplused and said, "Excuse me, I took them for her own children."

It was the time of the Durga Puja. After the noonday worship, we had our meal. The Mother was resting. I sat by her side and began to fan her. She said with great tenderness, "There is a pillow there. Bring it and lie down near me. I do not require any more fanning." I hesitated to use her pillow and brought one from Radhu's room. The Mother said with a smile, "This pillow belongs to Radhu's mother, that crazy woman. She will make a fuss. Please use my pillow. There is no harm in it." Then she said to Radhu, "Please come here and lie by your sister." The conversation drifted to the remarks of Chandra Babu's sister, narrated above. The Mother said, "Well, you could have easily replied that her husband is there in the shrine room, and that all of you are his children." I said, "All the men and women of the world are his children." The Mother laughed and remarked, "People come here with various selfish desires. Someone comes with a cucumber, offers it to Sri Ramakrishna, and prays for the fulfillment of selfish desires. This is the nature of average people."

After a little rest, we left the bed. A few women devotees were in the adjacent room. Two of them wore ocher robes. They prostrated themselves before the Mother. They brought some sweets for offering. We came to know that they were the disciples of Sri Narayan Paramahamsa of Kalighat. Their teacher was just then engaged in performing a grand sacrifice.

One of the nuns asked, "Is there any truth in image worship? Our teacher does not approve of it. He instructs people in the worship of the fire and the sun."

Mother: You should not doubt the words of your own teacher.

Why do you ask me about it when you have heard the opinion

of your guru in the matter?

The nun: We want to know your opinion.

The Mother refused to give any opinion, but the nun was stubborn and began to press for a reply. The Mother said at last, "If your teacher were an illumined soul—pardon me for the remark—then he would not have made such a statement. From time immemorial, innumerable people have worshiped images and thereby attained spiritual knowledge. Do you want to deny this fact? Sri Ramakrishna never cherished any such parochial and one-sided view. Brahman[9] exists everywhere. The prophets and incarnations are born to show the way to a benighted humanity. They give different instructions suited to different temperaments. There are many ways to realize truth. Therefore, all these instructions have their relative value. Take, for instance, a tree. There are many birds perched on its branches. They have different colors— white, black, yellow, red, etc. Their sounds are also different. But we say that these are the sounds of the birds. We never designate a particular sound as that of birds and refuse to acknowledge other sounds as such."

The nuns desisted from argument after some time. They then inquired about the Calcutta address of the Holy Mother and said that they would like to see her again. After they had left, the Mother said, "It does not become a woman to argue like that. Even the wise could hardly realize the nature of Brahman by argument. Is Brahman an object of discussion?"

A few days after, the Mother was to leave for Benares, and I might not meet her for some time. She was extremely kind to me when I took leave of her, and I was so overpowered by her love that I did not exchange a word with anyone that night.

January 31, 1913

The Holy Mother had returned from Benares. I went to her place one morning and found her absorbed in worship. After the worship was over, she left the seat and said, "I am glad to see you, my child. I was thinking of you and feared lest I should miss you again. We shall soon be leaving for our country home."

It was late in the morning. Radhu, her niece, was ready to go to the Christian missionary school of the neighborhood. Golap-Ma came and said to the Mother, "Radhu is now a grown-up girl. Why should she go to school anymore?" She asked Radhu not to go to school. Radhu began to cry. The Mother said, "She is not quite grown up. Let her go to school. She can do immense good to others if she gets an education and learns some useful arts at the school. She has been married in a backward village. Through education she will not only improve herself but be able to help others." So Radhu was allowed to go to school.

Annapurna's mother brought a girl with her to be initiated by the Holy Mother. She said, "Mother, this girl is harassing me for being taken to be initiated by you. I could not avoid her. Therefore I have brought her to you."

> Mother: How will it be possible to give initiation today? I have already taken my breakfast.[10]
>
> A.'s mother: But the girl is fasting. It does not matter at all if you have eaten anything or not.
>
> Mother: Is she ready for initiation?
>
> A.'s mother: Yes, Mother. She has come fully prepared for it.

The Mother agreed. After the initiation was over, Annapurna's mother began to talk about the girl and said, "She is not an ordinary girl. After reading about Sri Ramakrishna, she became eager for practicing spiritual austerities. She cut her long hair, dressed herself as a man, and set out on a pilgrimage. She went as far as Baidyanath, over two hundred miles from Calcutta. She entered a wood and was resting there when the guru of her mother happened to pass by that way. The guru inquired where she was staying and informed her father. In the meantime she was kept with the guru. Later on, her father went there and took back the girl."

The Mother heard these words in silence and then remarked, "Ah, what devotion." Other devotees present there said, "Goodness gracious, such a beautiful girl! How could she go out alone, even with all her eagerness and devotion?" Nalini said, "It would surely have created a great scandal in our part of the country." After the noonday meal, all of us lay down to rest in the adjacent room. The Mother also asked her new disciple to rest for a while. She said that she was not in the habit of lying down during the daytime. I said that she should obey the order of the Holy Mother. She agreed but after a few minutes left the bed and went to the porch. The Holy Mother remarked, "She is restless. That is why she left home." She asked the maid of the girl, "What is the occupation of her husband? Why does he not keep her near him?" "He gets a small salary," replied the maid. "Besides, there is no one in his family. He cannot keep the girl alone in the house; therefore she lives with her father. The husband visits the house of the father-in-law every Saturday and Sunday." Annapurna's mother said, "This girl says to her husband, 'You are not my husband. The Lord of the world alone is my lord.'" The Holy Mother kept quiet without giving any reply.

The women devotees were talking in the northern porch of the shrine room. That created a great deal of noise. The Mother told someone, "Go and ask them to talk in low tones. They are disturbing

Swami Saradananda." There was no one in the room. I asked her a few questions regarding spiritual practices. The Mother said, "Do not make any distinction between Sri Ramakrishna and me. Meditate on and pray to the particular aspect of the Divinity revealed to you. The meditation begins in the heart and ends in the head. Neither mantra nor scripture is of any avail; *bhakti* or devotion alone accomplishes everything. Sri Ramakrishna is everything—both guru and Ishtam. He is all in all."

Then the conversation drifted to Gauri-Ma and her disciple Durgadevi. The Mother spoke highly of both. She said, "Listen, my child. Many may take the name of God after their minds have been hardened by the contaminating influence of the world. But he alone is blessed who can devote himself to God from very childhood. The girl is pure like a flower. Gaurdasi has molded her character nicely. Her brothers tried their utmost to arrange for her marriage, but Gaurdasi took her from place to place and concealed her. At last she took her to Puri and made her exchange a garland with Jagannath and made her a nun. That is to say, she was married to Jagannath, the Lord of the universe. Thenceforth she has been leading the life of a nun. Such a nice, pure girl. She has been well educated. I have heard that she is preparing herself for a Sanskrit examination. I also heard from her many incidents of Gauri-Ma's early years and thus came to know that she also had to pass through a stormy life."

A little later, four or five women devotees came. They offered the Holy Mother green coconuts and some other fruits. One of them was about to approach and touch her feet. The Mother said, "Please salute me from a distance." They offered her a few coins. She forbade them to do so. They then wanted some spiritual instruction. The Mother replied with a smile, "What shall I instruct you about? The words of Sri Ramakrishna have been recorded in books. If you can follow even one of his instructions, you will attain to everything in life." After they had taken leave, the Holy Mother said, "Where is that competent student who can understand spiritual instruction? First of all, one should be fit; otherwise, the instructions prove futile."

Annapurna's mother entered the room and said, "Mother, I saw you in a dream asking me to take your *prasad*, which would cure me of my disease. But Sri Ramakrishna had forbidden me to eat the *prasad* of anybody. Still, I shall be glad if you will kindly give me a little of your *prasad*." The Mother refused to do so, but the woman began to insist upon it.

Mother: Do you want to disobey Sri Ramakrishna?

A.'s mother: Sri Ramakrishna's words were applicable so long as I made a distinction between him and you. But I now realize both of you to be identical. So please give me your prasad.

The Mother had to yield. A little later, we took leave of her.

Another day when I went to see the Holy Mother, she inquired about my husband. I said that he was not in very good health. She asked me to write a letter for her. She dictated it. After the noonday meal, the Mother had been resting for a while when a few women devotees came to her room. When the greetings were over, one of them said, "I have a nice goat. She gives four pounds of milk daily. I also keep three birds. I spend my time with these. I am now pretty old." I was reminded of the words of Sri Ramakrishna: "Mahamaya, the supreme power of cosmic illusion, makes us bring up a cat and thus forget God. This is how this world is going on." The Holy Mother simply nodded to the words of these devotees. Alas, what a great agony she had to bear for our sake! We did not allow her even to enjoy a little rest. We disturbed her with mere idle gossip. I took leave of her in the evening.

I saw the Mother one night. She was lying on her bed. Another woman was near her. She at once sat up in bed so that I might bow

The Nahabat (music tower) in which
Holy Mother lived at the Dakshineswar Temple Garden

before her. In the course of the conversation she said, "At the time of creation, people were born with the quality of *sattva*, light. They had wisdom from their very birth. Consequently they at once realized the unreal nature of the world. They renounced it and practiced austerity. They were liberated in no time. The creator found that the purpose of creation was going to be frustrated. These wise men, who were thus liberated, were unfit for the continuance of the play of the world. Then he again started the work of creation and mixed the qualities of *rajas* [activity] and *tamas* [inertia] with the *sattva*. Thus his purpose was fulfilled." Then she cited a popular verse bearing on the theme of creation and said, "In our young age we acquired these ideas from the country dramas. But now these have become rare."

Some of the young girls, relatives of the Holy Mother, were reading loudly from a book in another room. The Mother said, "Listen, how loudly they are reading. They have forgotten that there are many people on the ground floor."

Radhu's mother, the insane sister-in-law of the Holy Mother, entered the room and said, "Lakshmimani [Sri Ramakrishna's niece] is going to Navadvip on a pilgrimage. I wanted to go with her. But you have stood in my way." She left the room in a pique.

Mother: How can I allow her to go with Lakshmi? Lakshmi is a
devotee. She would sing and dance with other devotees. She
would not observe the distinction of caste and would dine with
others. But Radhu's mother would not understand this. She
hardly knows that the devotees need not observe caste rules
among themselves. So she would come back and criticize the
conduct of Lakshmi before others. Have you met Lakshmi?
Devotee: No, Mother.
Mother: She is in Dakshineswar. Visit her one day. Have you
been to Dakshineswar?
Devotee: Yes, Mother, I have visited the place many a time. But
I did not know she had been living there.

Mother: Have you seen the Nahabat at Dakshineswar, where I used to stay?

Devotee: Yes, Mother, I have seen it from the outside.

Mother: When you visit the place another day, go inside the room. When I stayed there, my entire world consisted of that small room. Have you seen Sri Ramakrishna's birthday festival at Belur?

Devotee: No, Mother. I have never been to the monastery at Belur. I have heard that the monks who live there do not like a crowd of women in the monastery; therefore I hesitate to go there.

Mother: Go there once and see the celebration of Sri Ramakrishna's birthday.

It was evening when I went to Baghbazar to see the Holy Mother. She was kind enough to ask me to spread her small carpet on the floor and fetch her beads. She soon became absorbed in her meditation. Across the lane there was an open space. A few laborers lived there with their families. One of the men began to beat a woman severely—probably his wife. Slaps and fisticuffs began to be showered upon her. Then he kicked her with such force that she was thrown to a distance with a child in her arms. Then he started kicking her again. The Mother could not proceed with her meditation anymore. Though she was extremely modest and would not usually talk even loudly enough to be heard by people on the ground floor, she now came to the porch of the second floor, stood by the iron railing, and cried aloud in a tone of sharp reprimand, "You rogue! Are you going to kill the girl outright? I am afraid she is already dead!" Hardly had the man looked at her than he became quiet like the snake before its charmer and released the woman. The sympathy of the Mother made the woman burst into loud sobs. We heard that her only fault was that she had not cooked in time. Afterward the man became his old self again and wanted to be at peace with the woman. The Holy Mother saw this and came back to her room.

Some time later, the voice of a beggar was heard in the lane. He was crying, "Radha Govinda, glory unto God! Please be kind to the blind." The Mother said, "This beggar passes the lane over there almost every night. At first he would cry, 'Please be kind to the poor blind.' But Golap one day rightly said to him, 'Please utter that, Radha-Krishna— the name of God. This will serve the double purpose of uttering the holy name and also of reminding the householders of God. Otherwise you will day and night think of your blindness alone.' Since that, the blind man, while passing this lane, shouts the name of God. Golap gave him a piece of cloth. He also gets alms in other forms."

I went to Baghbazar one evening and heard the Holy Mother saying, "New devotees should be given the privilege of service in the shrine room. Their new zeal makes them serve the Lord carefully. The others are tired of service. Service, in the real sense of the word, is not a joke. One should be extremely careful about making his service perfectly flawless. But the truth is, God knows our foolishness and therefore he forgives us." One woman devotee was near her. I do not know if these words were directed toward her. The Mother was asking her to be careful in picking the right kind of flowers and in making sandal paste for the purpose of worship, as also in not touching any part of the body, cloth, or hair while working in the shrine. "One must work in the shrine room with great attention," she said. "Offerings and the rest should be made at the proper time."

It was half past eight in the evening when I came to the place of the Holy Mother. She was absorbed in meditation in the porch to the north of the shrine room. We waited for a while in another room. The Mother came there and said with a smile, "I am glad to see you, my child."

Devotee: *I have brought my sister with me, Mother. Is aratri-*
ka[11] [the evening service] over?

Mother: *No. You may witness it now. I shall join you presently.*

The evening service soon commenced. Many ladies sat in the shrine room and began to pray. After the worship was over, we prostrated before the image and came to the adjacent room to meet the Holy Mother. While we were at her place, we were unwilling to lose sight of her even for a moment.

A few minutes later, the Mother came to the room. An old woman was learning a devotional song from another.

Mother: *I am afraid she may not be able to teach the song cor-*
rectly. Ah, what a great singer the Master was! His voice was
so sweet. While singing, he would be one with his song. His
voice is still ringing in my ears. When I remember it, other
voices appear so flat. But Naren also had a melodious voice.
Before leaving this city he came to see me and sang a few
songs. While taking leave of me he said, "Mother, if I can
return as a man in the true sense of the term, I shall see you
again; otherwise, goodbye!" "What do you mean, my child," I
cried. "Well," he replied, "I shall soon come back through your
grace." Girish Babu also had a sweet voice.

Radhu came to the room and asked the Mother to lie down by her. She said, "You go and lie on the bed. These devotees have come from a distance. I should like to sit with them for a while." Radhu still insisted. I said, "Let us also go to your room. You may lie there on your bed."

The Mother asked us to follow her. The Mother lay on her bed and began to talk to us about various things. I was fanning her. She said after a few minutes, "It is now cool. Please do not take any more trouble." I rubbed her feet. An old lady was explaining to another about the six centers as described in Yoga. Golap-Ma forbade her to do so, but still she continued. The Mother heard her words and said to me with a smile, "Sri Ramakrishna with his own hands drew for me the picture of the kundalini[12] and the six Yogic centers." I asked her if she still had the picture with her. The Mother replied, "No, my child. I had then no idea of the devotees coming to us. I have lost the paper."

It was eleven o'clock at night. We prostrated before her and took leave of her. The Mother sat on her bed and blessed us. She called me aside and said, "Spiritual progress becomes easier if husband and wife agree in their views regarding spiritual practices."

A few days later when I visited the Mother, I heard her saying, "One should tell even the guru what is right. It is perfectly proper for the disciple to do so. But the disciple must have unwavering devotion to his guru. The devotion to the guru, whatever may be his character, enables the disciple to attain to liberation. Look at the devotion of the disciples of Sri Ramakrishna to their Master. This love for their teacher makes them love everyone connected with Sri Ramakrishna's family. They love even the cat belonging to his village."

November 1913

We had plenty of flowers at our Ballygunj home. The Holy Mother was always pleased with flowers. One day I gathered a large quantity of them and came to see her. I found her just ready for the worship. I arranged the flowers, and she sat on the carpet before the image. I forgot to keep aside some flowers for worshiping the feet of the Holy Mother. So I was sorry to think that it would not be possible for me to worship her that day. But I soon found out that she had anticipated my secret desire. She herself had separated some flowers on the tray. After the worship was over, she said to me, "Now, my dear child, I have kept those flowers in the tray for you. Bring them here." Just then a devotee came to see the Mother with a large quantity of fruits. She was very pleased to see him. She put a mark of sandal paste on his forehead and kissed him by touching the chin. I had never seen her express her affection for any man devotee in such a manner. Next she asked me to hand over a few flowers to him. He accepted them. I found his whole body trembling with devotional fervor. With great joy he offered those flowers at her feet and left after accepting the *prasad*. She sat on the cot and invited me very tenderly to come to her. I worshiped her feet. With great love, she placed her hand on my head. I was deeply touched by her blessings.

After a while I found her on the roof drying her hair. She invited me to come near her and said, "Take off the cloth from your head and dry your hair, otherwise it may affect your health." Golap-Ma came to the roof and asked the Mother to make an offering of food in the shrine room. The Mother came down from the roof. I also followed her after a while to the shrine room. Like a bashful young bride, she was saying to Sri Ramakrishna in a soft voice, "Come now; your meal is ready." Then she came to the image of Gopala and said, "O my Gopala, come for your meal." I was just behind her. Suddenly she looked at me and said with a smile, "I am inviting them all to their noonday meal." With these words, the Holy Mother entered the room where the food was offered. Her earnestness and devotion made me feel that the deities, as it were, listened to her words and followed her to the offering room. I was pinned to the ground with wonder.

After the offering was over, we all sat together for our meal. Then the Mother asked me to rest for a while. A man came with a basket of fruits meant for offering. He asked the monks what he should do with the basket. They told him to throw it out in the lane. The Mother left her bed and went to the porch. She looked at the lane and said to me,

"Look there. They have asked him to throw away such a nice basket! It does not matter for them in the least. They are all monks and totally unattached. But we cannot allow such waste. We could have used the basket at least for keeping the peelings of the vegetables." She asked someone to fetch the basket and wash it. The basket was kept for some future use. I had my lesson from her words, but we are so slow to learn.

After some time, a beggar came to the house and shouted for some alms. The monks felt annoyed and said rudely, "Go away now. Don't disturb us." At these words the Holy Mother said, "Have you heard their remarks? They have driven away the poor man. They could not shake off their idleness and give something to the beggar. He only wanted a handful of rice. And they could not take the trouble to do this bit of work. Is it proper to deprive a man of what is his due? Even to the cow we owe these peelings of the vegetables. We should hold these near her mouth."

I went to see the Holy Mother again after many days. She had gone back to her country home and returned to Calcutta in the autumn, a few days before the Durga Puja. I visited her one afternoon and found a woman kneeling near her feet and begging with tears for initiation. The Mother was seated on her bedstead. She refused to comply with her prayer and said, "I have already told you that I would not be able to initiate you now. I am not well." The woman was insistent. The Mother felt annoyed and said, "You treat initiation very lightly. You are perfectly satisfied if you get the sacred mantra, but you never think of the consequence." But the woman was inexorable. All of us felt disgusted. The Holy Mother at last asked her to come another day. Then the woman asked her to ask one of the monks to give her initiation.

Mother: *They may not listen to me.*

Woman: *What do you mean, Mother? They must obey you.*

Mother: *In this matter they may refuse to comply with my request.*

Finding the woman unrelenting, the Mother said, "Well, I shall ask Swami Subodhananda. He will initiate you." But the woman started insisting again and said, "I shall be happy to be initiated by you. You can certainly fulfill my desire if you like." She brought out ten rupees and said, "Here is some money. You may purchase the necessary articles for initiation." We all felt mortified at her impudence. At last the Mother was angry and said severely, "What? Do you mean to tempt me with money? You cannot coax me with these coins. Take them back." The Holy Mother immediately left the room.

Being hard-pressed by the woman, the Holy Mother at last agreed to initiate her on the sacred Mahashtami day. She soon took leave of us. The Mother now found some leisure to talk to me.

I came to see the Mother after two and a half months. She cried, "Oh, it is almost an age since I have seen you." In the course of the talk, I asked her about the woman whom she had consented to initiate.

Mother: *She could not come here on the appointed day. I had said to her, "I am now ill. Let me be well and then I shall initiate you." My words came to be true. She could not come on the Mahashtami day, as she herself fell ill. She came here many days later and was initiated.*

Devotee: *That is right. The words that are once uttered by you cannot but be fulfilled. We suffer as we go counter to your wishes. Many a time, you initiate people even while you are ill and thus suffer all the more by transferring their sufferings to yourself.*

Mother: Yes, my dear child. Sri Ramakrishna also used to say, "Otherwise, why should this body have suffered at all?" The other day I was ill with an attack of diarrhea.

My sister-in-law was with me. Referring to her, the Mother said, "A very nice and quiet girl. There is only one dish of vegetable. If that be not palatable, then the whole dinner is spoiled." She meant that I had only one sister-in-law in the family. My life could have been made unhappy if she had not been good to me.

February 1914

I went to Baghbazar one morning with a basket of flowers. I offered it to the Holy Mother. She was exceedingly happy and began to decorate the image of Sri Ramakrishna with the flowers. Some of them were blue. She took these in her hands and said, "Ah, what a pretty color. There was a girl at Dakshineswar named Asha. One day, she came to the temple garden and picked a red flower from a plant with dark leaves. She cried, 'Dear me, such a red flower on a plant with dark leaves. Goodness gracious, what a strange creation of God!' Sri Ramakrishna saw her and said, 'My dear child, what is the matter with you? Why are you weeping like that?' She could hardly utter a word. She was weeping incessantly. Sri Ramakrishna at last pacified her."

The Holy Mother was in an exalted mood and said, "Look at these flowers with a blue color. How can one decorate God without such fine flowers?" She took a handful of them and offered them to the image of Sri Ramakrishna. A few flowers dropped at her feet before they were offered. She cried, "Dear me, how they have dropped at my feet before I could offer them to the Lord!" "It is very nice," I said. Then I thought, "To you, Sri Ramakrishna may be a higher being; but we do not make any distinction between you and him."

A widowed woman came into the room. I asked the Mother about her. The Mother said, "She took initiation from me about a month ago. She had accepted another guru before. She later felt that it was a mistake and came here for initiation. I could not convince her that all teachers are one. The same power of God works through them all."

In the afternoon, the conversation again turned to flowers.

Mother: One day while living at Dakshineswar, I made a big garland of seven strands with some jasmine and red flowers. I soaked the garland in water in a stone bowl, and quickly the buds turned into full blossoms. I sent the garland to the Kali temple to adorn the image of the Divine Mother. The ornaments were taken off from the body of Kali, and she was decorated with the garland. Sri Ramakrishna came to the temple. He at once fell into an ecstatic mood to see the beauty of Kali so much enhanced by the flowers. Again and again he said, "Ah, these flowers are so nicely set off against the dark complexion of the Divine Mother! Who made the garland?" Someone mentioned me. He said, "Go and bring her to the temple." As I came near the steps I found some of the men devotees there—Balaram Babu, Suren Babu, and others. I felt extremely bashful and became anxious to hide myself. I took shelter behind the maid, Brinde, and was about to go up the temple by the back steps. Sri Ramakrishna noticed this instantly and said, "Don't try those steps. The other day a fisherwoman was climbing those steps and slipped. She had a terrible shock, fractured her bones, and died. Come by these front steps." The devotees heard those words and made way for me. I entered the temple and found Sri Ramakrishna singing, his voice trembling with love and emotion.

A few women devotees now entered the room, and the conversation stopped. It was time for me to take leave. Again the Mother began to talk about God-realization.

Mother: Do you know, my child, what it is like? It is just like a candy in the hand of a child. Some people beg the child to part

*with it. He does not care to give it to them. But he easily hands
it over to another whom he likes. A man performs severe austerities throughout his life to realize God, but he does not succeed;
whereas another man gets his realization practically without any
effort. It depends upon the grace of God. God bestows grace
upon anyone he likes. Grace is the important thing.*

1917

I went to see the Holy Mother in the evening. I had been residing at
our Baghbazar house at that time, and I visited her almost every day.
Finding her alone, I narrated to her a dream and said, "Mother, one
night I saw Sri Ramakrishna in a dream. You had been living then at
Jayrambati. I saluted him and asked, 'Where is the Mother?' He said,
'Follow that lane, and you will find a thatched cottage. She is seated in
the front porch.'" The Holy Mother was on her bed. With great enthusiasm she sat up and said, "You are quite right. Your dream is true." "Is
it, then, true?" I said in surprise. "I had the idea that your home at
Jayrambati is a brick building. But in the dream I saw the earthen floor,
thatched roof, etc., and therefore concluded that it was all illusory."

In the course of conversation regarding austerity for the realization of God, she said, "Golap-Ma and Yogin-Ma devoted a great deal
of their time to meditation and the repetition of God's name. Yogin-
Ma practiced the greatest austerities. At one time she lived only on
milk and fruits. Even now she spends much of her time in spiritual
practices. The mind of Golap-Ma is hardly affected by external things.
She does not even hesitate to eat cooked vegetables purchased from
the market, which a brahmin widow would never touch."

It was arranged to have devotional songs on the goddess Kali sung
that evening at the house of the Holy Mother. The monks of the Belur
Math would take part in it. The music commenced at half past eight
in the evening. Many of the women devotees sat on the verandah to

hear the music. I was rubbing oil on the Mother's feet and could hear the songs from the room. I had heard them many times before, but that day, those songs coming from the mouths of the devotees had a novel charm. They were thrilling and full of power. My eyes became moist. Now and then they sang those songs Sri Ramakrishna had himself sung. At such times the Holy Mother would cry out with enthusiasm, "Yes, Sri Ramakrishna would sing this song!" They commenced the song whose first line runs thus: "The bee of my mind has become fascinated with the blue lotus of the Divine Mother's feet!"

The Holy Mother could not lie down anymore. A few teardrops trickled down her cheeks. She said, "Come, darling. Let us go to the verandah." After the singing was over, I saluted the Mother and returned home.

July 22, 1918

It was half past seven in the evening when I arrived at the house of the Holy Mother. Only two months earlier she had returned from her village home, emaciated by a protracted attack of malaria. She greeted me with her usual smile.

Mother: *It is a very warm day. Take a little rest and refresh your-*
self. What about your sister? Has she reached home?
Devotee: *Yes, Mother. I started after she had reached home.*
Mother: *Take this fan for Radhu and rub this medicated oil on*
my back. There are heat blisters all over my body.

As I started rubbing the oil, the bell rang for evening worship. The Holy Mother sat on her bed and saluted God with folded hands. Other devotees went to the shrine room to witness the worship.

Mother: *Everybody says regretfully, "There is so much misery in*
the world. We have prayed so much to God, but still there is
no end of misery." But misery is only the gift of God. It is the
symbol of God's compassion. Is it not so?

That day, my mind had been greatly troubled. Did she really know it and therefore address those words to me?

> Mother: *Who has not suffered from misery in this world?*
> *Brinde, the woman devotee of Krishna, said to him, "Who*
> *says that you are compassionate? In your incarnation as Rama*
> *you made Sita weep for you all through her life. And in this*
> *incarnation of Krishna, Radha has been weeping on your*
> *account. Your parents suffered extreme agony in the prison of*
> *Kamsa and cried day and night, uttering your name. Then*
> *why do I repeat your name? It is because your name removes*
> *all fear of death."*

Referring to a woman, the Holy Mother said, "People of that appearance are generally devoid of *bhakti*, devotion to God. I have heard it from Sri Ramakrishna."

> Devotee: *Yes, Mother, I have read in the Kathamrita[13] that he*
> *used to say that people who are not frank cannot make real*
> *spiritual progress.*
> Mother: *Oh, you are referring to that. He said those words in*
> *the house of a devotee named Naren.*
> *Once a man had a mistress. She came to Sri Ramakrishna and*
> *said with repentance, "That man ruined me. Then he robbed*
> *me of my money and jewels." Sri Ramakrishna was aware of*
> *the innermost contents of people's minds. But still he would like*
> *to hear about things from their own mouths. He said to that*
> *woman, "Is it true? But he used to give us tall talks about*
> *devotion." Then he described the traits that stand in the way of*
> *spirituality. In the end the woman confessed to him all her sins*
> *and was thus released from their evil effects.*
> Nalini: *How is it possible, Mother? How can one be absolved*
> *from sin by simply expressing it in words? Is it possible to wash*
> *away sin in this manner?*
> Mother: *Why not, my dear child? Sri Ramakrishna was a perfect*

soul. Certainly one can be free from sin by confessing it to one like him. Listen, if at a certain place people talk of virtue and vice, those present there must take a share of those qualities.

Nalini: How is this possible?

Mother: Let me explain. Imagine that a man confessed to you his virtue or vice. Whenever you will think of that man, you will remember his virtuous or sinful acts. And they will thus leave an impression upon your mind. Is it not true, my child?

Again the talk turned to human misery, affliction, and worry.

Mother: Many people come to me and confess their worries. They say, "We have not realized God. How can we attain to peace?" Thereupon the thought would flash in my mind: "Why do they say so? Am I then a superhuman being?" I never knew what worry was. And the vision of God—it lies, as it were, in the palm of my hand. Whenever I like it, I can have it.... The Kathamrita by M. is very nice. This is because he has put down the exact words of the Master. How sweet are those words! I hear that he has enough material for four or five books like that. But now he is old. I doubt if he will be able to undertake the task of bringing it all out as books. He has amassed a great deal of money from the sale of the book. The amount has been kept in deposit. He has given one thousand rupees for building my house at Jayrambati, besides meeting other incidental expenses. He also sends me ten rupees every month. He gives twenty rupees or more when I stay in Calcutta. Formerly he used to give me two rupees a month. He was then a school teacher.

Devotee: I hear that Girish Babu contributed in the beginning a large amount of money for the maintenance of the monks.

Mother: Not a large amount. Suresh Mitra was rather munificent in his contribution. Girish also gave money now and then.

*He at one time defrayed all my expenses for a year and a half.
How could he make a large contribution? He was never a rich
man. The early part of his life was not very clean. He lived in
bad company and acted on the stage. But he was a man of
wonderful faith; therefore he received the grace of Sri
Ramakrishna. In this incarnation Sri Ramakrishna has
redeemed Girish. The life of each incarnation of God is
marked by similar incidents. Gauranga saved the two brothers,
Jagai and Madhai. Again, Sri Ramakrishna once remarked that
Girish had within him the trait of Siva.*

*What is there in money, my child? Sri Ramakrishna could not
touch it. His hand would recoil before money. He said, "This
world is illusory. Had I known it to be otherwise, I would have
covered your Kamarpukur with leaves of gold. But I know the
world to be impermanent. God alone is real."*

Maku, her niece, said sorrowfully, "I could not settle myself at one
place." The Mother replied, "How is that? Wherever you live, you
must feel quite at home. You think that you will be happy at your husband's place. How is that possible? He gets a small salary. How can you
manage with such a pittance? You are staying with me. It is just like
your father's place. Married girls sometimes live with their parents, do
they not? Can't you practice renunciation a little?"

Yogin-Ma was then standing by the window, and I was talking to
her. The Mother said, "Come in. I seldom see you nowadays." Yogin-
Ma laughed and entered the room. Her foot touched my body. As she
was about to salute me with folded hands, I interrupted her and prostrated myself before her. "What is this, Yogin-Ma?" said I. "I am not
even fit to take the dust of your feet. Why should you salute me if your
foot touched my body?" In reply Yogin-Ma said, "Why not? A snake,
whether big or small, is a snake all the same. You are all devotees and
therefore worthy of our respect." I looked at the Mother. The same
compassionate smile lit her face. I took leave of her late at night.

July 28, 1918

It was evening when I visited the Holy Mother at her Baghbazar home. Just before the evening service, an elderly widow came and saluted the Mother by placing her head on the feet of the Mother. The Mother was greatly annoyed and said, "Why do you touch the feet with the head? I am not doing well at all. This sort of thing makes me worse." The Holy Mother washed her feet after the widow had left the place.

Later, while I was rubbing the Mother's body with medicated oil, the conversation drifted to Lalit Babu, a great householder devotee.

Devotee: He was at one time fatally ill. But I heard that he recovered through your grace.

Mother: He had many unfulfilled desires. He was very seriously ill with dropsy and was on the point of death. He said to me in a very plaintive voice, "Mother, I have a great desire to build temples and hospitals at Kamarpukur and Jayrambati. But this great desire is not going to be fulfilled." Ah, Sri Ramakrishna saved his life that time. Now he wants to carry out his plans. Let him try. He has bought a tank for me.

July 30, 1918

Swami Premananda, a disciple of Sri Ramakrishna, passed away in the evening. I went to see the Mother at dusk.

Mother: Come in, my child. Take your seat. Today my Baburam [Swami Premananda] has passed away. I have been weeping since morning.

She again burst into tears.

Mother: Baburam was dearest to my heart. The strength, devotion, rationality, and all the virtues of the Belur Math were embodied in him. He was the very light of the Math. His mother was a poor woman. She inherited her father's property, and she became a little proud of it. She herself confessed it to me and

said, "I had some gold ornaments, and I thought of the world as
a mere mud puddle." She left behind four children. The fifth
one she lost before her own death.

After a while I saw the Holy Mother placing her head at the feet of the
picture of Sri Ramakrishna hung on the southern wall of the room and
uttering in a heartrending voice, "Lord, you have taken away my
Baburam!" I could hardly restrain my tears. Golap-Ma was also seriously ill with blood dysentery. She was almost on her deathbed.

July 31, 1918

It was half past seven in the evening. The Holy Mother was seated in
the shrine room. This day, too, her conversation turned on the late
Swami Premananda. She said, "My child, in the body of Baburam
there was neither flesh nor blood after his last illness. It was a mere
skeleton." Chandra Babu came to the room and joined in our talk. He
told the Mother that some devotees gave sandalwood, butter, flowers,
incense, etc., worth four or five hundred rupees for the cremation of
the swami's body.

> *Mother: Their money is, indeed, blessed. They have spent it for*
> *a devotee. God has given them abundantly and will give them*
> *more.*

Chandra Babu left the room.

> *Mother: Listen, my child. However spiritual a man may be, he*
> *must pay the tax for the use of the body to the last farthing.*[14]
> *But the difference between a great soul and an ordinary man is*
> *this: the latter weeps while leaving this body, whereas the for-*
> *mer laughs. Death seems to him a mere play.*
> *Ah, my dear Baburam came to Sri Ramakrishna while he was a*
> *mere boy. Sri Ramakrishna used to make great fun with the*
> *boys. Naren [Swami Vivekananda] and Baburam would roll*
> *on the ground with sidesplitting laughter. While living in the*

Cossipore garden, I was once climbing the steps, carrying a
pitcher with five pounds of milk. I felt giddy, and the milk
spilled on the ground. My heels were dislocated. Naren and
Baburam ran there and took care of me. There was a great
inflammation of the feet. Sri Ramakrishna heard of the accident and said to Baburam, "Well, Baburam, it is a nice mess I
am now in. Who will cook my food? Who will feed me now?"
He was then ill with cancer in the throat and lived only on farina
pudding. I used to make it and feed him in his room in the
upper story of the house. I had, then, a ring in my nose. Sri
Ramakrishna touched his nose and made the sign of the ring by
describing a circle with his finger, in order to indicate me. He
then said, "Baburam, can you put her (making the sign) in a
basket and carry her on your shoulder to this room?" Naren
and Baburam were convulsed with sidesplitting laughter. Thus
he used to cut jokes with them. After three days the swelling
subsided. Then they helped me to go upstairs with his meals.
Baburam used to tell his mother, "How little you love me! Do
you love me as Sri Ramakrishna does?" "How foolish!" she
would reply, "I am your mother, and I do not love you? What
do you mean?" Such was the depth of Sri Ramakrishna's love.
While four years old, Baburam would say, "I will not marry,
or else I will die." When Sri Ramakrishna was suffering from
cancer in the throat and could not swallow his food, he said
one day, "I shall eat later on in my subtle body through a million mouths." Baburam, replying, said, "I do not care for your
million mouths or your subtle body. What I want is that you
should eat through this mouth and that I should see this gross
body."
Sri Ramakrishna never accepted anyone with numerous children.
A man begetting twenty-five children! What a shame! Is he a
man? No self-control! He is a veritable beast!

Golap-Ma had been suffering from an attack of blood dysentery. She was slightly better today. The doctor observed that it would take three months to be cured completely.

> Mother: *Blood dysentery is not a simple disease. Sri Ramakrishna would often be down with that disease. It happened frequently during the rainy season. At one time he was rather seriously ill. I used to attend on him. A woman from Benares had come to Dakshineswar. She suggested a remedy. I followed her directions and the Master was soon cured. The woman could not be seen anymore. I never met her again. She had really helped me a great deal. I inquired about her at Benares but could not find her. We have often seen that whenever Sri Ramakrishna felt the need, people would come of themselves to Dakshineswar and then disappear just as suddenly.*
>
> *I also suffered from dysentery, my child. The body became a mere skeleton. I would lay myself down near the tank. One day I saw my reflection in the water and noticed that all that remained of my body was only a few bones. I thought, "Dear me, what is the use of this body? Let me give it up. Let me leave it here." A woman came and said, "Hallo, Mother! Why are you here? Come, let us go home." She took me home.*

Late at night, I took my leave of the Holy Mother.

August 1, 1918

Today I found the Mother alone and therefore had a long talk with her. Our conversation mainly drifted to the monastic disciples of Sri Ramakrishna. Perhaps, on account of the passing away of Swami Premananda, the Mother had been continually thinking of these monks.

> Mother: *Sri Ramakrishna accepted his disciples after thoroughly examining them. What an austere life they led at the*

Baranagore monastery after his passing away. Niranjan [Swami Niranjanananda] and others often starved themselves. They spent all their time in meditation and prayer. One day, these young monks were talking among themselves: "We have renounced everything in the name of Sri Ramakrishna. Let us see if he would supply us with food if we simply depend upon him. We will not tell anybody about our wants. We will not go out for begging." They covered their bodies with sheets of cloth and sat down for meditation. The whole day passed. It was late at night. They heard somebody knocking at the door. Naren left the seat and asked one of his brother monks, "Please open the door and see who is there. First of all, notice if he has anything in his hand." As soon as the door was opened, it was found that a man was standing there. He had brought some delicious food from the temple of Gopala on the bank of the Ganges. They were exceedingly happy and felt convinced of the protecting hand of Sri Ramakrishna. They offered that food to Sri Ramakrishna at that late hour of the night and partook of the prasad. *Such things happened many a time....*

Now the monks do not experience any such difficulty. Alas, what hardship Naren and Baburam passed through. Even my Rakhal, who is now the president of the Ramakrishna Mission, had to cleanse the pots and kettles many a day. At one time Naren was traveling as an itinerant monk in northern India. He did not get any food for two days and was lying down under a tree. He found a man standing near him with delicious food and a jar of water in his hands. The man said, "Here is the prasad of Rama. Please accept it." Naren said, "You do not know me, my good friend. You have made a mistake. Perhaps you have brought these articles for someone else." The man said with the utmost humility, "No, revered sir. I have

brought this food solely for you. I was enjoying a little nap at
noontime when I saw a man in a dream. He said, 'Get up
quickly. A holy man is lying under the tree over there. Give
him some food.' I dismissed the whole thing as a mere dream.
Therefore I turned on my side and again fell asleep. Then I
again dreamed of the man, who said, giving me a push, 'I am
asking you to get up, and still you are sleeping? Carry out my
order without any more delay.' Then I thought that it was not
an illusory dream. It was the command of Rama. Therefore in
obedience to his command I brought these articles for you, sir."
Naren realized that it was all due to the grace of Sri
Ramakrishna and cheerfully accepted the food.

A similar incident happened another day. Naren was traveling
in the Himalayas for three days without any food. He was
about to faint when a Muslim fakir gave him a cucumber. It
saved his life that time. After his return from America, Naren
was one day addressing a meeting at Almora. He saw that
Muslim seated in a corner. Naren at once went to him, took
him by the hand, and made him sit in the center of the gather-
ing. The audience was surprised. Naren said, "This gentleman saved my life once." He then narrated the whole
incident. He also gave the fakir some money, but at first the
fakir refused to accept the gift. He said, "What have I done
that you are so anxious to make me a gift?" Naren did not
yield and pressed some money into his pocket.

Naren took me to the Belur Math at the time of the first Durga
Puja festival and through me gave twenty-five rupees to the
priest as his fee. They spent fourteen hundred rupees on that
auspicious occasion. The place became crowded with people.
The monks worked hard. Naren came to me and said,
"Mother, please make me lie down with fever." No sooner had
he said this than he was laid down with a severe attack of

fever. I thought, "Goodness gracious, what is this? How will he be cured?" "Do not be anxious, Mother," said Naren, "I have myself begged for this fever. My reason is this. The boys are working hard. But if I see the slightest mistake, I shall fly into a rage and abuse them. I may even give them slaps. It will be painful to them as well as to me. Therefore I thought it would be better to lie down with fever for some time." When the day's function was over, I came to him and said, "Dear child, the work is over now. Please get up." Naren said that he was all right and got up from bed.

Naren also brought his own mother to the Math at the time of the Durga Puja. She roamed from one garden to another and picked chilies, eggplants, etc. She felt a little proud, thinking that it was all due to her son, Naren. Naren came to her and said, "What are you doing there? Why do you not go and meet the Holy Mother? You are simply picking up these vegetables. Maybe you are thinking that your son has done all this work. No, mother. You are mistaken. It is he who has done all this. Naren is nothing." Naren meant that the Math was founded through the grace of Sri Ramakrishna. What great devotion....

My Baburam is dead! Alas, who will look after the Durga Puja this year?

August 6, 1918

When I went today to see the Holy Mother, I found her in the porch, absorbed in meditation. Some time afterward, five or six women devotees came to her to pay their respects. They prostrated themselves before the image of Sri Ramakrishna in the shrine room. The Mother asked them about themselves. Nalini introduced them. One of them had come to Calcutta for treatment. The doctor had diagnosed her trouble as a tumor in the abdomen and had asked her to be operated on.

She was extremely nervous about the operation. The Holy Mother did not allow any of them to touch her feet. I do not know the reason. They begged her again and again to let them take the dust of her feet. The Mother firmly asked them to bow to her from a distance. They pointed to the sick girl and said, "Please bless her so that she may be cured. May she be able to pay her respects to you again." The Mother answered them, saying, "Bow down before Sri Ramakrishna and pray to him sincerely. He is everything." The Holy Mother appeared to be restive and said to them, "Goodbye, my children. It is getting late for you."

After they had left, the Mother said, "Please sweep the room and sprinkle it with Ganges water. It is now time for food-offering for the Lord." Her order was at once carried out.

She lay down on the bed and gave me a fan.

Mother: My child, please fan me a little. The whole body is burning. My salutation to your Calcutta! People come here and lay before me the catalogue of their sorrows. Again there are others who have committed many sinful acts. There are still others who have procreated twenty-five children! They weep because ten of them are dead! Are they human beings? No! They are veritable beasts. No self-control! No restraint! It is therefore that Sri Ramakrishna used to say, "One seer of milk mixed with five seers of water! It is so difficult to thicken such milk. My eyes have become swollen by constantly blowing the fire to keep it burning. Where are my sincere children who are ready to renounce everything for God? Let them come to me. Let me talk to them. Otherwise life is so unbearable."

These words are so true. Please move the fan, dear child. People have been streaming here today since four o'clock in the afternoon. I cannot bear the misery of people anymore.

The wife of Balaram also came here today. She is the sister of my Baburam. She wept bitterly for him. She said, "Was he only an ordinary brother to me? He was a veritable God."

August 14, 1918

I found the Holy Mother engaged in conversation with a widow, the sister of Dr. Durgapada Babu. The doctor's sister had become widowed at an early age. There were some troubles regarding the property left by her husband. She could not secure the probate of the will. They were talking about these things, and at last the Holy Mother said to the widow, "As you have no right to sell the property, I would advise you to place it under the care of a good man. A worldly-minded person can never be trusted in money matters. Only a real monk can resist the temptation of money. Please do not worry so much, my child. Let the will of God be done. You have been following the right path. The Lord will never put you to any difficulty. Goodbye. Write to me now and then, and come again."

After the widow had left, Shyamadas, the Ayurvedic physician, came to see Golap-Ma. The Holy Mother waited a while for him, but when she found that he had left the house, she lay down on her bed and, looking at me, said, "Now do your duty." I began to rub her body with the medicated oil.

> *Mother: The sister of Girish Ghosh was very fond of me. She would always keep apart for me a little of all the articles of food she cooked at home and send them here. A brahmin would bring them, and she would sit by me as I ate them. Her love for me was deep. She had been married in an aristocratic family and owned considerable wealth, but her relatives had squandered away the money. Atul, the brother of Girish, started a business with five thousand rupees. Besides, she had had to spend a large amount of money for her husband's illness, which lasted for a year. In her will, she expressed her desire to leave a hundred rupees for me. While alive, she was ashamed to give me this amount. She thought one hundred rupees was too small an amount! After her passing, her brother came here and gave it to me. She had come to see me on the day previous to the*

Durga Puja. As long as she stayed, she never left me even for a second. I planned to go to Benares immediately after the Durga Puja. I was a little busy arranging my things and was moving from room to room. At last she said, "May I take my leave now?" I was a little absent-minded and said, "Yes, go." She hurried down the stairs. As soon as she left, I said to myself, "What a foolish thing have I done! Did I say to her, 'Go'?"[15] *Never before did I say such a thing to anybody. And, alas, she never came back.*[16] *I do not know why such words came out of my mouth.*

I went to the Udbodhan Office in the evening. The Mother was lying in bed. Radhu also was lying by her side on another mat and was pressing her to tell a story. The Mother asked me to tell one instead. I was in a quandary. I did not know what to say. I knew the story of Mirabai, the great Vaishnava saint. I narrated it. As I recited the song of Mirabai that ends in the line "God cannot be realized without love," the Mother cried out in an exalted mood, "Yes, it is very true. Nothing can be achieved without sincere love." But Radhu did not appreciate the story very much. Sarala at last came to my rescue. She told a story from the fairy tales. That pleased Radhu. The Holy Mother was very fond of Sarala. She had to nurse Golap-Ma, who was ill, and so left the room after a while. Then Radhu asked me to massage her feet, but she was not pleased with my doing so and requested me to give her a harder massage. The Mother said, "Sri Ramakrishna taught me the art of massaging by massaging my own body. Let me see your hand." I stretched out my hand toward her. She showed me how to massage. Radhu fell asleep very soon. The Mother said, "The mosquitoes are biting my feet. Please pass your hand gently over them." She was quiet for a while and then said, "This year is a very bad one for the Belur Math. Baburam, Devavrata, and Sachin have passed away."

I had heard that Swami Brahmananda had seen disembodied spirits in the Udbodhan Office a few days before the death of Devavrata Maharaj. I asked her about the incident.

Mother: *Please talk softly, my child; otherwise they will be frightened. Sri Ramakrishna also often saw many such spirits. One day he had been to the garden house of Benipal with Rakhal. He was strolling in the garden when a spirit came to him and said, "Why did you come here? We are being scorched. We cannot endure your presence. Leave this place at once." How could it stand his purity and blazing holiness? He left the place with a smile. He did not disclose this to anybody. Immediately after supper he asked someone to call for a carriage, though it had been previously arranged that he would spend the night there. A carriage was brought, and he returned to Dakshineswar that very night. I heard the sound of the wheels near the gate. I strained my ears and heard Sri Ramakrishna speaking with Rakhal. I was startled. I thought, "I do not know if he has taken his supper. If not, from where can I get any food at the dead of night?" I always used to keep something in the store for him, at least farina. He would ask for food at odd hours. I had been quite sure of his not coming back that night, and so my store was empty. All the gates of the temple garden were barred and locked. It was one o'clock in the morning. He clapped his hands and began to repeat the names of God. The entrance gate was opened. I was thinking anxiously what to do about his food in case he was hungry. He shouted to me, "Don't be anxious about my food. I have finished my supper." Then he narrated to Rakhal the story of the ghost. Rakhal was startled and said, "Dear me, it was really wise of you not to have told me about it at that time.*

Otherwise my teeth would have been set on edge through fear.
Even now I am seized with fear."

The Mother ended the story with a hearty laugh.

Devotee: *Mother, those spirits must have been foolish. Instead of*
asking him for their liberation, they told him to go away.

Mother: *They will, no doubt, be liberated. His presence cannot be*
in vain. Once Naren liberated a disembodied spirit in Madras.

I narrated one of my dreams to the Mother.

Devotee: *Mother, I once dreamed that I was going to some place*
with my husband. We came to a river, the other bank of which
could not be seen. We were going by the shady track along the
river when a golden creeper so entwined my arms that I could
not free them from it. From the other side of the river came a
dark-complexioned boy with a ferryboat. He said, "Cut off the
creeper from your arm, and then only will I take you across the
river." I cut off almost the whole creeper, but the last bit I could
not get rid of. In the meantime my husband also disappeared. In
despair I said to the boy, "I cannot get rid of this bit. You must
take me to the other side." With these words I jumped into the
boat. It sailed and my dream vanished.

Mother: *The boy whom you have seen is none other than*
Mahamaya, the great cosmic illusionist. She took you across
the waters of the world in that form. Everything—husband,
wife, or even the body—is only illusory. These are all shackles
of illusion. Unless you can free yourself from these bondages,
you will never be able to go to the other shore of the world.
Even this attachment to the body, the identification of the self
with the body, must go. What is this body, my darling? It is
nothing but three pounds of ashes when it is cremated. Why so
much vanity about it? However strong or beautiful this body
may be, its culmination is in those three pounds of ashes. And
still people are so attached to it. Glory be to God!

> *Once I spent a couple of months at Kailwar in the District of Arah. It is a very healthy place. Golap-Ma, Baburam's mother, Balaram's wife, and others were with me. The country abounded in deer. A herd of them would roam about in the form of a triangle. No sooner had we seen them than they fled away like birds. I had never before seen anything running so swiftly. Sri Ramakrishna would say, "Musk forms in the navel of the deer. Being fascinated with its smell, the deer run hither and thither. They do not know where the fragrance comes from. Likewise, God resides in the human body, and man does not know it. Therefore he searches everywhere for bliss, not knowing that it is already in him." God alone is real. All else is false. What do you say, my child?*

The Holy Mother had pimples all over her body. She said, "I have been suffering from this ailment for the last three years. I do not know for whose sins I have been suffering in this body. Otherwise, how is it possible for me to get any disease?"

August 22, 1918

It was evening when I went to see the Holy Mother. She was lying on a mat on the floor near her couch. I prostrated myself before her and asked her in the course of our conversation, "Mother, it is a long time since I have been to our home at Kalighat. Should I go there now?"

> *Mother: Why don't you stay here for a few days more? Once you go to Kalighat, you will not be able to come here so frequently. If you fail to come for one day, I become very anxious. You were not here yesterday. I was worried to think that you might be unwell. If you had failed to come today, I would have sent someone to inquire about you. But if your husband is ailing, if you think that he wants your presence there, then you will have to go to Kalighat.*

When I told her that there was no such difficulty and that all I feared was popular criticism for staying too long with my sister, she asked me not to mind it and advised me to stay on at Calcutta for a month more. A *brahmachari* came up and said to the Mother that a certain woman devotee wanted to see her. The Mother was dead tired and lay on her bed. She was evidently annoyed and said, "Dear me, am I to see another person? I shall die!" She sat on her bed. A little later, a well-dressed woman entered the room and bowed down to her, touching the Mother's feet with her head.

"You could salute from a distance," said the Mother. "Why do you touch the feet?" The Mother asked her about her welfare.

> Devotee: You know, Mother, that my husband has been ailing
> for some time past.
> Mother: Yes, I have heard of that. How is he now? What is the
> trouble with him? Who is treating him?
> Devotee: He has been suffering from diabetes. His feet have
> swollen. The doctors say that it is a dangerous disease. But I
> do not care for their opinions. You must cure him, Mother.
> Please say that he will be cured.
> Mother: I do not know anything, my child. The Master is every-
> thing. If he wills, your husband will be all right. I shall pray to
> the Master for him.
> Devotee: I am now very happy, Mother. Sri Ramakrishna can
> never disregard your prayer.

She began to weep, putting her head on the feet of the Holy Mother. The Mother consoled her.

> Mother: Pray to the Master. He will cure your husband. What
> is his diet now?
> Devotee: He takes luchi and such other things as are prescribed
> by the physician.

She soon took leave of the Holy Mother and went to see Swami Saradananda.

"I am burning day and night with the pain and misery of others," said the Mother, and she took off the cloth from her body. I was about to rub her body with the medicated oil when a relative of the woman devotee who had just left entered the room to salute her. She had to get up again. No sooner had he left the room than the Holy Mother lay down again and said, "Let anybody come. Whoever he may be, I am not going to get up again. What a trouble it is, my child, to get up again and again with my aching feet. Besides, I feel the burning sensation on my whole back, caused by pimples. Please rub the oil well."

As I was rubbing the oil, the talk turned to the woman who had left. The Mother said, "Her husband is so dangerously ill. She has come here to pray to God for his recovery. Instead of being prayerful and penitent, she has covered herself with perfumes. Does this become one who comes to a shrine? Ah, such is the nature of your modern people!"

As I was going to take leave of her, the Mother asked someone to give me *prasad*.

August 23, 1918

I went to see the Mother in the evening. Referring to a woman devotee, she was saying, "She imposes very strict discipline upon her daughter-in-law. She should not go to such excess. Though she has to keep an eye upon her, she should also give her a little freedom. She is only a young girl. Naturally she likes to enjoy some nice things. If the lady becomes overstrict, she may go away from home or even commit suicide. What can she do then?" Looking at me, she said, "She had painted her feet a little. Is it a crime to do so? Alas, she cannot even see her husband. The husband has become a monk. I saw my husband with my own eyes, nursed him, cooked for him, and went near him whenever he permitted me."

Another day I had been to the Holy Mother's place when a monk came and prostrated before her.

Monk: Mother, why does the mind become so restless every now and then? Why can't I constantly meditate on you? Many worthless thoughts disturb my mind. Useless things we can easily obtain if we simply want them. Shall I never realize the Lord? Mother, please tell me how I can attain peace. Nowadays I seldom have visions. What is the use of this life if I cannot realize him? It is better to die than to lead such a worthless life.

Mother: What are you talking of, my child? Do not even think of such things. Can one have the vision of God every day? Sri Ramakrishna used to say, "Does an angler catch a big carp every day the moment he sits with his rod? Arranging everything about him, he sits with the rod and concentrates. Once in a while a big carp swallows the hook. Many a time he is disappointed. Don't relax the practices for that reason. Do more japa [repetition of the name of God].

Yogin-Ma: Yes, that is true. The name is identical with Brahman. Even if the mind is not concentrated at the outset, you will succeed ultimately.

Monk: Please tell me, Mother, how many times I should repeat the name. That may help me to get concentration.

Mother: Ten thousand times, or even twenty thousand times, or as many times as you can.

Monk: One day, Mother, I was kneeling in the shrine and weeping when I suddenly saw you standing by my side. You said to me, "What do you want?" "I want your grace, Mother," I replied, "as you bestowed it on King Suratha."[17] Then I added, "No, Mother, that was done by you as Durga. I do not care for that form. I want to see you as you are at present." With a smile you disappeared. My mind became all the more restless. Now nothing satisfies me. Often I think, "If I cannot realize her, then what is the use of this life?"

Mother: *Why are you so restless, my child? Why don't you stick to what you have received? Always remember, "I have at least a Mother, if none else." Do you remember those words of Sri Ramakrishna? He said he would reveal himself to all who take shelter under him—reveal himself at least on their last day. He will draw all unto him.*

Monk: *I have been staying with a householder who is a great devotee. His wife comes from a very aristocratic family. She spends much money for me.*

Mother: *Ask her not to spend much money for you. The money of the devoted householders is for the benefit of the monks. Their money enables the monks to stay at a place for four months together during the rainy season. It is very inconvenient for them to go out [at that time] for begging.*

The monk prostrated himself before the Mother and left the room.

September 3, 1918

I was in indifferent health for a few days. When I felt better, I went to see the Holy Mother one evening. In the course of conversation the Mother began to speak of Sri Ramakrishna.

Mother (to me): *What a good time of it we had yesterday. Sarala read about Sri Ramakrishna. How fine his teachings were. How could we know then that things would take this turn? What a great soul was born! How many people are illumined by his words! He was the embodiment of bliss itself. All the twenty-four hours of the day were devoted to devotional music, merriment, laughter, teaching, and storytelling. So far as I remember, I never saw him worried by anything. Often he would tell me nice words of advice. If I had known how to write, I would have noted them down. Well, Sarala, please read something today.*

Sarala began to read from the *Kathamrita*.

> Mother: Do you notice those words, which he addressed to
> Rakhal's father: "A good apple tree begets only good apples"?
> In this way he would satisfy him. When he came to
> Dakshineswar, Sri Ramakrishna would carefully feed him with
> delicious things. He was afraid lest he should take the boy
> away. Rakhal had a stepmother. When the father came there,
> he would say to Rakhal, "Show him everything. Take good
> care of him."

Sarala was now reading about Brinde, the maidservant.

> Mother: She was by no means an easy woman. A fixed number
> of luchis was set aside for her lunch. She would be extremely
> abusive if that was found wanting. She would say, "Look at
> these sons of gentlemen! They have eaten my share also. I do
> not get even a little of the sweets." Sri Ramakrishna was afraid
> lest those words should reach the ears of the young devotees.
> One day, early in the morning, he came to the Nahabat and
> said, "Well, I have given Brinde's luchis to others. Please pre-
> pare some for her. Otherwise she would indulge in abuse. One
> must avoid wicked persons." As soon as Brinde came, I said to
> her, "Well, Brinde, there is no lunch for you today. I am just
> preparing luchis." She said, "That's all right. Please do not
> take the trouble. You may give me raw foodstuffs." I gave her
> flour, butter, potato, and other vegetables.

After finishing a chapter, Sarala went away to attend Golap-Ma, who
was ill.

The Holy Mother began to speak in a low voice.

> Mother: Do you notice this human body? Today it is, and
> tomorrow it is not. And this world is full of misery and pain;
> why should one worry about taking another birth? The body is
> never free from its accompanying troubles. The other day Bilas
> said to me, "Mother, we are to be always very alert. We

*always tremble with fear lest we should think any unholy
thought." That is very true. A monk is like a bleached cloth,
and the householder is like a black one. One does not notice
the spots in a black cloth so much, but even a drop of ink looks
so prominent on white linen. The monk's life is always beset
with dangers. The whole world is engrossed in lust and gold.
The monk must always practice renunciation and dispassion.
Therefore Sri Ramakrishna used to say, "A monk must be
always alert and careful."*

In the meantime Harihar Maharaj came to the shrine for offering food.
Pointing to him, the Mother said to me, "Look at this child who has
renounced the world. He has left everything behind in the name of Sri
Ramakrishna."

*Mother: The worldly men beget children without number, as if
that is their only duty in this world. Sri Ramakrishna used to
say, "One must practice self-control after the birth of one or
two children." I have heard that the Englishman begets children
according to the amount of his property. After the birth of the
children they want, the husband and wife live separately, each
one busy with his or her own work. And look at our race!*

*(with a smile) Yesterday a young woman came to see me. She
had a lot of children, some hanging from her back and some
clinging to her arms. She could hardly manage them. Can you
imagine what she told me? She said, "Mother, I do not at all
enjoy this worldly life." I said, "How is that, my child? You
have got so many young ones." She replied, "That is the end of
it. I will not have them anymore." I said, "It would be well if
you could carry out your intention."*

The Mother began to laugh.

*Devotee: Well, Mother, according to our Hindu conception, the
husband is our most adorable guru. The scriptures say that by
serving him, one can go to heaven and even be united with*

God. Now, if a wife, somewhat against the will of the husband, tries to practice self-control through prayer and spiritual
pursuits, is she committing a sin?

Mother: Certainly not. Whatever you do for the realization of
God cannot have any sinful effect. Self-control is absolutely
necessary. All the hard disciplines enjoined upon Hindu
widows are meant to help them practice self-control. All the
acts of Sri Ramakrishna were directed to God alone. He once
performed the Shodasi Puja, making me the object of worship.
I asked him what I should do with the bangles, the clothes, and
other articles of worship. After a little thought, he said that I
could give them all away to my mother. My father was alive
then. Sri Ramakrishna said to me, "When you present your
mother with these articles, don't think that she is an ordinary
human being. Think of her as the direct embodiment of the
Divine Mother of the universe." I acted accordingly. That was
the nature of his teaching.

September 4, 1918

The Mother was seated on her meditation carpet, counting beads. The
evening service was over. A woman devotee, a sister-in-law of the
Mother, came there and said to her, "Please set my mind right. I am
full of worries. I do not wish even to live for a day. I shall make a will
and leave all my property to you. After my death, you execute my
will." The Mother laughed and said, "When are you going to die?"
Suddenly, she became grave and reprimanded her for her foolish
thoughts, which she attributed to a heated brain and idle life.

Looking at me, the Mother smiled and said: "Do you notice, my
child, the inscrutable play of Sri Ramakrishna? Look at my own relatives.
See the evil company I am in. One is already mad, and this one also is
verging on insanity. And look at the third one. How much care I took

to train her up, but all to no effect. She does not have the slightest trace of wisdom. Look there. She is standing in the porch, leaning against the railing and wistfully looking forward to the return of her husband. She is afraid that her husband may enter the house where that music is going on. Day and night she has been trying to keep him within her sight. What an inordinate attachment! I could never dream that she would be so much attached."

The woman relative of the Mother left the place with a sorrowful air, and she lay down on her bed.

> Mother: My child, you have been extremely fortunate in getting this human birth. Have intense devotion to God. One must work hard. How can one achieve anything without effort? You must devote some time for prayer, even in the midst of the busiest hours of the day. I used to be very busy during my days at Dakshineswar; yet I did my prayer and meditation.... Let my sister-in-law, who complains of mental worry, do likewise. Let her get up from bed at three o'clock in the morning and sit in the porch adjoining my room for meditation. Let me see whether she can still have any worry of mind. She will not, however, do that but only talk about her troubles. What is her suffering? I never knew, my child, what mental worry was. But now I have been suffering day and night for my relatives. It was an unlucky time when this sister-in-law came to our family; all my sufferings are due to my efforts to bring up her daughter Radhu. Let them all go away. I do not want anybody. Just look at these girls. They never listen to me. Such disobedient women!

> Golap-Ma: Just see how they decorate their bodies. They think that is how they will get the love of their husbands.

> Mother: Ah, how kindly Sri Ramakrishna treated me! Not even one day did he utter a word to wound my feelings. He would tell me, "One should always be active. One should

never be without work. For when one is idle, all sorts of bad
thoughts crop up in one's mind."

My child, this mind is just like a wild elephant. It races with the
wind. Therefore one should discriminate all the time. One should
work hard for the realization of God. What a wonderful mind I
had at that time. Somebody used to play on the flute at night at
Dakshineswar. As I listened to the sound my mind would be
extremely eager for the realization of God. I thought the sound
was coming directly from God, and I would enter into samadhi.
I experienced the same ecstasy at Belur, also. The place was then
very peaceful, and I was constantly in a mood of meditation.
Therefore Naren intended to build a house there for me. The
land on which this house stands was given by Kedar Das. But
now the price of land has soared high; it is impossible to purchase
a place now. All this has been done through the grace of God.

Just at that time, Maku, her niece, entered the room with her child in
her arms and left the boy there, saying, "Mother, what shall I do? He
does not sleep at all." The Mother said, "The child has the quality of
sattva; therefore he does not sleep."

The Mother had been suffering terribly from the pain caused by
pimples. At her bidding, I rubbed her with medicated oil.

One day the Mother was seated upstairs in the northern porch of her
house. She was still suffering terribly from pimples, which had per-
sisted for so many days. She said that that was because of several devotees touching her and their sins being transferred to her in the form of
illness. The conversation then turned to Sri Ramakrishna.

Mother: Once when Sri Ramakrishna was lying ill at Cossipore,
a few devotees brought some offerings for Mother Kali of the

Dakshineswar temple. On hearing that the Master was at Cossipore, they offered all the things they had brought before a picture of the Master and then partook of the prasad. On hearing about this Sri Ramakrishna remarked, "All these things were brought for the great Mother of the universe. And they have offered them all here [meaning himself]!" I was frightened very much at this and thought, "He is suffering from this dangerous disease. Who knows what might happen?" What a calamity! Why did they do it?[18]

The Master too referred to this incident again and again. Afterwards, at a late hour in the night, he said to me, "You will see how in course of time I will be worshiped in every house. You will see everyone accepting this [meaning himself]. This is surely going to happen." This was the only day I heard him using the first personal pronoun with reference to himself. Usually he would speak of himself not as "I" or "me" but as "case" or as "belonging to this," pointing to his body.

After the Master's passing, there was a quarrel as to who should get possession of some of the valuable things like his woolen wrapper, shawl, and other garments. After all, it is the devotees who would look upon them as invaluable possessions and preserve them for all time. And it was they who finally gathered them in a box and kept them in the drawing room of Balaram Babu's house. But, O my daughter, who knew the Master's will? In Balaram Babu's house a servant stole away most of the things and either sold them or disposed of them in some other way. It was not proper to keep such things in the drawing room of a house. They ought to have been kept in the inner apartments of the house. What was left of those garments and other things of the Master is now being preserved at the Belur Math.

My father-in-law [Sri Ramakrishna's father] was a pious and spirited brahmin. He never received gifts from anyone. He even prohibited his people from accepting any gift brought to his house in his absence. But as regards my mother-in-law, if anyone made a private gift to her, she would accept it, cook it, offer it to the deity, and then give it to others as prasad. My father-in-law used to get angry if he happened to know it. He possessed a burning devotion. That was why the Master was born in his family.

A woman named Hari Dasi wanted to go on a pilgrimage to Navadvip. She did not, however, actually reach there but stopped at Kamarpukur. She loved me very much. She was a woman of great faith. She kept with her some dust gathered from the Master's birthplace and would remark, "This itself is my Navadvip. Gauranga himself was born here. Why should I then go to Navadvip?" What a tremendous faith!

After the Master's passing, a sadhu, hailing from Orissa, was staying at Kamarpukur. I used to give him rice, pulses, and other necessaries. I used to visit him both morning and evening and ask, "Revered sir, how do you do?" Ah, with what great difficulty I built a thatched hut for him. Every day the sky would be overcast with clouds, and it would seem as if it were going to rain just then. I would therefore pray with folded hands, "O Lord, wait a while, wait a while. Let me finish the cottage, and then let it rain in torrents if necessary." The people of the village helped me in the work by giving timber, straw, and other necessary materials. Somehow the cottage was completed, but unfortunately it so happened that a few days after, the sadhu passed away in that cottage.

Sri Ramakrishna used to say that his body had come from Gaya. When his mother passed away, he asked me to offer pindam [funeral cakes] at Gaya. I replied I was not entitled to perform those rites when the son himself was alive. The Master replied, "No, no, you are entitled to do it. Under no circumstances *can I go to Gaya. If I go, do you think it will be possible for me to return?*"[19] So I did not want him to go there. And later on, I performed the rites at Gaya.

September 28, 1918

It was morning when I went to the Udbodhan Office. The Holy Mother was peeling fruits for worship. As soon as her eyes fell on me, she said, "I am so glad to see you here. It is the day of the Bodhan.[20] (I had entirely forgotten about it.) Please arrange these flowers for the worship of Sri Ramakrishna, and keep the fruit tray on this side." I obeyed her orders. I then combed her hair. While I was combing, a number of her hairs came out. The Mother said, "Here they are. Preserve these." I felt myself really blessed. I had a strong desire for some of her hair.

Shyamadas Kaviraj, the celebrated physician, came to examine Radhu. When the examination was over, the Mother asked Radhu to bow before the physician. Radhu did as she was asked. After the physician had left the place, someone inquired, "Is the physician a brahmin?"

Mother: No, he is a vaidya.

Devotee: Why, then, did you ask Radhu to bow down before him?

Mother: Why should I not do so? The physician is so full of wisdom. He is equal to a brahmin. To whom should one bow down if not to him? What do you say, my child?

September 30, 1918

It was the sacred day of the Mahashtami. My sister and I arrived at the Udbodhan Office early in the morning. After a while, a few women devotees brought some flowers. They worshiped the Holy Mother and went to the Ganges for their bath. The Mother asked me, "Will you stay here today? It is the day of the Mahashtami, the second day of the Durga Puja." I answered in the affirmative. A few moments later, revered Sarat Maharaj [Swami Saradananda] came there to salute the Mother. We retired into the next room. The Mother was seated on her bed with her feet resting on the ground. Many devotees came and bowed before her.

Later on, we went to take our bath in the Ganges in the company of Maku and other women devotees. The Mother said she would finish her bath at home, as rheumatism prevented her from bathing in the Ganges every day. After returning, we saw many women devotees worshiping the Holy Mother. Many of them brought new cloths as offerings. After the worship, they wrapped the body of the Mother with the cloths, as they do with the image of Kali at Kalighat. Then she laid the cloths aside, one by one. To some devotees the Mother would say, "It is a nice piece of cloth."

A *brahmacharin* came to the room and said that the men devotees would come now to bow down before the Mother. What an impressive sight! With flowers, full-blown lotuses, and bel leaves in their hands, they came there one by one and, after worship and salutation, went away. Some time passed in this manner. The members of Balaram's family came and worshiped the Holy Mother. I was the last to go to her. After the worship, I wrapped her body with a cloth when she said suddenly, "I will wear this cloth, as today I must put on a new one." She at once put on the cloth given by me. This brought tears to my eyes. After all, it was an ordinary piece of cloth. There were so many costly cloths around her. I was the poor daughter of the Mother. Her excessive affection for me made me bashful. The Mother said, "What a fine border this cloth has."

A woman dressed in an ocher robe worshiped Mother and placed two rupees near her feet. The Mother said, "Goodness, why should you do that? You have just put on the ocher robe. You have *rudraksha* beads on your arm." The Mother asked her about her spiritual teacher.

In reply, the woman said that she had not been initiated. "Without initiation," said the Mother, "and without any spiritual realization, you have put on this sacred robe. This is not proper for you. The robe you have put on is very holy. I was about to salute you with folded hands. All will bow down at your feet. You must acquire the power to assimilate the honor." The woman said, "I have a desire to be initiated by you." The Mother replied, "How is it possible?" But the woman insisted. Golap-Ma supported her. The Mother seemed to yield a little. She said, "We shall think about it."

Gauri-Ma came with the girls of her ashrama. They all worshiped the Mother, took *prasad*, and went away.

After finishing the worship in the shrine room, Bilas Maharaj came there and whispered to the Holy Mother, "I do not know, Mother, if Sri Ramakrishna has accepted the food offering today. An impure leaf, carried by the wind, dropped on the food. Why was it so? Many devotees brought offerings from home. I do not know what has happened." The Mother asked if he had sprinkled the water of the Ganges over the food. He answered in the affirmative and went away. I felt troubled in mind to hear this.

The worship of the Holy Mother went on in the same way. No sooner had one heap of flowers and bel leaves been removed than a fresh pile was formed near her feet.

It was the time of the noonday worship when a party of three men and women from a distant part of the country came to pay their respects to the Holy Mother. They were very poor, all their possessions consisting of one piece of cloth each. They begged their passage to Calcutta. One of the party—a man devotee—was having a private talk with the Mother. There seemed to be no end to the conversation. The time for the noonday worship was passing, and the Mother must perform it. The inmates of the Udbodhan Office became annoyed. One of them said to the devotee in unmistakable language, "If you have anything more to say, you had better come downstairs and talk to the senior monks." But the Mother declared with some firmness, "It does not matter if it gets late. I must hear what they have to say." She continued to listen to him with great patience. In a whisper she gave him some instructions. Then she sent for his wife as well. We inferred that they must have experienced something in a dream. Later on we came to learn that they had received a sacred mantra in a dream. After about an hour they took leave of the Mother. The Mother said, "Alas, they are very poor. They have come here with great hardship."

After the noonday worship, we had our meal. The Holy Mother now wanted to have a little rest, and we retired into the adjoining room.

It was four o'clock in the afternoon. After the worship in the shrine, Rashbehari Maharaj said, "A European woman has come to pay her respects to you. She has been waiting for a long time." The Mother asked him to bring the woman to her. As she bowed down before the Mother, the latter clasped her hand as one does in shaking hands. The words of the Master—that one should behave according to time and circumstance—were verified in this instance. Then she kissed the woman by touching the chin. The latter knew Bengali and said, "I hope I have not inconvenienced you by this visit. I have been waiting for a long time downstairs to see you. I am in great difficulty. My only daughter, a very good girl, is dangerously ill, so I have come here to crave your favor and blessings. Please be gracious to her, so that she may be cured. She is such a nice girl. I praise her because one seldom finds nowadays a good woman among us. I can vouch that many of them are wicked and evil-minded; but my daughter is of quite a different nature. Please be kind to her." The Mother said, "I shall pray for your daughter. She will be cured."

The European woman was much encouraged by this assurance from the Holy Mother and said, "When you say that she will be cured, she shall be cured. There is no doubt about it." She spoke these words thrice with great faith and emphasis. The Mother, with a kindly look, said to Golap-Ma, "Please give her a flower from the altar. Bring a lotus." Golap-Ma brought a lotus with a sacred bel leaf. The Mother took the lotus in her hand and closed her eyes for a few moments. Then she looked wistfully at the image of Sri Ramakrishna and gave the flower to the woman, saying, "Please touch your daughter's head with it." She accepted the flower with folded hands and bowed down before the Mother. "What shall I do with the flower after that?" she asked.

Golap-Ma: *When it is dried, throw it into the Ganges.*

Woman: *No, no! This belongs to God. I cannot throw it away. I shall make a bag out of a new piece of cloth and preserve the flower in it. I shall touch my daughter's head and body every day with it.*

Mother: *Very well, do that.*

Woman: *God is the Supreme Reality. He exists. I want to tell you something. A few days ago, a baby was bedridden with fever in my house. With great fervor I prayed to God, "O Lord, I feel that you exist, but I want an actual demonstration." I wept and laid my handkerchief on the table. After a long time I was surprised to find three sticks in its folds. I gently touched the body of the baby thrice with the three sticks. Soon it was cured of the fever.*

As she narrated the incident, teardrops trickled down her cheeks. She said, "I have taken much of your valuable time. Please forgive me." "No," said the Mother, "I am greatly pleased to talk to you. Come here again on Tuesday." The woman bowed down and took leave of her.

When I went to the Mother a few days after, I learned that the European woman had gone to see her on Tuesday. The Mother had shown her special favor and initiated her. Her daughter, too, was cured of her illness.

March 24, 1920

The Holy Mother had been staying in her country home at Jayrambati. After about a year she returned to Calcutta in the spring. She was extremely unwell, having been in the grip of malarial fever for a long time. I prostrated myself before her, and she blessed me by placing her hand on my head. She asked me how I was. I offered her a little money for her expenses, and she accepted it. At the sight of her emaciated body, I lost all power of speech. I looked at her face wistfully and thought, "Alas, how pale and weak her body is." My sister's maidservant was with me. She was about to touch the Mother's feet in salutation, but she said to her, "You may bow from a distance." The maid bowed from near the doorsill and went away.

The Mother was so weak that she felt it painful even to utter a word. I was seated on the floor. In the meantime, Rashbehari Maharaj came up and asked me not to talk much with her; but the Mother now and then asked me about various things. I gave her very short replies. Then Radhu came with her child. I took him in my arms and gave him some cash as a present. Radhu insisted on his not accepting it. The Mother said, "What is this, Radhu? She is your sister. Why should you not accept the present when she gives it with so much love?" The Mother accepted the money herself. She felt so sorry for the sufferings of the child caused by his mother's and grandmother's negligence. Radhu protested in bitter words. The Mother said, "There is no use talking to her," and kept quiet. After a while, Sarala and a few women devotees came there to see the Mother. She was lying in bed. She began talking with them.

March 30, 1920

I went to pay my respects to the Holy Mother after five or six days. She had had no fever for the previous two or three days, but she was much worried on account of Radhu and her incapacity to look after her little child. Moreover, today Radhu's hand had bumped against an iron railing, and with the swollen hand dressed in a dirty linen soaked in castor oil, she came to the Mother's room to consult Dr. Kanjilal, who had come to examine the Mother.

After Radhu's hand was properly dressed, the Mother lay down on her bed and asked me to rub her feet. While rubbing, I asked her whether I could question her about something and if it would inconvenience her. The Mother said, "No, not at all. Speak what you have to."

I spoke to her about some experience I had had, and at this the Mother remarked, "Ah, my daughter, can one experience such delight everyday? Everything is real. Nothing is untrue. The Master is all—he is Prakriti, he is Purusha. Through him you will achieve everything."

> *Disciple: Mother, one day while doing* japa *with great concentration, a long period of time passed quite unobserved. I therefore had to get up and attend to my household duties without carrying out the other items of spiritual practices that you had instructed me to do. Was it wrong on my part to have done so?*
>
> *Mother: No, no. There is nothing wrong in it.*
>
> *Disciple: Someone told me that while meditating at the dead of night, he hears a mystic sound. Generally he experiences it as coming from the right side of the body; sometimes, when the mind is working on a lower plane, it comes also from the left side.*
>
> *Mother (after thinking a while): Indeed, the sound comes from the right side. Only when there is body-consciousness it comes from the left side. Such things happen when the power of the kundalini is awakened. The sound that comes from the right side is the real one. In time, the mind itself becomes the guru. To pray to God and meditate on God for even two minutes with full concentration is better than doing so for long hours without it.*

I did not feel inclined to question the Mother on the significance of body-consciousness, for the Mother was not doing well.

I was about to take leave. Instantly the Mother raised her head from the pillow and said, "Well, my daughter, I have raised my head." She did so because it is not the custom for a devotee to bow down to one lying down. When I bowed down, she said "Come again. Come a little earlier in the evening. Can't you finish your household duties a little earlier and come?"

Then, uttering the name of Durga as a prayer for my safety, she bade me adieu. Even after I had come to the verandah, I heard her uttering the name of Durga in a compassionate tone. What an unbounded love! So long as we were by her, we forgot all the sorrows and sufferings of worldly life.

The Mother's illness showed no signs of improvement. Her body was getting weaker and weaker. I went to see her one afternoon. She was about to go for her evening wash. She asked me to help her to get up. She said, "I am getting fever very often, and the body has become very weak."

April 14, 1920

The evening *aratrika* in the shrine was over. The Mother had fever. Rashbehari Maharaj was rubbing her hands and Brahmachari Varada her feet. They were taking her temperature, and the Mother was lying with her eyes closed. I stood by her side. Once the Mother asked, "Who is there?" Rashbehari Maharaj replied to her in a low voice. I heard that the temperature was 100.1 degrees.

Sister Sudhira was giving a treat to the girls of the Nivedita School, as it was the New Year's Day. So Sarala, the disciple who was attending the Mother, had gone to the school. The Mother asked Brahmachari Varada to bring Sarala from there; for she had to feed Radhu's child. It was not yet time to feed the child, but as he was weeping, Radhu wanted to feed him just then. The Mother tried to dissuade her. This only enraged Radhu, who began to abuse the Mother. She said, "May you die, and I shall light your funeral pyre!" We were deeply pained to hear this. The Mother was so badly ill, and Radhu was abusing her in such a fashion at that time! Radhu, however, went on shouting out many more abusive words. Such conduct on her part was seen quite frequently. The Mother, who had unbounded patience, would put up with such behavior on all occasions. But this time, because of her protracted illness, she too got annoyed and remarked, "You will realize the consequences of this afterwards! What a sad plight you will be in after my death; you will understand! I do not know how many kicks and thrashings with broomstick are in store for you!"

At this, Radhu became still more irritated and abusive. After a time Sarala arrived and fed the child. The experience of that day cast a gloom over my mind. The Mother asked me to rub her feet.

Just then Rashbehari Maharaj entered the room and began to fit up the mosquito netting. So I took leave of her, and the Mother said by way of bidding farewell, "Come." This was the last command and last word I heard from her.

I had to go to Kalighat that day. Afterward, for several days, I could get no opportunity to visit her because of the illness of many at home and other difficulties. I used to get regular information about her health and came to know that she was sinking day by day. At the earliest opportunity I went to see her, my heart filled with the fear that we were to lose our most precious possession in life very soon. I was, however, still hoping against hope.

Holy Mother at age 52

Swami Arupananda and Sarajubala Devi

3

Conversations from the Diary of a Monastic Disciple, Swami Arupananda

Jayrambati
1909

Uncle Varada said to me, "The Mother has sent for you."

I went inside the inner apartment and found the Holy Mother standing at the door of her room waiting for me. As I saluted her, she asked, "Where do you come from?" I told her the name of the district of my native village.

Mother: I suppose you are now reading the teachings of the Master.

I did not reply to these words. She spoke to me as if we had known each other for a long time. I still remember her tender and affectionate look.

Mother: Do you belong to the Kayastha caste?

Disciple: Yes.

Mother: How many brothers have you?

Disciple: Four.

Mother: Sit down and take some refreshments.

With these words, the Mother spread a small carpet on the floor of the verandah and gave me some luchis and sweets that had been offered in the shrine on the previous night.

I told the Mother that I had walked all the way from Tarakeswar on the previous day, spending the night in the village of Deshra, to the northwest of Jayrambati, in the house of a young man whom I had met at the railway station of Haripal. The Mother listened to all this and said to me after I had finished my refreshments, "Don't bathe now; you have walked a great deal." Then she gave me a betel leaf to chew.

She sent for me again after the noonday worship. After the offerings were over, she first of all served me food. She served it with her own hands, on a shal leaf, on the porch of her room. "Eat well and remember: don't feel shy!" she said to me as I was enjoying the meal. Afterward she gave me a betel leaf.

I went to the Holy Mother again at three or four o'clock in the afternoon and found her kneading dough for bread. She was seated on the floor facing the east, her legs stretched out in front of her. The oven stood near her. Casting a benign glance upon me, she said, "What do you want?"

Disciple: I want to talk to you.

Mother: What do you want to talk about? Sit down here.

She gave me a seat.

Disciple: Mother, people say that our Master is God eternal and absolute. What do you say?

Mother: Yes, he is God eternal and absolute to me.

As she had said "to me," I went on.

Disciple: It is true that to every woman her husband is God eternal and absolute. I am not asking the question in that sense.

Mother: Yes, he is God eternal and absolute to me as my husband, and in a general way as well.

Then I thought that if Sri Ramakrishna were God eternal, then she, the Holy Mother, must be the Divine Power, the Mother of the universe. She must be identical with his divine consort. She and he are like Sita and Rama, Radha and Krishna. I had come to the Holy

Mother cherishing this faith in my heart. I asked her, "If that be the case, then why do I see you preparing bread like an ordinary woman? It is maya, I suppose, is it not?"

> Mother: *It is maya, indeed! Otherwise, why should I fall into such a state? But God loves to sport as a human being. Sri Krishna was born as a cowherd boy and Rama as the child of Dasaratha.*
>
> Disciple: *Do you ever remember your real nature?*
>
> Mother: *Yes, I recall it now and then. At that time I say to myself, "What is this that I am doing? What is all this about?" Then I remember the house, buildings, and children* (pointing with the palm of her hand to the houses), *and forget my real self.*

I used to visit the Mother almost daily in her room. She would lie down on her bed and talk to me, Radhu lying asleep by her side. An oil lamp would cast a dim light in the room. On some days a maidservant rubbed her feet with medicated oil for rheumatism.

One day, she said to me in the course of conversation, "Whenever the thought of a disciple comes to my mind and I yearn to see him, then he either comes here or writes a letter to me. You must have come here prompted by a certain feeling. Perhaps you have in your mind the thought of the Divine Mother of the universe."

> Disciple: *Are you the Mother of all?*
>
> Mother: *Yes.*
>
> Disciple: *Even of these subhuman beings, birds and animals?*
>
> Mother: *Yes, of these also.*
>
> Disciple: *Then why should they suffer so much?*
>
> Mother: *In this birth, they must have these experiences.*

One evening I had the following conversation with the Holy Mother in her room:

> Mother: *You all have come to me, because you are my own.*
>
> Disciple: *Am I your own?*

Mother: Yes, my own. Is there any doubt about it? If a man is the very own of another, they remain inseparably connected in the successive cycles of time.

Disciple: All address you as "apani" but I cannot do so. I cannot utter that word. I address you as "tumi."[1]

Mother: That is good, indeed. It denotes an intimate relationship.

In the course of our talk, I said to her, "You must have taken the responsibilities of those whom you have initiated with the sacred mantra. Then why do you say when we request you to fulfill a desire, 'I will speak to the Master about it'? Can't you take our responsibility?"

Mother: I have, indeed, taken your responsibility.

Disciple: Please bless me, O Mother, that I may have purity of mind and attachment to God. Mother, I had a classmate in school. I would be grateful if I could bestow upon Sri Ramakrishna a fourth of the love with which I cherished my friend.

Mother: Ah me, that is true, indeed! Well, I shall speak to the Master about it.

Disciple: Why do you only say that you will speak to the Master? Are you different from him? My desire will certainly be fulfilled by your blessings alone.

Mother: My child, if you can get perfect knowledge through my blessings, then I bless you with all my heart and soul. Is it ever possible for a man to free himself unaided from the clutches of maya? It was for this that the Master performed spiritual austerities to the utmost extent and gave the results thereof for the redemption of mankind.

Disciple: How can one love Sri Ramakrishna without seeing him?

Mother: Yes, that's true. Can one ever have an intimate relationship with a mere airy being?

Disciple: When shall I have the vision of the Master?
Mother: You shall certainly see him. You shall see the Master at
the right time.

One day the Mother lay on her bed while Kamini, the maid, was rubbing her knee with some medicated oil for rheumatism. The Mother
said to me, "The body is one thing and the soul another. The soul pervades the whole body; therefore I have been feeling the pain in my leg.
If I should withdraw my mind from the knee, then I would not feel any
pain there."

Referring to initiation by mantra, I said to her, "Mother, what's
the need of taking the mantra from a teacher? Suppose a man does not
repeat his mantra; will it not do for him if he simply repeats: Mother
Kali, Mother Kali?"

Mother: The mantra purifies the body. Man becomes pure by
repeating the mantra of God. Listen to a story: One day,
Narada went to Vaikuntha to see the Lord and had a long con-
versation with him. Narada had not, at that time, been initiated.
After Narada left the place, the Lord said to Lakshmi, "Purify
the place with cow dung." "Why, Lord?" asked Lakshmi.
"Narada is your great devotee. Why, then, do you say this?"
The Lord said, "Narada has not, as yet, received his initiation.
The body cannot be pure without initiation."

One should accept the mantra from a guru at least for the purifi-
cation of the body. The Vaishnava, after initiating the disciple,
says to him, "Now all depends upon mind." It is said, "The
human teacher utters the mantra into the ear; but God
breathes the spirit into the soul." Everything depends upon
one's mind. Nothing can be achieved without purity of mind. It

is said, "The aspirant may have received the grace of the guru,
the Lord, and the Vaishnava; but he comes to grief without the
grace of one." That one is the mind. The mind of the aspirant
should be gracious to him.

When the Master passed away, I also wanted to leave my body.
He appeared before me and said, "No, you must remain here.
There are many things to be done." I myself realized later on
that this was true; I had so many things to do. The Master
used to say, "The people of Calcutta live like worms swarming
in darkness. You will guide them." He said that he would live
for three hundred years in a subtle body in the hearts of the
devotees. He further said that he would have many devotees
among white people.

After the passing away of the Master, I was at first greatly
frightened, for I used to put on a sari with thin red borders
and wear gold bangles on my wrist, which made me afraid of
people's criticism.[2] Gradually I got rid of that fear. One day,
the Master appeared before me and asked me to feed him
with khichuri. I cooked the dish and offered it before
Raghuvir[3] in the temple. Then I mentally fed the Master
with it....

Balaram Babu used to refer to me as the "great ascetic, the
embodiment of forbearance." Can you call him a man who
is devoid of compassion? He is a veritable beast. Sometimes
I forget myself in compassion. Then I do not remember
who I am.

Finally the Holy Mother said to me, "I feel very free with you. See me
in Calcutta and stay with me."

At that time I lived in the world with my people, though I had
been cherishing an intense desire to embrace the monastic life. I said
to myself, "Perhaps in the future it will be possible for me, through her
grace, to be a monk and live near her."

When I was in Jayrambati, Radhu's mother, Surabala, was mentally deranged. She had taken to her father's house all the jewelry of her daughter Radhu. Taking advantage of her insane condition, her father snatched away all the jewelry. That made her even more distracted. On her return to Jayrambati, Radhu's mother wept in the temple of Simhavahini, praying for the jewelry. It was dusk. I was talking to the Holy Mother in her room when suddenly she said to me, "My child, I must go now. That crazy sister-in-law of mine has none else to call her own but me. She is weeping before the deity for the jewelry." With these words, the Mother left the room. But I could not hear any sound of weeping, nor was it possible to do so at such a distance; yet she had recognized the voice. She returned with Radhu's mother. The latter said to her, "O sister-in-law, you have put away my jewelry. You have deprived me of it." The Mother said, "Had these ornaments belonged to me, then I would have thrown them away at once like the filth of a crow." Referring to Radhu's mother, she said to me, laughing, "Girish used to say that she is my mad companion."

At first I used to hesitate to address the Holy Mother as *Mother*. My own mother had died during my childhood. One morning, the Holy Mother sent me to a certain person on an errand. As I was about to leave, she asked me, "What will you say to him?" I said, "Why? I shall say to him: She asked me to tell you, etc." "No, my child," said the Holy Mother, "tell him: the *Mother* asked me to tell you." She emphasized the word *Mother*.

One morning I was reading aloud to the Mother and several devotees on the porch of her room. I was reading a life of Sri Ramakrishna entitled *Ramakrishna Punthi* written in verse. In the chapter on her marriage with Sri Ramakrishna, the author eulogized her greatly and referred to her as the "Mother of the Universe." As I read that passage the Mother left the porch. A few minutes earlier I had read to her some pages from the Udbodhan, in which had been published a

portion of the *Kathamrita* by M. No one else was present then. I had
been reading the following passage:

> Girish: I have a desire.
> Master: What is it?
> Girish: I want love of God for the sake of love.
> Master: That kind of love is possible only for the
> Isvarakotis. Ordinary men cannot achieve it.

I asked the Holy Mother, "What does the Master mean by that?"
> Mother: The Isvarakotis have all their desires fulfilled in God.
> Therefore they have no worldly desires. Love for the sake of
> divine love is not possible so long as a man has any desire.
> Disciple: Mother, do your own brothers belong to the same level
> as these Isvarakotis?

I thought that, as they were her brothers, they must have the same spiritual capacities as the monastic disciples of Sri Ramakrishna. At this
the Mother simply looked scornfully, as if she were going to say, "What
a comparison! What can one achieve by simply being my brother? To
be the intimate disciple of the Master is quite a different thing."

One morning, the Holy Mother was assisting in husking paddy. It
was almost her daily job. I asked her, "Mother, why should you work so
hard?" "My child," said she in reply, "I have done much more than is
necessary to make my life a model."

One night, all were asleep in the house of the Holy Mother when
the husband of Nalini, a niece of the Holy Mother, arrived unexpect-
edly with a bullock cart to take Nalini to his house. Nalini had
returned from her husband's place and did not want to go back.
Hearing of her husband's intention, Nalini shut the door of her room
and threatened suicide if her husband forced her to go back with him.
The Holy Mother, however, assured her that she would not have to go
back with her husband, and she opened the door. There was confusion

in the family for the whole night, and the Holy Mother sat through the night on the porch of Nalini's room. She put out the lamp at dawn and repeated to herself, "Ganga, Gita, Gayatri, Bhagavata, Bhakta, Bhagavan, Ramakrishna!"

One day, the Holy Mother sent me with an old servant of the family to Pagli's [the mad sister-in-law's] father to persuade him either to come to Jayrambati or to return the ornaments he had taken from his daughter. After a great deal of persuasion he accompanied us, but he did not bring the ornaments with him. The Mother begged him to return them and thus free Pagli from her mental agony, but the greedy brahmin turned a deaf ear to her request.

I intended to return home on the day before the Sivaratri, as I wanted to attend Sri Ramakrishna's birthday celebration at Belur Math, which occurred two days after the Sivaratri. I told the Mother about it. She asked me to go to Kamarpukur first. I had left home with a great yearning to see the Holy Mother alone, and in my eagerness I had forgotten to take my umbrella or an extra piece of cloth. At the request of the Mother, I agreed to visit the birthplace of the Master. She gave me a fresh piece of cloth to put on and asked me to take it with me.

Mother: *Have you any money with you? You will require carriage hire. Take the money from me.*

Disciple: *I have money with me. I have not to take it from you.*

Mother: *Write to me after you reach home. Ah, I could not feed my son properly. I could not prepare anything good for him.*
This was because at that time there was great confusion in the family on account of Nalini and Pagli.

I prostrated myself before her and set out with tears in my eyes. The Holy Mother accompanied us for some distance and then watched us till we disappeared. I could not refrain from weeping out of devotion for her till I had reached Kamarpukur.

After my arrival at Kamarpukur, I was shown the room where the Holy Mother had lived. There I saw a picture of the Mother, which made me still more restless to see her again. The next day, M. and Prabodh Babu went to Jayrambati by way of Kamarpukur, halting at the latter place for a few hours. In the evening, Lalit Babu, a disciple of the Mother, arrived there, dressed in turban, trousers, and a long toga. He was on his way to Jayrambati. As it would be difficult for me to go from Jayrambati to Calcutta alone, a devotee suggested that I might revisit Jayrambati and go to Calcutta in the company of Lalit Babu. So I went with him to Jayrambati once again and said to the Mother, "I am here again." The Mother was greatly pleased and said, "That's very good. You can go to Calcutta with Lalit."

After the Sivaratri festival was over, the devotees sat down for their meal. They were served some *prasad* on leaf plates. I asked them what it was. They said it was the *prasad* of the Holy Mother. I also partook of it. Later on, I said to the Mother, "They all enjoyed your *prasad*. But you never offered it to me." "My child," said the Mother, "you never asked for it. How could I suggest it?" What great humility, I thought.

The next day, Lalit Babu was sent in a palanquin to get Radhu's ornaments from her grandfather. Lalit posed as a government official and carried a letter with him supposed to have been written by a high police officer of Calcutta. The Holy Mother asked M. to accompany Lalit Babu lest the latter, a young man, should use insulting language when speaking to the old brahmin. However, he succeeded in bringing Radhu's grandfather with the ornaments to Jayrambati in the afternoon. At about two o'clock in the morning, we heard that the Mother was spending a sleepless night. She was feeling nervous. M. and I entered the inner apartments. While all were looking for medicines, I asked Mother the cause of her ailment. She said, "After they had left to fetch the ornaments, I felt worried and feared that they might insult the old brahmin. That made me nervous." I was amazed to see the compassion of the Mother for the brahmin who was at the root of all these troubles.

The next afternoon, I left with the party for Calcutta. The Mother had told Lalit Babu about me: "He is very devoted to God. Please take him with you." We all prostrated ourselves before the Mother. Her eyes became filled with tears. She was moved to tears as she accompanied us to the outer gate of the house. At Vishnupur, on our way to Calcutta, M., Prabodh Babu, and others visited the shrine of Mrinmayi, an aspect of the Divine Mother. But Lalit Babu and I directly went to the railway station and boarded the train. M. sent Prabodh Babu to ask us also to visit the shrine, but we did not care to see Mrinmayi [lit., made of earth], as we had seen Chinmayi [a living goddess]. I arrived at the Belur Math and, after witnessing Sri Ramakrishna's birthday festival, returned home.

Udbodhan Office, Calcutta
1909

The next winter I came to Calcutta to pay my respects to the Holy Mother. On the first day I went to see her, she was still staying at the house of Balaram Bose, but by the time of my second visit, she had shifted to her newly constructed house in Calcutta [i.e., the Udbodhan Office]. On entering the house I saw Doctor Kanjilal reading a newspaper. In answer to my query he said, "The Mother had an attack of pox. She has not yet completely recovered. You may see her after two weeks." I had not been aware of her illness. Swami Saradananda said to me, "Come tomorrow; you may see her then. Also, take your meal here." When I came the next day, the Mother showed me the pox marks. Most of them had disappeared. Through her blessings and the arrangement made by Swami Saradananda, I was staying in the Belur Math. On being informed of this, the Holy Mother said to me, "That's good. He has fallen a victim to the influence of monastic life. Live in the Belur Math. May you get love for the Master! You have my blessings."

I used to take milk for the Mother now and then from the Belur Math. That would also give me the opportunity to pay my respects to her. One day, while entering her house with milk, I saw her preparing betel leaf, assisted by Nalini, her niece. Seeing me, Nalini was about to leave the room. The Mother checked her and said, "Don't go away. He is my child. Sit here." In the course of conversation, she referred to the relatives of Maku's husband [Maku was another niece], and said, "I have to take special care of them, otherwise they feel offended and hiss. But you are my children. You are satisfied with whatever I do for you. You do not mind if I cannot always show you attention. But those relatives feel very much offended if I do not give them the best of everything, or if I fail in the least in attending to them."

After a while I asked her, "Mother, how does one get purity of mind and yearning for God?"

> Mother: Oh, you will certainly have these. As you have taken
> refuge in the Master, you will achieve all. Pray to him
> sincerely.
> Disciple: I can't do it. Please do pray for me.
> Mother: I always pray to Sri Ramakrishna to make your mind
> pure and holy.
> Disciple: Yes, Mother, I shall have everything if you but pray
> for me.

After a few months I was sent to Ghatal, not very far from Jayrambati, to give relief to the flood-stricken people of that place. I took leave for three days and visited the Holy Mother at Jayrambati on the occasion of the Jagaddhatri Puja. Atul was with me. This was his first visit to the Mother. We went to Jayrambati through Kamarpukur, and as soon as we reached her home, Ashu Maharaj, an attendant of the Holy Mother, said, "It is nice that you have come. The Mother has been sad because of not seeing any devotee for some time past." The Mother asked us to stay for the meal and fed us sumptuously. Early next morn- ing, we had to return to the relief work. While taking leave of the

Mother, I said to her, "I shall come again." Atul said, like a schoolboy, "Please remember."

After finishing the relief work at Ghatal, I again returned to Jayrambati. It was winter. On reaching the house of the Holy Mother in the evening, I found her seated on the porch, applying medicine to her leg. She was suffering from rheumatic pains in her knees.

Disciple: What is this medicine?

Mother: Someone suggested this leaf. Have you been starving for the whole day?

Disciple: No, but I have not taken any food on the way.

Mother: Why did you not buy some refreshments? There are stores on the way.

I had with me only a rupee I had saved to make an offering at Belur Math. However, I did not tell her about it. She served me with a hot meal, which I ate heartily. She gave me a blanket and asked me to use it during the night. I asked her, "Whose blanket is this?" She told me, "It is mine. I use it myself."

The next day's mail brought a letter to her from one of my brothers, asking her to persuade me to return home. Though short, the letter was written in a good style and contained beautiful sentiments. The Mother said, "Ah, what a nice letter." Then she said, addressing me, "Why don't you return home? Live in the world, earn money, and bring up a family." She was testing me. "But, Mother," said I, "please do not say that."

I began to weep. The Mother then said to me with great tenderness, "My child, please do not weep. You are a living God. Who is able to renounce all for his sake? Even the injunctions of destiny are canceled if one takes refuge in God. Destiny strikes off with her own hand what she has written about such a person. What does a man become by realizing God? Does he get two horns? No. What happens is that he develops discrimination between the real and the unreal, gets spiritual consciousness, and goes beyond life and death. God is realized in spirit. How else can one see God? Has God talked to anybody devoid of ecstatic fervor? One sees God in spiritual vision, talks to him, and establishes a relationship with him in spirit."

Disciple: No, Mother. There is something else besides. One gets a direct vision of the spirit.

Mother: That Narendra [Swami Vivekananda] alone had. The Master kept with himself the key to Narendra's liberation. What else is spiritual life besides praying to the Master, repeating his name, and contemplating on him? (with a smile) And the Master? What is there after all in him? He is our own eternally!

Disciple: Mother, please see that I realize the right thing—just that Sri Ramakrishna is our own.

Mother: Must I repeat it? (firmly) You will certainly realize it. Certainly.

It was the evening of the following day. I was talking to the Mother in her room. She was lying on her bed. The conversation drifted to Vedanta. I said to her, "Nothing exists in the world except name and form. It cannot be proved that matter exists. Therefore the conclusion is that God and such other things do not exist."

My idea was that such things as the Master and the Holy Mother were also illusory. She at once understood my thought.

Mother: Narendra once said to me, "Mother, the knowledge that explains away the lotus feet of the guru is nothing but ignorance. What is the validity of knowledge if it proves that the guru is naught?" Give up this dry discussion, this hodgepodge of philosophy. Who has been able to know God by reasoning? Even Siva and sages like Suka and Vyasa are like big ants at the most.

> Disciple: I want to know. I understand a little too. How can one
> stop reasoning?
> Mother: Reasoning does not disappear as long as one has not
> attained to perfect knowledge.

I asked her about *japa* and other spiritual practices. The Mother said,
"Through these spiritual disciplines, the ties of past karma are cut
asunder. But realization of God cannot be achieved without ecstatic
love [*prema bhakti*] for him. Do you know the significance of *japa* and other
spiritual practices? By these, the power of the sense organs is subdued."

Referring to Lalit Chatterjee, who had been dangerously ill, the
Mother said, "Lalit used to give me great financial help. He would take
me out in his carriage. He gives much for the divine service in the
shrines at Kamarpukur and Jayrambati. My Lalit has a heart worth a
million rupees. There are again people who are miserly in spite of their
wealth. The rich should serve God and his devotees with money, and
the poor worship God by repeating his name."

Referring to ecstatic love, the Mother said, "Did the cowherd boys
of Vrindavan get Sri Krishna as their *own* through *japa* or meditation?
They realized him through ecstatic love. They used to say to him, as to
an intimate friend: Come here, O Krishna. Eat this! Take this!"

> Disciple: How can one yearn for God without seeing the mani-
> festation of his love?
> Mother: Yes, you can do so. There lies the grace of God.

Jayrambati
December 1909

It was about nine in the morning. The Holy Mother had been preparing betel leaves when I came to see her. Soon we were engaged in
conversation.

> Disciple: Mother, I have seen and heard so much; still I cannot
> recognize you as my own mother.

Mother: Otherwise why should you come here so often? You will
   know your own mother in proper time.

After a while I said to her, referring to my own parents and brothers,
"My parents brought me up. I do not know where they are now [after
their death] or how they live. Please give your blessings that my brothers may have good tendencies."

Mother: Do most people ever want God? There are so many
   people in this very family; but do all want the Lord? (after a
   few minutes) Don't worry. Don't lead a married life. What
   should you fear if you are a celibate? Wherever you may live,
   you will be free.

Disciple: But, Mother, I have fear.

Mother: No, have no fear. All depends upon the will of the
   Master.

Disciple: The mind is the whole thing. If it be in a pure state, it
   does not matter where I live. Please see, Mother, that my mind
   always remains pure.

Mother: May it be so.

It was the birthday of the Holy Mother. A few days before, Prabodh
Babu had come to Jayrambati and given five rupees to the brothers of
the Holy Mother for special worship on her birthday. The Mother said
to them, "You are not to do anything special today. I shall wear a new
cloth, the Master will be worshiped with a sweet offering, and I shall
partake of it later on. That's all for this occasion."

After the worship in the shrine, the Holy Mother sat on her
couch with her feet hanging down. She had put on a new piece of
cloth. Prabodh Babu offered some flowers at her feet. I stood on the
porch near the door. The Mother said to me, "What? Won't you offer
some flowers? Here they are. Take them." Then I also offered flowers
at her feet. We enjoyed a sumptuous feast at midday. Afterwards
Prabodh Babu left for Calcutta; but as I was indisposed, I remained at
Jayrambati.

December 1909

In the course of conversation, the Mother said, "Can you tell me whether anyone could bind God? Mother Yasoda could bind Krishna because he himself allowed her to do so. The cowherd boys and the milkmaids of Vrindavan also realized God."

Mother: As long as a man has desires, there is no end to his transmigration. It is the desires alone that make him take one body after another. There will be rebirth for a man if he has even the desire to eat a piece of candy. It is for this reason that a variety of foodstuffs are brought to Belur Math. Desire may be compared to a minute seed. It is like a big banyan tree growing out of a seed, which is no bigger than a dot. Rebirth is inevitable so long as one has desires. It is like taking the soul from one pillowcase and putting it into another; only one or two out of many men can be found who are free from all desires. Though one gets a new body on account of desires, yet one does not completely lose spiritual consciousness if one has merits from a previous birth to one's credit. A priest in the temple of Govinda in Vrindavan used to feed his mistress with the food offerings of the deity. As a result of this sin, he got the body of a ghoul after his death. But he had served God in the temple. As a result of his merit, one day he appeared before all in his own physical body. It was possible for him to do so on account of his past good actions. He told people the cause of his inferior birth and said to them further, "Please arrange a religious festival and music for the redemption of my soul from this state. That will free me."

Disciple: Is it possible to be freed from such states through religious festivals and music?

Mother: Yes; that is enough for the Vaishnavas. They do not perform such obsequies as sraddha and so forth. Once I visited the image of Jagannath at Puri at the time of the Car Festival.

*I wept in sheer joy to see so many people having a view of
the image of the deity. "Ah," I said to myself, "it is good.
They will all be saved." But later on I realized that it was
not so. Only one or two who were absolutely free from
desires could attain their salvation. When I narrated the
incident to Yogin-Ma, she corroborated this by saying, "Yes,
Mother, only people who are free from desires attain liberation [mukti]."*

One morning, while taking my breakfast on the verandah of the Holy
Mother's room, I asked her, "Mother, will I have to be initiated into
sannyasa if I am to live in Belur Math?"

Mother: *Yes, my child.*

Disciple: *But, Mother, the monastic life begets a terrible vanity.*

Mother: *Yes, that is true. A monk may become very vain. He
may think, "See, he does not respect me. He does not bow
down before me, and so on."* (pointing to her own white
cloth) *One should rather live thus [meaning possessed of inner
renunciation].*[4] *Gaur Siromani*[5] *took to the monastic life in his
old age when his sense organs had become dull. Is it possible,
my child, to get rid of vanity—vanity of beauty, vanity of
virtue, vanity of knowledge, and vanity of a holy life?*

The Holy Mother exhorted me to make ready for the life of renunciation. "Go home," said she, "and tell your brothers once and for all: I
will not accept any job; I will not be a slave to anyone since my mother
is dead; I will not do anything of that sort. You be happy with your
householder's duties."

The Mother and I were engaged in conversation in the evening.

Disciple: Mother, one gets spiritual realization at any time if the grace of God descends on him. Then he does not have to wait for the right time.

Mother: That is true; but can the mango that ripens out of season be as sweet as the one that ripens in the month of Jaishtha—that is, the proper season? People are trying to get fruits out of season. You see, nowadays one gets mangoes and jackfruits even in the month of Asvin [autumn]. But these are not as sweet as those found in the proper season. This is also true of the efforts that lead to God-realization. Perhaps you practice some japa and austerities in this life; in the next life you may intensify the spiritual mood, and in the following life you advance further.

Referring to one's attaining spiritual realization suddenly, the Mother said, "God has the nature of the child. One man does not ask for it, yet he gives it to him; whereas another man asks for it and God will not give it to him. It is all his whim."

Another day, while the Holy Mother was seated on her porch preparing betel leaf, I said to her, "In the future, how many will practice spiritual disciplines to propitiate you!" Mother said with a smile, "What do you say! All will say: Ah, the Mother had such a gout, she used to limp like this!"

Disciple: You may say that.

Mother: That's good. That is why the Master used to say when he was lying ill at the Cossipore garden, "Those who came to me expecting some earthly gain have disappeared saying, 'Ah, he is an incarnation of God? How can he be ill? This is all maya.'

But those who are my own, have been suffering a great deal in seeing this misery...."

Udbodhan Office, Calcutta
1910

On the day previous to my initiation, I said to the Holy Mother, "Mother, I want to be initiated." Mother said, "Have you not been initiated?" I answered in the negative. "I thought that you had been initiated," she said. After initiating me, she blessed me, saying, "May your body and mind become pure by repeating the name of God."

Disciple: What is the need of repeating the mantra with the fingers? Is it not enough to do so mentally?

Mother: God has given the fingers that they may be blessed by repeating his name with them.

The Mother was engaged in a conversation with me in the morning.

Disciple: Mother, if there exists some being called God, why is there so much suffering and misery in the world? Does he not see it? Has he not the power to remove it?

Mother: The creation itself is full of misery and happiness. Could anyone appreciate happiness if misery did not exist? Besides, how is it possible for all persons to be happy? Sita once said to Rama, "Why don't you remove the suffering and unhappiness of all your subjects? Please make all the inhabitants of your kingdom happy. If you only will, you can easily do it." Rama said, "Is it ever possible for all persons to be happy at the same time?" "Why not?" asked Sita. "Please supply from the royal treasury the means of satisfying everyone's wants." "All right," said Rama, "your will shall be carried out." Rama sent for Lakshmana and said to him, "Go and notify everyone in my empire that he may get whatever he wants from the royal treasury." At this, the subjects of Rama came to the palace and told their wants. The royal treasury began to flow without stint. When everyone was spending his days joyously, through the maya of Rama, the roof of the building in which Rama and Sita lived started to leak. Workmen were sent for to repair the building. But where were workmen to be had? There was not a laborer in the kingdom. In the absence of masons, carpenters, and artisans, all buildings went out of repair, and work was at a standstill. The subjects of Rama informed the king of their difficulties. Finding no other help, Sita said to Rama, "It is no longer possible to bear the discomfort of the leaking roof. Please arrange things as they were before. Then all will be able to procure workmen. Now I realize that it is not possible for all persons to be happy at the same time." "Let it be so," said Rama. Instantaneously all things were as before, and workmen could once more be engaged. Sita said to Rama, "Lord, this creation is your wonderful sport!" No one can suffer for all time. No one will spend all his days on this earth in suffering. Every action brings its own result, and one gets one's opportunities accordingly.

Disciple: Is everything then due to karma?

Mother: If not, to what else? Don't you see the scavenger carrying the tub on his head?

Disciple: Where does one first get the propensity that leads him to an action, good or bad? You may say, as an explanation of the propensities of this life, that they are due to the actions of the previous life, and the propensities of that life to the preceding one. But where is the beginning?

Mother: Nothing can happen without the will of God. Not even a straw can move. When a man passes into a favorable time, he gets the desire to contemplate God. But when the time is unfavorable, he gets all the facilities for doing evil actions. Everything happens in time according to the will of God. It is God alone who expresses his will through the actions of man. Could Naren [Swami Vivekananda] by himself have accomplished all those things? He was able to succeed because God worked through him. The Master has predetermined what he is going to accomplish. If anyone surrenders himself totally at the Master's feet, then the Master will see that everything is set right. One must bear with everything, because all our facilities are determined by actions [karmas]. Again, actions can be canceled by actions.

Disciple: Can action ever cancel action?

Mother: Why not? If you do a good action, that will counteract your past evil action. Past sins can be counteracted by meditation, japa, and spiritual thought.

I had heard that a boy in the Mirzapur Street was possessed by a ghost. Some members of the Udbodhan Office had visited the boy yesterday.

Disciple: How long does one live in the spirit body?

Mother: All people, excepting highly evolved souls, live in the spirit body for a year. After that, food and water are offered in Gaya for the satisfaction of the departed souls, and religious festivals are arranged. By this, the souls of the departed are released from their spirit body. They go to other planes of existence and experience pleasure or pain and, in the course of time, are born again in human forms according to their desires. Others attain salvation from those planes. But if a person has some meritorious action to his credit in this life, he does not lose spiritual consciousness altogether in his spirit body.

Here the Mother again referred to the priest of the Govinda temple in Vrindavan.

Disciple: Is it possible for one to attain to a higher state if one's
sraddha *ceremony is performed in Gaya?*

Mother: Yes, that is true.[6]

Disciple: Then what is the necessity of spiritual practices?

Mother: These dead souls, no doubt, attain to a higher state and
live there for some time, but afterwards they are again born in
this world according to their past desires. After their birth in a
human body, some of them obtain salvation in this life; whereas
others take inferior births to reap the results of their karma. This
world is moving around like a wheel. That, indeed, is the last
birth in which one gets completely rid of all desires.

Disciple: You just referred to the dead souls attaining to a divine
state. Do they go there by themselves, or does someone lead them?

Mother: No, they go by themselves. The subtle body is like a
body made of air.

Disciple: What happens to those for whom no sraddha *ceremony*
is performed in Gaya?

Mother: They live in the spirit body until some fortunate ones
born in their family perform the sraddha *ceremony in Gaya or*
some other forms of obsequies.

Disciple: We hear of ghosts and spooks. Are they the attendants
of Siva or simply spirits? Or are they the spirits of dead people?

Mother: They are the spirits of the dead. The spirit attendants of
Siva belong to a special group. One must live very carefully.
Every action produces its result. It is not good to use harsh
words toward others or be responsible for their suffering.

Disciple: Mother, a margosa tree does not produce a mango, nor
does a mango tree produce a margosa fruit. Everyone reaps the
result of his own karma.

Mother: You are right, my child. In course of time one does not
feel even the existence of God. After attaining wisdom [jnana],
one sees that gods and deities are all maya. Everything comes

*into existence in time and also disappears in time.... Deities and
such things really disappear at the dawn of knowledge. The
aspirant then realizes that the Mother alone pervades the entire
universe. All then become one. This is the simple truth.*

The Holy Mother was sorting bel leaves for the daily worship when I
showed her one of the photographs of her that had been printed
recently. I asked if it was a good likeness of her.

Mother: *Yes, this is a good picture, but I was stouter before it
was taken. Jogin [Swami Yogananda] was very ill at that time.
Worrying about him, I became emaciated. I was very unhappy
then. I would weep when Jogin's illness took a turn for the
worse, and I would feel happy when he felt better. Mrs. Sarah
Bull took this photograph. At first I did not agree to it; but she
insisted and said, "Mother, I shall take this picture to America
and worship it." At last the picture was taken.*

Disciple: *Mother, that photograph of Sri Ramakrishna which you
have with you is a very good one. One feels it when one sees
the picture. Well, is that a good likeness of the Master?*

Mother: *Yes, that picture is very, very good. It originally
belonged to a brahmin cook. Several prints were made of his
first photograph. The brahmin took one of them. The picture
was at first very dark, just like the image of Kali. Therefore it
was given to the brahmin. When he left Dakshineswar for
some place—I do not remember where—he gave it to me. I
kept the photograph with the pictures of other gods and goddesses
and worshiped it. At that time I lived on the ground floor of the
Nahabat. One day the Master came there, and at the sight of
the picture he said, "Hallo, what is all this?" Lakshmi and I*

had been cooking under the staircase. Then I saw the Master take in his hand the bel leaves and flowers kept there for worship and offer them to the photograph. He worshiped the picture. This is the same picture. That brahmin never returned; so the picture remained with me.

Disciple: Mother, did you ever see the face of the Master to be pale at the time of his samadhi?

Mother: Why, I don't remember to have seen it so. On the other hand, I always saw a smile on his face in his ecstatic mood.

Disciple: It is possible to have a smile during the state of emotional ecstasy [bhava samadhi]; but regarding the photograph of his sitting posture, the Master said that it was a picture of a very exalted state. Is it possible to have a smile in that state?

Mother: But I have seen him smile in all states of samadhi.

Disciple: Of what complexion was he?

Mother: His complexion was like the color of gold—like that of harital [yellow orpiment]. His complexion blended with the color of the golden amulet he wore on his arm. When I used to rub him with oil, I could clearly see a luster coming out of his entire body.... When he came out of his room in the temple, people used to stand in line and say to one another, "Ah, there he goes!" He was fairly stout. Mathur Babu gave him a low stool to sit on. It was a rather wide stool but not quite big enough to hold him comfortably when he squatted on it to take his meals. People would look at him wonderstruck when he went with slow, steady steps to the Ganges to take his bath.

When he was at Kamarpukur, men and women looked at him with mouths agape whenever he chanced to come out of the house. One day as he went out for a walk in the direction of the canal known as Bhutir Khal, the women who had gone there to fetch water looked at him agape and said, "There the

Sri Ramakrishna's parental home in the village of Kamarpukur

Master goes!" Annoyed at this, Sri Ramakrishna said to
Hriday, "Well, Hridu, please put a veil on my head at once."
I never saw the Master sad. He was joyous in the company of
everyone, whether a boy of five or a man of ripe old age. I
never saw him morose, my child. Ah, what happy days those
were! At Kamarpukur he would get up early in the morning
and tell me, "Today I shall eat this particular green; please
cook it for me." With the other women of the family, I would
accordingly arrange for his meal. After a few days he said,
"What has come over me? The moment I get up from sleep I
say, What shall I eat? What shall I eat?" Then he said to me,
"I have no desire for any particular food. I shall eat whatever
you will cook for me."
He used to go to Kamarpukur to get relief from severe diarrhea,
from which he was suffering at Dakshineswar. He used to say,
"Goodness, my belly is filled only with filth. There is no end to
it!" Suffering thus, he developed a kind of hatred for the body,
and thereafter he did not pay much heed to it....
Nowadays you see so many devotees everywhere. There is so
much excitement and noise. But during the illness of the
Master, one of the devotees ran away in order to avoid giving
twenty rupees. The expenses for the treatment of the Master
during his illness were raised by subscription, and this devotee
had been asked to contribute that sum. Now it is not at all difficult to serve the Master. For though food is offered to him, it
is really eaten by the devotees. If you make the Master sit, he
will sit. If you make him lie down, he will remain in that position. After all, he is now a picture!
The Master saw [in a vision] Balaram Babu with a turban on,
his head and his hands folded, standing by the image of Kali.
After that, Balaram always remained with folded hands before
the Master. He never saluted the Master by touching his feet.

> The Master understood his thought and said to him one day,
> "O Balaram, my foot is itching; kindly massage it gently."
> Immediately Balaram sent for Naren or Rakhal or someone
> else among the boys who attended the Master and asked him to
> massage his feet.
>
> Disciple: Once I asked Swami Brahmananda about Sri
> Ramakrishna's complexion. He said, "The Master's complex-
> ion was like mine [i.e., dark]."
>
> Mother: Yes, he looked like that when Rakhal and other disciples
> met him. At that time he had lost his former good health and
> complexion. For example, look at me and see my complexion
> and health. Did I use to look like this formerly? No, I was very
> pretty then. I was not stout, but later on I became so....

It was the time of worship. The Mother made herself ready to go to the shrine room. I came downstairs. After the worship was over, I went upstairs again to bring the *prasad* for the devotees. As I took the leaves containing the sweets and fruits, suddenly my elbow touched the Holy Mother's feet. "Ah!" said the Mother, and saluted me with folded hands. "That's nothing," said I. But she was not satisfied with merely bowing down before me and said, "Come, my child, let me kiss you." She touched my chin with her hand and kissed her hand, and so became pacified. Thus she used to respect her disciples as the manifes-tations of God, and at the same time show her affection to them as a mother does to her own children.

October 29, 1910

It was early in the morning. I was seated near the Mother's bed. She began to talk to me about the Master.

> Disciple: Does the Master really live in the picture?
>
> Mother: Of course he does. The body and the shadow are the
> same.[7] And what is his picture but a shadow?

Disciple: Does he live in all the pictures?

Mother: Yes. If you pray to him constantly before his picture, then he manifests himself through that picture. The place where the picture is kept becomes a shrine. Suppose a man worships the Master there (pointing to a plot of land north of the Udbodhan); then the place is associated with his presence.

Disciple: Well, good and bad memories are associated with all places.

Mother: It is not exactly like that. The Master will pay special attention to such a place.

Disciple: Does the Master really partake of the food that you offer him?

Mother: Yes, he does.

Disciple: But we do not see any sign of it.

Mother: A light comes out of his eyes and licks all the articles of food. Why? Does the Master require any food? He doesn't. He eats the food offering only for the gratification of the devotees. The sacred prasad purifies the heart. The mind becomes impure if one eats food without first offering it to God.[8]

Disciple: Does the Master really partake of the food offering?

Mother: Yes. Do I not notice whether he partakes of the food or not? The Master takes his seat before the plate and then partakes of the food.

Disciple: Do you then actually see it?

Mother: Yes. In the case of some offerings, he actually eats, and in other cases he merely looks at them. Take your own case. You don't like to eat all things at all times. Nor do you relish the food offered by anyone and everyone. It is like that. One's love of God depends entirely upon one's inner feeling. Love of God is the essential thing.

Disciple: How does one get love of God? If one's own son is brought up by someone else, he does not recognize his own mother as his mother.

Mother: Yes, that is true. The grace of God is the thing that is needful. One should pray for the grace of God.

Disciple: How can one speak of deserving grace or not deserving it? Grace is the same for all.

Mother: One must pray sitting on the bank of the river. He will be taken across in proper time.

Disciple: Everything happens when the proper time comes. Then where does God's grace come in?

Mother: Must you not sit with the fishing rod in your hand if you want to catch the fish?

Disciple: If God be our own, why then should one sit and wait?

Mother: That is true. It may happen even out of season. Don't you see nowadays how people get fruits like mango and jackfruit out of season? Many mangoes grow nowadays in the month of Bhadra.

Disciple: Is this our limit—that he sends us away by giving us what we desire? Or, can one get him as one's very own? Is God my very own?

Mother: Yes, God is one's very own. It is the eternal relationship. He is everyone's own. One realizes him in proportion to the intensity of one's feeling for him.

Disciple: Intense feeling is like a dream. A man dreams what he thinks.

Mother: Yes, it is a dream. The whole world is a dream; even this [the waking state] is a dream.

Disciple: No, this is not a dream, for then it would have disappeared in the twinkling of an eye. This state exists for many, many births.

Mother: Let it be so; still, it is nothing but a dream. What you *dreamed last night does not exist now. [As a matter of fact, on the previous night the disciple had an amazing dream.] A farmer who lost a son dreamed at night that he was a king and the father of eight sons. When the dream vanished, he said to his wife, "Shall I weep for those eight children or for this one?"*

After arguing thus with the Mother, I said, "Mother, I don't really bother my head about what I just said to you. All that I want to know is whether there is anyone whom I may call my *own*."

Mother: Yes, such a one exists.

Disciple: Surely?

Mother: Yes.

Disciple: If he be really our own, *then why should we pray unto him in order to see him? One who is truly my own would come to me even if I did not call on him. Does God do things for us as our parents do?*

Mother: Yes, that is true, my child. He himself has become our father and mother. He himself brings us up as our parents. It is he alone who looks after us. Otherwise, where were you, and where are you now? Your parents brought you up, but at last realized that you did not belong to them. Have you not seen a cuckoo brought up in the nest of a crow?[9]

Disciple: Shall I realize God as really my own?

Mother: Yes, surely you will realize him. Whatever you think, you will get. Did not Swamiji [Swami Vivekananda] realize him? You will realize him as Swamiji did.

Disciple: Mother, please see that I am not overcome by fear or slackening of faith.

Mother: There is no such danger for you. For I myself have hooked the fish.

Disciple: That is good. We all shall enjoy it.

Mother: Yes, that is right. One makes the mold and many others make their images from it.

Disciple: Yes, we shall get everything if you only work for us.
   You cannot set us aside.
Mother: Yes, my child, you will have all if I do it for you.

In the forenoon, a devotee had arrived from Shillong. Doubtful about the divine nature of the Mother, he had taken a vow that he would not visit her unless he had seen her in a dream seven times. He had the requisite visions. Therefore, he had gone to Jayrambati to pay his respects to her. In the afternoon, as he was about to take leave of her, he said, "Mother, I shall say goodbye now. Do I need anything else?"

Mother: Yes, surely. You must have your initiation.

Devotee: I may have it at Baghbazar in Calcutta.

Mother: Better finish that task, my child. Have your initiation
   today.

Devotee: But I have eaten the prasad.

Mother: That doesn't matter.

After the initiation, the devotee departed.

Earlier in the morning, another devotee, an eccentric young man, had come and clamored before the Mother for *sannyasa*. He also demanded that the Mother should make him "mad" and give him the vision of the Master immediately. The Mother somehow pacified him for the time being and sent him home. The mental state of the eccentric devotee took a turn for the worse after he returned home from Jayrambati. He became restless for the vision of the Master and felt piqued to think that though the Holy Mother could, by her mere will, make him get a vision of Sri Ramakrishna, she refused to do so. In a very angry state of mind he came back to Jayrambati and said to her, "Mother, won't you enable me to see the Master?" The Mother said tenderly, "Yes, you will see him; don't be so restless." He could not stand it any longer. He said in an angry voice, "You are only deceiving me. Here is the rosary you gave me. Take it back. I don't care for it anymore." With these words he threw the rosary at her. "All right," said the Mother, "remain forever the child of Sri Ramakrishna." He left the place at once.

Afterward the devotee really went mad. He began writing abusive letters to the swamis of the Ramakrishna Mission and did not spare even the Holy Mother in this respect.

One day, referring to this devotee, I asked the Holy Mother, "Did he also return the mantra? He threw away his rosary. Can anyone ever return the mantra?"

Mother: *Can that ever be possible? The word of the mantra is living. Can anyone who has received it give it back? Can he, once having felt attraction for the guru, get rid of him? Someday in the future this man will come round and fall at the feet of those whom he now abuses.*

Devotee: *Why does such a thing come to pass?*

Mother: *One sees such things. One guru may initiate many disciples, but can they all be of the same nature? Spiritual life manifests in a devotee according to his nature. He once said to me, "Mother, make me mad." "Why?" said I. "Why should you be mad, my child? Can anyone, without committing much sin, ever be mad?" He said, "My younger brother has seen the Master. Please let me also have a vision of him." I said in reply, "Who can ever see him with the physical eyes? But one may do so by closing one's eyes. Your brother is a child. He may have visualized the Master with his eyes closed, but he thinks that he has seen him with his eyes open." I asked him to continue his spiritual life—to practice spiritual disciplines and pray to the Master—and told him that he also would have the vision. Man knows in his own mind how far he has advanced and how much knowledge and consciousness of God he has attained. He knows in his innermost soul how much of God he has realized. Besides, who has been able to see God with his physical eyes?*

This devotee, after having been scolded at the Udbodhan Office, used to live on the bank of the Ganges. Sometimes he would sit on the doorsill of the Udbodhan Office and would take his meal there. After some time, he was brought once to the Holy Mother with her permission. She tried to pacify him in various ways and said, "The Master used to say, 'At the time of death I shall have to stand by those who pray to me.' These are words from his own mouth. You are my child. What should you be afraid of? Why should you behave like a madman? That will disgrace the Master. People will say that his devotee has become mad. Can you conduct yourself in a way that will discredit the name of the Master? Go home and live as others do. Eat and live like them. At the time of your death, he will reveal himself to you and will take you to him. Can you tell me if anyone ever got a vision of him with physical eyes? It was only Naren who saw him thus. That happened in America when he had intense yearning for him. Naren used to feel that the Master was grasping his arm then. That vision also lasted only for a few days. Now go home, and live there happily. How miserable are the worldly people. The other day Ram's son passed away. You can at least sleep with an easy heart."

The devotee was much pacified by the Holy Mother's consolation and words of instruction. He took his meal at the Udbodhan Office and later returned to his native village. He gradually regained his normal state of mind.

Jayrambati
May 26, 1911

The Holy Mother returned to Calcutta from her pilgrimage to Rameswaram and after a few days went back to Jayrambati. One evening, while seated on the porch of her old house, she asked me about a monastic devotee.

Mother: *What did he say?*

Disciple: *He felt a yearning for you for three or four months.*

Mother: *How strange. A sannyasin must sever all bondage of maya. A golden chain is as good a shackle as an iron one. A sannyasin must not entangle himself in any form of maya. Why should he constantly say, "Oh, Mother's love! Mother's love! I am deprived of it!" What ideas! I do not like men constantly hanging on me. At least he has the form of a man; I am not talking of God. And I am to move about with women. Ashu also used to come to me frequently to make sandal paste or on some other pretext. One day I warned him.*

Disciple: *Will the sannyasins who profess the ideals of Vedanta attain to nirvana?*

Mother: *Surely. By gradually cutting off the bonds of maya, they will realize nirvana and merge themselves in God. This body is, no doubt, the outcome of desires. The body cannot live unless there is a trace of desire. All comes to an end when one gets rid of desires completely.*

Children [i.e., devotees] come here, eat their meals, enjoy themselves, and then go away. Why should I be attached to them? One day Hazra said to the Master, "Why do you constantly long for Narendra and other youngsters? They are quite happy by themselves, eating, drinking, and playing. You had better fix your mind on God. Why should you be attached to them?" At these words, the Master took his mind away from the young disciples completely and merged it in the thought of God. Instantaneously he entered into samadhi; his beard and hair stood straight on end like the kadamba flower. Just imagine what kind of a man the Master was! His body became hard like a wooden statue. Ramlal, who was attending on him, said

Swami Vivekananda, during his wandering days in India

repeatedly, "Please be your former self again." At last the mind came down to the normal plane. It was only out of compassion for people that he kept his mind on the material plane.

At the time of death, Jogin [Swami Yogananda] wanted nirvana. Girish Babu said to him, "Look here, Jogin! Don't accept nirvana. Don't think of the Master as pervading the entire universe, the sun and the moon forming his eyes. Think of the Master as he used to be to us, and thus thinking of him, go to him." Deities and angels, whoever they be, are born again on this earth. They do not eat or talk in their subtle bodies.

Disciple: If they neither eat nor talk, then how do they spend their days?

Mother: Immersed in meditation, they remain where they are like wooden images for ages. Like the images of the kings I saw at Rameswaram, standing there dressed in royal robes. When God needs them, he brings them down from their respective places. There are different heavenly planes such as the Yama-loka, Satya-loka, and Dhruva-loka. The Master said that he had brought down Narendra [Swami Vivekananda] from the plane of the Seven Sages [Saptarishis]. His words are verily the words of the Vedas. They can never be untrue.

Disciple: Must we also, then, live like images of wood or clay?

Mother: Oh, no, you will serve the Master. There are two classes of devotees. One class devotes itself to the service of God, as on this earth; and another group is immersed in meditation for ages, like the images.

Disciple: Well, Mother, the Master used to say that the Isvarakotis can come back to the relative plane of consciousness even after the attainment of nirvana; others cannot do so. What does that mean?

Mother: The Isvarakoti, even after the attainment of nirvana, can gather back his mind from it and direct it to the ordinary plane of consciousness.

Disciple: How can the mind that has merged itself in God be brought back again to the world? How can one ever separate a jar of water from the water of the lake if it has been poured into it?

Mother: Not all can do so. Only the paramahamsa can. A hamsa can separate the milk from a mixture of water and milk and drink only the milk.[10]

Disciple: Can all get rid of desires?

Mother: If they could, then this creation would have come to an end. The creation is going on because all cannot be free of desires. People with desires take their births again and again.

Disciple: Suppose a man gives up his body standing in the waters of the Ganges.

Mother: Freedom from birth is possible only when there is no trace of desire. Otherwise, nothing else is of any avail. If one does not get rid of desires, what will one gain, even if this be one's last birth in this world?

Disciple: Mother, infinite is this creation; who can tell what is happening in a remote plane? Who can say if any living beings inhabit any of those innumerable stars and planets?

Mother: It is possible only for God to be omniscient in this realm of maya. Perhaps there is no living being in those planets and stars.

One day in the rainy season of the same year, 1911, Swami Saradananda, Yogin-Ma, Golap-Ma, and several other devotees went to Kamarpukur from Jayrambati. Yogin-Ma slipped on the road and cut some parts of her body, and blood flowed. I returned to Jayrambati ahead of the party and told the Holy Mother about Yogin-Ma's accident. The Mother said sadly, "Golap said before they set out, 'Yogin is going with us; let us see how often she slips on the road.' Yogin fell down to vindicate Golap's words. After all, those were the words of a spiritual woman. She practices spiritual disciplines; therefore her words must bear fruit. Hence, a holy person must not say anything bad about anyone."

Udbodhan Office, Calcutta
January 16, 1912

I was with the Holy Mother in the morning in her room.

> *Disciple: Mother, Sri Chaitanya one day blessed Narayani, saying, "May you have devotion to Krishna." The words had such a magical effect that the girl, only three or four years old, rolled on the ground, uttering, "Ah, Krishna! O Krishna!" We have read a story about Narada. After he had realized God, he one day felt compassion for an ant. He said to himself, "I have attained to perfection as the result of practicing austerities through many human births, and this poor ant will have to wait so long, even before it is born as a man." Tenderly he blessed the ant, saying, "Be free!" Immediately the ant assumed such nonhuman forms as birds, beasts, and so forth, and gradually took the body of a man. It passed through many human births, enjoyed the experiences associated with them, and step by step directed its attention to spiritual disciplines. It worshiped God and attained salvation. Narada saw in the twinkling of an eye all these events of innumerable births. Therefore one may get liberation instantaneously through the grace of a great soul.*

Mother: That is true.

Disciple: But I have also heard that one cannot keep one's body long if one accepts the burden of the sins of others. The body that might have been instrumental in getting salvation for many withers away for the sake of one sinful person.

Mother: That's also true. Further, a great soul thus loses his power. The power of austerities and spiritual disciplines that might have been used for the liberation of many souls is spent for the sake of one person. The Master used to say, "I have all these physical ailments because I have taken upon myself the sins of Girish." But now Girish is also suffering.

Disciple: Mother, one day I had a dream. I saw that a man with shaggy hair came to you and insisted that you must do something for him at once. He had previously been initiated by you, but he himself would not practice any spiritual discipline. You said, "If I do something for him, then I shall not live; my body will fall off immediately." With all the earnestness I could command, I forbade you to show any kindness to this man and said, "Why should you do anything for him? He will achieve his own salvation. Let him practice sadhana." As he insisted again and again, you became disgusted with him, did something to him by touching his chest and neck, and said repeatedly, "If I do something for him, then I shall not live; my body will fall off immediately." Then my dream disappeared. Well, is it true that one's power becomes limited when one is born in a physical body?

Mother: Yes, that is so. Many a time, disgusted with the repeated requests of some persons, I think, "Well, this body will die someday. Let it fall off this moment. Let me give him salvation."

Disciple: Mother, does the vision of God mean the attainment of knowledge [jnana] and spiritual consciousness [chaitanya]? Or does it signify something else?

Mother: What else can it mean except the attainment of these?
Does anybody mean to say that a man of realization grows two
horns?

Disciple: Many of your devotees explain the vision of God differ-
ently. They believe that one sees God with physical eyes and
talks to him.

Mother: Yes, they say, "Please show us the Father." But he [Sri
Ramakrishna] is nobody's father. The three words—guru,
master, and father—pricked him like thorns. How many sages
practiced austerities for ages and ages? Still they could not
realize God. And now people will not practice disciplines or
undergo austerities—but they must be shown God immediately!
I can't do it. Can you tell me if he [Sri Ramakrishna] had
shown God to anyone?

Disciple: Well, Mother, we hear that some seek but do not get,
while others do not seek but get. What does this mean?

Mother: God has the nature of a child. Some beg but he does not
give them, while others do not want but he asks them to
accept. Perhaps the latter had many meritorious acts to their
credit in their past births. Therefore God's grace descends on
them.

Disciple: Then there is discrimination even in the grace of God.

Mother: Yes, that's true. Everything depends upon karma. The
moment one's karma comes to an end, one realizes God. That
is one's last birth.

Disciple: I admit that the cessation of actions, spiritual disciplines, and time are the factors in the attainment of spiritual
knowledge and consciousness. But if God be our very own,
then can't he reveal himself to his devotees by his mere will?

Mother: That is right. But who has this faith that he is his own?
All practice these or those disciplines because they think it their
duty to do so. But how many seek God?

Disciple: Once I said to you that the child does not recognize
even its own mother if it is deprived of her care and love.

Mother: Yes, you have spoken truly. How can one love another
unless one sees him? You see, you have seen me. I am your
Mother and you are my child.

February 1, 1912

It was about half past nine in the evening when I went to the Holy
Mother. I had not seen her for the whole day.

Mother: Where have you been the whole day?

Disciple: I have been busy downstairs with the accounts.

Mother: Yes, Prakash told me so. Can anyone who has
renounced the world relish these things? Once there was a
mistake in the accounts relating to the salary of the Master. I
asked him to talk to the manager of the temple about it. But
he said, "What a shame ... shall I bother myself about
accounts?" Once he said to me, "He who utters the name
of God never suffers from any misery. No need to speak
about you!" These are his very words. Renunciation was
his ornament.

February 9, 1912

Girish Chandra Ghosh had given up his body on the previous night.
Referring to him, I asked the Holy Mother, "Well, Mother, do those
who give up their bodies in a state of unconsciousness attain to a higher
spiritual state afterwards?"

Mother: The thought that is uppermost in mind before one loses
consciousness determines the course of one's soul after death.

Disciple: Yes, that is true. A little after six o'clock in the
evening, Girish Babu exclaimed, "Jai Ramakrishna!" and

then fell unconscious. Afterwards he never regained his consciousness. A few minutes before, he had been constantly saying, "Let us go, let us go.... Hold me a little, my son!" and so forth. I said to him, "Why do you only say: Let us go, let us go?[11] *You had better repeat the name of Sri Rama-krishna, which will do you real good." I had said that a couple of times when Girish Babu replied, "Do I not know that?" I said to myself, "Now see, he is fully conscious within."*

Mother: *He remained immersed in the thought that was in his mind when he became unconscious. They [Sri Ramakrishna's disciples] all have come from him and will go back to him [the Master]. They all have come from him—from his arms, feet, hair, and so forth. They are his limbs and parts.*

February 21, 1912

It was seven o'clock in the morning. The Holy Mother was seated on the floor near her couch. Swami Nirbhayananda, who had gone to Dwaraka on pilgrimage, sent the Mother some *prasad* from the shrine of Dattatreya in the Girnar Hills.[12] The Mother asked, "Who was Dattatreya?"

Disciple: *He, like Jada Bharata and others, was a great sage—an Isvarakoti.*[13]

Mother: *Like some of the children of the Master?*

Disciple: *Well, how is it that some of the Isvarakotis among the Master's disciples are thus immersed in worldliness with their wives and children?*

Mother: *Yes, they are rotting there. Purna was forced to marry. His relatives threatened him, saying, "If you go to him [Sri Ramakrishna], we will smash his carriage with stones and brickbats when he comes to Calcutta."*

Disciple: Well, they might have married. Nag Mahasay also
married. But to have children and lead a worldly life!

Mother: Perhaps they had some such desires. Let me tell you one
thing. There is great complexity in this creation. The Master
does one thing through one person and another thing through
another person. Oh, it is so inscrutable! But even a householder
can be an Isvarakoti. What is the harm?

Radhu was ill. She had pain and a fever. The Mother was worried
about her and said, "She cannot get well when I am alive. Who will
look after her when I am gone? Will she live then?"

Disciple: What a crowd of devotees the whole day. You could not
get a moment's respite.

Mother: Day and night I say to the Master, "Please lessen this
rush. Let me have a little rest." But I hardly get it. It will be
like this for the few days I am in this body. The message of the
Master has spread everywhere; therefore so many people come
here.... Such crowds used to visit the Master also during his
last days. I try to persuade people so earnestly, saying, "Have
initiation from your family preceptor. They expect something
from you. I do not expect anything." But they will not leave
me. They weep, and it moves my heart. Well, I am nearing
the end; the few days I shall live will be spent in this manner.

Disciple: Oh, no, Mother, why should you say that? You are
well. You have no particular ailment. Why do you, then, want
to leave this world? Never say that again.

At that time the Mother appeared very sad and indifferent about
things.

During the noontime, a hotheaded man had come to the Holy
Mother and created a row. Referring to this, she said, "The Master did
not let anybody know of my existence. He protected me always with
infinite care. Now the thing has gone to the other extreme; they are
advertising me, as if by the beat of a drum in a marketplace. M. is at

the root of it all. People are beside themselves after reading *The Gospel of Sri Ramakrishna*. Girish Babu enforced his demands on the Master and abused him; now people are doing the same thing with me.

"Why should they always bother me about initiation? There are my children [referring to the direct disciples of the Master] at the Belur Math. Have they no power? Everyone is being sent here. I went so far as to tell people that they would be incurring great sin if they give up their hereditary preceptor. But still they would not leave me alone."

> Disciple: You initiate the devotees because you desire to do so.
>
> Mother: No, I do so out of compassion. They won't leave me. They weep. I feel compassion for them. Out of kindness, I give them initiation. Besides, what do I gain by it? When I initiate devotees, I have to accept their sins. Then I think, "Well, this body will die anyway; let them realize Truth."

May 1, 1912

In the forenoon, I went upstairs to read letters to the Holy Mother.

> Disciple: The daughter of a devotee has written from her father-in-law's place that she would like to come here to see you. She has sent you her salutations. She has further requested you to be careful so that her husband's relatives might not know about her writing to you.
>
> Mother: Then do not write any reply to her. Again she wants me to conceal it from her relatives. I do not know such a game of hide and seek. At Jayrambati, Jogindra, the postal deliverer, used to write letters for me. Many complained, saying, "Does the postman see our letters?" They did not like my asking a man in a humble position to write my letters for them. Why? There is no deceit in me. Anybody who likes may see my letters.

Another devotee inquired as to when the Holy Mother would return to Jayrambati. I asked her, "May I tell the devotee that you will return there in autumn at the time of the Jagaddhatri Puja?"

>Mother: Oh, no, no! Can one be sure of it? As to where I shall be, that remains entirely in the hands of God. Today man is, and tomorrow he is not.

>Disciple: O Mother, why should you talk like that? It is because you are alive that so many people are able to see you and get peace of mind.

>Mother: Yes, that is true.

>Disciple: Please do live for our sake.

In a tender voice, choked with emotion, she said, "Alas, how fond they are of me.... I am also very fond of them." Her eyes were moist with tears. The disciple was fanning her. She said to him in a most compassionate voice, "My child, I bless you from my heart that you live long, attain devotion, and enjoy peace. Peace is the principal thing. One needs peace alone."

>Disciple: Mother, one idea crops up in my mind constantly: Why do I not get the vision of the Master? As he is our very own, why does he not reveal himself to us? Can't he do so by his mere will?

>Mother: That is true. Who can say why he does not reveal himself when you suffer from so many miseries and sorrows? Once Balaram's wife was ill. The Master said to me, "Go to Calcutta and visit her." "How can I go?" I said. "I don't see any carriage or other conveyance here." The Master replied in an excited voice, "What? Balaram's family is in such trouble and you hesitate to go? You will walk to Calcutta. Go on foot." At last a palanquin was brought, and I set out from Dakshineswar. Twice I visited her during her illness. On another occasion, I went on foot at night from Shyampukur. Where, indeed, will we be if God does not protect us in our trouble?

Disciple: I know sorrows and sufferings are inevitable so long as one lives in the physical body. I do not ask the Master to remove the sufferings. But can't he console us by revealing himself to us in the midst of our troubles and sorrows?

Mother: You are right, my child. The only son of Ram [Balaram's grandson] died the other day. Ram's wife and mother came to me for peace of mind. They were relieved of their grief to some extent. I used to speak to the Master of such things, and he would say, "I have millions of them. I shall cut my goat at the tail or through the back and then kill it. It is my sweet will."

Disciple: Does he not see our suffering?

Mother: But he has so many like you. He used to tell me, "It is the ocean of consciousness and bliss. How many waves crop up and disappear! There is no end, no limit."

Disciple: Someone in the street whose spiritual consciousness has not been awakened at all is quite happy. But those whose consciousness has been partially awakened and who want to realize God suffer a great deal if they do not see him. They alone know how much they suffer.

Mother: Ah, how true it is. Ordinary people are quite happy. They eat, drink, and make themselves merry. The devotees alone know no end of suffering.

Disciple: Don't you suffer at the suffering of the devotees?

Mother: Why should I? He who has created the world looks after all.

Disciple: Don't you want to come back to this earth in a human form for the sake of the devotees?

Mother: Oh, such suffering in a human body. No more, no more! May I not be born again. At the time of his illness, the Master expressed the desire to eat an amalaka fruit. Durgacharan procured some after searching for them for three *days without food and sleep. The Master asked him to take his meal and himself took some rice in order to turn the food into prasad. I said to the Master, "You are taking rice quite well. Why, then, should your meal consist only of farina pudding? You should take rice rather than pudding." "No, no," said he, "I would rather take farina during these last days of my life." It was such an unbearable suffering for him to eat even the farina. Every now and then he would throw it out through his nose.*

The Master used to say, "I have been suffering for you all. I have taken upon myself the miseries of the whole world." The Master suffered, as he had taken on himself the sins of Girish.

All our sufferings are on this earth. Is there anything elsewhere? People suffer from endless miseries on account of their egoism, and at last they say, "Not I, not I; it is Thou, O God. It is Thou."

Disciple: Will you keep us in your mind hereafter?

Mother: Perhaps not when I enjoy divine bliss after my passing away. My child, time alone is the principal thing. Who knows what will happen in course of time?

Disciple: True, Mother. Everything, no doubt, happens under the dominance of time; but there is also a subduer of time.

Mother: Yes, that is true.

Disciple: Please keep yourself well; then everything will be all right.

It was eight o'clock. The Mother asked, "Is it eight o'clock? Perhaps it is. It is time for worship in the shrine room. Let me go now."

I went upstairs with her mail.

One of her disciples had passed away at Benares. The Mother heard the news and remarked, "All must die someday. Instead of dying in a pool or on the bank of a lake, he has died in Benares."

Her brothers had written to her asking for money, also telling about their family quarrels. I said to her, "Please see that they get plenty of money. Please tell the Master about it. Let them enjoy the material life and come to satiety."

Mother: *Will they ever be satiated? Nothing can satisfy them—*
no, not even if they have plenty. Are the worldly people ever
satiated with enjoyments? They always spin out the tale of their
woe. It is Kali [one of her brothers] who always wants money.
Now Prasanna [another brother] imitates him. Varada [a third
brother] never asks for money. He says, "Where will sister get
money from?"

Disciple: *What about that insane lady? Does she want money?*

Mother: *She won't accept it even when offered.*

Disciple: *Why were you born in that family?*

Mother: *Why not? My father and mother were very good*
people.

May 2, 1912

Disciple: *Mother, I feel it is purposeless to live unless we have a*
direct vision of God. Once I asked a fakir, "A man sits with
an angling rod on the bank of a lake or a river in the expecta-
tion of catching fish. He never does so near a mud puddle.
Have you gotten a glimpse of that for which you have become
a religious mendicant?"

Mother: *What did he say?*

Disciple: *What could he say?*

Mother (after a little reflection): *You have said the right thing.*
That is true. What does it avail a man unless he gets some
kind of realization? But one should continue to have faith in
things spiritual.

Disciple: The other day Sarat Maharaj said that Swamiji [Swami Vivekananda] also had remarked, "Suppose there is a lump of gold in the adjoining room, and a thief sees it from this room. There is an intervening wall that prevents him from taking possession of this precious metal. Under that condition, can the man ever sleep? All the time he would be thinking of how he might get at that lump of gold. In the same way, if a man is firmly convinced that there is such a thing as God, can he ever indulge in worldly life?"

Mother: That is true indeed.

Disciple: Whatever you may say, Mother, renunciation and dispassion are the chief things. Shall we ever acquire them?

Mother: Certainly you will. You will gain everything if you but take refuge in the Master. Renunciation alone was his splendor. We utter his name and eat and enjoy things because he renounced all. People think that his devotees must also be very great, as he was a man of such complete renunciation.

Ah, me.... One day he went to my room in the Nahabat. He had no spices in his small bag. He used to chew them now and then. I gave him some to chew there and also handed over to him a few packed in paper to take to his room. He proceeded; but instead of going to his room, he went straight to the embankment of the Ganges. He did not see the way, nor was he conscious of it. He was repeating, "Mother, shall I drown myself?" I became restless with agony. The river was full to the brim. I was then a young woman and would not go out of my room. I could not see anyone about. Whom could I send to him? At last I found a brahmin belonging to the Kali temple coming in the direction of my room. Through him I called Hriday, who was then taking his meal. He left his plate, ran to the Master, caught hold of him, and brought him back to his room. A moment more and he would have dropped into the Ganges.

Disciple: Why did he go south of the river?

Mother: Because I put a few spices in his hand, he could not find
  his way. A holy man must not lay things by. His renunciation
  was a hundred percent complete.

Once, a Vaishnava sadhu came to the Panchavati. At first he
  showed a great deal of renunciation. But, alas, like a rat he
  finally began to pull and gather various things—pots, cups,
  jars, grain, rice, pulses, and so forth. The Master noticed it
  and said one day, "Poor thing. This time he is going to be
  ruined." He was about to be entangled in the snare of maya.
  The Master advised him strongly about renunciation and fur-
  ther asked him to leave the place. Then he went away.

A devotee came to salute the Mother. As he was about to take his
leave, she said, "I was once deceived by showing Harish my affection.
Therefore I do not nowadays show a person my feelings toward him."

June 25, 1912

It was morning. The Mother was seated near the bedstead in the room
adjacent to the shrine. We were engaged in conversation.

Disciple: Some say that it is not good for the sadhus [of the
  Ramakrishna Order] to work in the sevashrams [homes of ser-
  vice] and dispensaries or to be preoccupied with selling books,
  accounting, and so forth. Did the Master ever undertake such
  activities? Works of this kind are thrust upon the seekers who
  enter the Order with a yearning for the realization of God. If
  anyone must do some work, it must be worship in the shrine,
  meditation, japa, and devotional music. Activities other than
  these entangle one in desires and turn one away from God.

Mother: You must not listen to those who talk in that manner.
  What will you do day and night if you are not engaged in
  work? Can one practice meditation and japa for twenty-four

hours? You referred to the Master. His case was different. Mathur used to supply him with the proper diet. You are able to get your food because you are doing some work. Otherwise you would have to roam from door to door begging for a morsel of food. Perhaps you would fall ill. Besides, where are people today to give alms to the sadhus? Never pay any heed to such words. Things will go on as the Master directs. The Math will be run on these lines. Those who cannot adjust themselves will go away. One day Mani Mallick visited a sadhu and reported it to the Master. "Well," said the Master, "how did you like him?" "Yes," said Mani, "I saw the sadhu, but—" "But what?" the Master asked. "All want money," Mani Mallick replied. The Master said, "How much does a holy man want? Perhaps a small amount for tobacco or ganja. That's all. You need your cups of ghee and milk, a mattress, and such things; and the sadhus want a little for their smoke. Should they not have it?"

Disciple: Enjoyments come from desire alone. A man may live in a four-story mansion; but he does not really enjoy anything if he has no desire for it. And a man may live under a tree, but if he has desire, he gets all enjoyments from that alone. The Master used to say, "A person may have no relatives anywhere; but Mahamaya may cause him to keep a cat and thus make him worldly. Such is her play!"

Mother: That's true. Everything is due to desire. What bondage is there for a man who has no desire? You see, I live with all these things, but I do not feel any attachment. No, not in the least.

Disciple: Indeed, you can have no desires. But how many insignificant desires crop up in our minds. How can we get rid of them?

Mother: In your case these are no real desires. They are nothing.

They are mere fancies that appear and disappear in your mind. The more they come and go, the better for you.[14]

Disciple: *Yesterday I thought how I could fight with my mind unless God assured me of his protection. The moment one desire disappears, another crops up.*

Mother: *So long as the ego exists, desires also remain. But those desires will not injure you. The Master will be your protector. It will be a heinous sin on the part of the Master if he does not protect those who have taken shelter at his feet, who have taken refuge in him renouncing all, and who want to lead a good life. You must live in a spirit of self-surrender to him. Let him do good to you if he so desires, or let him drown you if that be his will. But you are to do only what is righteous, and that also according to the power he has given you.*

Disciple: *Have I, O Mother, surrendered to him to that extent? Sometimes I feel that I can depend upon him to a small extent, and the next moment it disappears. What will be the way for us if he does not protect us? Sometimes I think that because you, O Mother, are alive, we can report our dangers and difficulties to you and gain peace by a look at your face. Who will protect us after your leaving us? We shall feel safe if you give us assurance.*

Mother: *Don't be afraid, my child. You have nothing to fear. You will not lead a worldly life with wife and children. You will have none of these. Why should you fear? And in the meantime, before my death, you will be able to build up a secure foundation for your spiritual life.*

Disciple: *What will japa and austerities avail us if God does not cast his benign look upon us? We shall be protected only if he protects us.*

Mother: *You have nothing to fear. The Master will certainly protect you. Don't worry.*

July 7, 1912

Disciple: Mother, was it not arranged that you would visit Puri at the time of the Car Festival?

Mother: Is it good to go there when there is such a rush of people? Perhaps there will be an epidemic of cholera then. Lakshmikanta, the priest, said, "Even now all the rooms and houses are rented. There is no place to stay. Even the small rooms have been rented for ten rupees each. Please come during the winter months."

Disciple: How many temples, gods, and goddesses the Muslims have destroyed! They have cut off the noses of some of the images and the ears of others. There is the temple of Somanath in Gujarat. The priests, in former times, used to bathe the deity daily with water from the Gangotri. Every day, people used to carry water from the Himalayas in pots on their heads. Sultan Mohammed demolished the image and carried away the temple doors that were made of sandalwood. Why should that happen?

Mother: The wicked do not feel the divine presence in the image. The deity disappears, as it were, before them. He can do whatever he likes by his mere will. This also is a sport of God.

Disciple: Can the effect of karma be made null and void? The scriptures say that knowledge alone can destroy karma. Still, one must reap the result of prarabdha karma.[15]

Mother: Karma alone is responsible for our misery and happiness. Even the Master had to suffer from the effect of karma. Once his elder brother was drinking water while delirious. The Master snatched the glass out of his hand after he had drunk just a little. The brother became angry and said, "You have stopped me from drinking water. You will also suffer likewise. You will also feel such pain in your throat." The Master said, "Brother, I did not mean to injure you. You are ill. Water will harm you. That is why I have taken the glass away. Why have you, then, cursed me in this manner?" The brother said, weeping, "I do not know, brother. These words have come from my mouth. They cannot but bear fruit." At the time of his illness, the Master told me, "I have this ulcer in my throat because of that curse." I said to him in reply, "How can man possibly live if such a thing as this can happen to you?" The Master remarked, "My brother was a righteous man. His words must come true. Can the words of anyone and everyone be thus fulfilled?"

The result of karma is inevitable. But by repeating the name of God, you can lessen its intensity. If you were destined to have a wound as wide as a ploughshare, you will get a pinprick at least. The effect of karma can be counteracted to a great extent by japa and austerities. This was the case with King Suratha. He had worshiped the goddess by slaughtering one hundred thousand goats. Later on, these goats killed the king with one stroke of the sword; he did not have to be born one hundred thousand times. That was because he had worshiped the Divine Mother. Chanting God's holy name lessens the intensity of karmic effects.

Disciple: If that be so, then the law of karma is supreme in this world. Then why should one believe in God? The Buddhists accept the law of karma but not God.

Mother: Do you mean to say that there are no deities like Kali, Krishna, Durga, and the like?

Disciple: Is the effect of karma destroyed by austerities and japa?

Mother: Why not? It is good to do the right kind of work. One feels happy in doing good, and one suffers by doing evil....

Disciple: Many devotees used to visit the Master. Where are they now? None of them come to see you.

Mother: Oh, they are all leading happy lives.

Disciple: What? Happy!

*Mother: You are right. How can a man be happy in this world
with his wife and children? They have forgotten themselves
in lust and gold. Everything in the world results in suffering
after all.*

Disciple: Besides, the mind has outgoing propensities.

*Mother: Kali, the Mother of the universe, is the Mother of all. It
is she alone who has begotten both good and evil. Everything
has come out of her womb. There are different kinds of perfect
souls—perfect from their very birth, perfect through spiritual
disciplines, perfect through the grace of the teacher, and made
perfect all of a sudden.*

Disciple: What is the meaning of "made perfect all of a sudden"?

*Mother: It is like suddenly becoming wealthy by inheriting the
riches of another.*

Just then, Nalini, the Mother's niece, entered the room after a bath in
the Ganges. Finding the water closet a little dirty, she had washed it
with a few pots of water and hence had taken a bath in the Ganges for
purification. The disciple and the Mother opined that she need have
bathed under the tap alone.

Nalini: How is that enough? A water closet?

*Mother: I too had to purify myself for coming into contact with
filth on several occasions. But I only chanted the name of
Govinda[16] a few times and felt pure. The mind is everything.
It is in the mind alone that one feels pure and impure. A
man, first of all, must make his own mind guilty and then
alone he can see another man's guilt. Does anything ever
happen to another if you enumerate his faults? It only injures
you. This has been my attitude. Hence I cannot see anybody's faults. If someone does a trifle for me, I try to remember the person even for that. To see the faults of others—one
should never do it. I never do so. Forgiveness is tapasya
[austerity].*

Disciple: Swamiji [Swami Vivekananda] used to say, "Suppose a thief entered the house and stole something. The idea of a thief would flash in your mind. But a baby has no such idea; therefore it would not see anyone as a thief."

Mother: That's true, indeed. One who has a pure mind sees everything pure.... One could be born with a pure mind if one had performed many austerities and spiritual practices in a previous birth.

Disciple: Mother, my mind does not feel joy in doing japa or spiritual practices.

Mother (smiling): Why? Not a little even?

Disciple: Oh, I do a little rather halfheartedly. The next moment I think, "What is the use of mumbling? If God exists, then he is; let me rather try meditation."

Mother: Can you meditate?

Disciple: No, I cannot do even that. I understand everything; but I cannot practice it all and get peace. You know the road to Dakshineswar very well, but can you walk all the way?

Lalit Babu entered the room and saluted the Mother. They became engaged in conversation, the disciple joining in now and then.

Mother: The Master used to say, "The way is extremely difficult, like the sharp edge of a razor." (after a little pause) But he has kept you in his arms. He is looking after you.

Lalit: The Master will take us in his arms after death; is there anything great in that? If he would only do so while we are in this body.

Mother: He is holding you in his arms even in this body. He is above our head. Truly he is holding you.

Disciple: Does he really hold us? Are you telling the truth?

Mother (firmly): Yes. Really. Truly.

The Mother finished the morning worship and distributed prasad in shal leaves to the devotees. Then she swept the room. As she took the dirt in her hand, a pin entered her little finger. The finger bled, and the Mother suffered terribly from pain. As soon as the disciple heard about it, he ran upstairs. Someone asked him to apply hot lime. That greatly relieved the pain. The Mother said to him affectionately, "My child, you are my own. Truly you are my very own."

Benares
November 1912

The Holy Mother was on a visit to the sacred city of Benares, where the following conversation took place:

> Disciple: All the pilgrims touch the image of Visvanatha [Siva]. Therefore it is bathed in the evening. Afterwards, the priests worship the deity and give the food offering.

> Mother: The priests allow people to touch the image out of greed for money. Why should they do so? It is enough to see the image from a distance. Otherwise people of immoral character would touch the image. There are some people whose very touch creates a burning sensation in the body. It is so painful; therefore I wash my hands and feet after they touch me. Fortunately the rush of people here is less than in Calcutta.

> Disciple: One can see you here only after obtaining the permission of the senior swamis. This arrangement has been made in order to lessen the rush.

> Mother: Who cares to hold court, as it were, at different places?

Her lunatic sister-in-law tormented her even in Benares. Referring to this, she said: "Perhaps I worshiped Siva with bilva leaves having thorns. Therefore, I have this thorn in my life in the shape of this sister-in-law."

> Disciple: How is that? What's the harm in offering thorny bilva leaves to Siva unknowingly?

Mother: No, no. It is extremely difficult to worship Siva. It
harms a person even if he makes a mistake unconsciously. But
the fact is that those who are having their last birth suffer from
the effects of past karma in this one.

I do not remember having committed any sin since my very
birth. I touched the Master at the age of five. I might not have
understood him at that time, but he undoubtedly touched me.
Why should I suffer so much? By touching him, all others are
being freed from maya; why should I alone have so much
entanglement? Day and night my mind wants to soar high. I
force it down out of compassion for people. And yet I am so
tormented.

Disciple: Let them do whatever they like. Please bear with us all.
A person cannot be angry so long as he is conscious of himself.

Mother: Right you are, my child. There is no other virtue higher
than forbearance. This is a body of flesh and blood. Sometimes
I may say something in a fit of anger.

Then the Mother added, saying to herself, "He who warns in time is a
true friend. What's the use of saying 'Ah!' when the right time has
passed?"

December 11, 1912

The Holy Mother, while in Benares, used to listen to the reading of the
Kashi Khanda.[17] One evening, after the reading of the book, she was
engaged in conversation with the disciple.

Disciple: Do all that die in Benares gain liberation?

Mother: The scriptures say yes.

Disciple: What is your direct experience? The Master saw that
Siva himself whispers the holy word into the ears of the dead.

Mother: I don't know about it, my child; I have not seen any-
thing of this kind.

Disciple: I cannot believe unless I hear something from you on
this point.

Mother: I shall tell the Master, "Rashbehari does not want to
believe. Please show me something about it."

I referred to the destruction of temples in many places in India during
the Muslim rule and said, "There was so much oppression. What did
God do to prevent it?"

Mother: God has infinite patience. People worship Siva by pour-
ing water in jugs over the head of the deity day and night. Does
it affect him in the least? Or they worship him covering the
image with dry cloths. Does it trouble him at all? God's
patience knows no limit.

The following morning, the Holy Mother said to Khagen Maharaj,
"Yesterday night I lay awake on my bed when I suddenly saw the image
of Narayana of the Seth's temple of Vrindavan standing by my side.
The garland of flowers around the neck of the deity hung to the feet.
The Master stood with folded hands in front of the image. I thought,
'How could the Master come here?' I said, 'Rashbehari does not want
to believe.' The Master said, 'He must. This is all true.' He meant that
one dying in Benares gains liberation. That Narayana image said to me
two things. One was: can one ever get the knowledge of reality unless
one knows the truth about God? The other thing I do not recall."

Khagen Maharaj: Why did the Master stand with folded hands
before the image of Narayana?

Mother: That was the characteristic attitude. He was humble
before all.

I called on the Mother in the morning and asked her, referring to the
conversation of the previous day, "Please tell me if one dying in
Benares gains liberation. What have you seen?"

Mother: The scriptures say so. Besides, so many people come
here with this faith. What else can happen to one who has
taken refuge in the Lord?

Disciple: It is, of course, true that one who has taken refuge in God will be liberated. But take the case of those who have not surrendered themselves to God, who are not his devotees, or who belong to other faiths—will they also get liberation by dying at Benares?

Mother: Yes, they too. Benares is permeated with the spirit of God. All living beings of this place, even the moths and insects, are filled with divine consciousness. Any being that dies here—be it a devotee, an atheist, one belonging to another religion, or even an insect or moth—will surely be liberated.

Disciple: Are you speaking the truth?

Mother: Yes, it is true, indeed. Otherwise, how can you explain the glory of the holy place?

Nearby there were some sweets that had been offered to the Lord. A fly, buzzing about, sat on my arm. Pointing to it, I said, "Even this fly?"

Mother: Yes, even that fly. All living beings of this place are filled with the spirit of God. Bhudev wanted to take home two young pigeons that had been caught in the niche over the staircase. I said to him, "No, no, you must not take them away. They are inhabitants of Benares." The women coming from East Bengal live in the Bangalitola. Have they no love for their homes and properties, friends and relatives? But they have all settled down here in order to breathe their last in Benares. They have such wisdom. They are without attachment.

Disciple: You see, how spiritual are the people of East Bengal!

Mother: Yes, that's true. People of our district are devoid of spiritual wisdom. Take the case of the father-in-law of Radhu. His family owns a house in Benares. Still, the members of the family are frightened at the very mention of Benares. They fancy that they will not die if they cling to their native village. Death, however, moves with us as our shadow.

Disciple: Are you really speaking the truth when you say that one dying here gains liberation?

Mother (sharply): I cannot swear before you thrice. Swearing once is bad enough. Swearing three times! And that, too, in Benares!

Disciple (smiling): Please see that I do not die in Benares. In that case, where shall I be and where will you be? We shall not see each other.

Mother (smiling): How stupid! He says that he does not want to die in Benares.

Disciple: Mother, seeing is believing. One believes in a statement when it can be corroborated by direct perception.

Mother: What else shall you do if you do not believe in the words of high-souled men? Is there any other way except the one trodden by sages and seers and other holy men?

Disciple: None, indeed. What else can I do but listen to the seers who have had direct perception? That is why I have put the question to you. I shall let you go only when you will give me a direct reply.

Mother: Does it matter in the least to God whether you believe or not? Even the sage Sukadeva was to him like a big ant at the most. Infinite is he. How much can you understand of him? Our Master was a man of direct perception. He saw everything; he knew everything. His words are the words of the Vedas. What will you do if you do not believe in his words?

Disciple: The scriptures differ. Some scriptures say this and others that. Which shall we accept? That is why I am bothering you.

Mother: That's true, indeed. The almanac makes a forecast of rain. But you do not get a drop by squeezing its pages. Besides, the scriptures are filled with many useless things. One cannot observe the injunctions of the scriptures to the letter. The

Master used to say, "The bhakti hedged around by the scriptural injunctions hardly justifies the name." In this Kali Yuga, one attains to God if one simply sticks to truth. The Master used to say, "He who speaks nothing but truth is lying on the lap of God." During the Master's illness at Dakshineswar, I used to boil and condense milk for him and take to him two pounds of milk, saying that it was one. I would not tell him the correct quantity. One day he came to know about it and said, "What is this? Stick to truth. You see, I have bowel complaints on account of my taking a large quantity of milk." Surprisingly enough, that very day he suffered from disorder of the bowels. He had all powers, but it is not so with us.

Disciple: My asking you all these questions or talking in this manner is not really meant for me. I do not worry about myself. I have a different feeling about it. What I want to know is this: I address you as my mother. Are you really my mother?

Mother: Who else am I? Yes, I am your own mother.

Disciple: You may say so. But I do not clearly see this. Naturally and spontaneously I know the mother who gave birth to my body as my own mother. But can I think of you likewise?

Mother: Alas, it is true, indeed.

A few moments later, she added, "My child, he alone is our father and mother. He alone has become our father and mother."

December 1912

Disciple: What is the need of tapasya?

Mother: It is very necessary. Look at Yogin-Ma. How much does she fast even now? She practices intense austerities. Golap is an adept in japa. One day Naren's mother came to visit me.

Naren said to her, "Perhaps you had practiced austerities;
therefore you got Vivekananda as your son. Repeat them and
then you may get another." The Master practiced all kinds of
disciplines. He used to say, "I have made the mold; now you
may cast the image."

Disciple: What is the meaning of casting the image?

Bhudev: It means to meditate on the Master and mold yourself
after him.

Mother: Yes, he has understood it. To cast the image means to
meditate and contemplate on the Master, to think of the various
incidents of his life. By meditating on him, one gets all the spiritual moods. He used to say, "One who remembers me never
suffers from want of food or from other physical privations."

Maku: Did he himself say this?

Mother: Yes, these are the very words from his mouth. By remem-
bering him, one gets rid of all sufferings. Don't you see that all
his devotees are happy? Elsewhere you will not find devotees like
those of the Master. Here in Benares I see so many holy men,
but can you point out one who is like his devotees?

Disciple: There is a reason for that, Mother. About him we feel
as if the market has just come to a close. All the signs of the
market are there. People are still moving about. The devotees
and the intimate disciples of the Master are still alive. We feel
that the Master, as it were, is very near us. He has not gone
away to any great distance. We shall get the response if we but
call on him.

Mother: Yes, many people do get it.

Disciple: Krishna, Rama, and others seem to belong to a bygone
age. They are not near enough to respond to our prayer.

Mother: Yes, that is true.

Referring to the Cossipore Garden, the disciple said, "It is a sacred
place, and now a European gentleman lives there."

Mother: At the Cossipore Garden, the Master spent the last days of his life. The place is associated with so much meditation, samadhi, and the practice of austerities. It is the place where the Master entered into mahasamadhi. It is a place permeated with intense spiritual vibration. One realizes God-consciousness by meditating there. The place may be acquired if the Master commands its owner through a dream to hand it over to the Belur Math.

Then the Mother talked about the disciples of the Master, whereupon the disciple asked her, "Please tell me who these disciples of the Master are. We cannot recognize them."

Mother: What do I know? But it is true that those who were born with the Master in his previous incarnations have accompanied him this time also.

Disciple: I do not have any such desire as to see a four-handed deity and the like. I am quite satisfied with what we have.

Mother: That is also the case with me. What shall we gain by these supernatural visions? For us the Master exists. He is everything.

Jayrambati
March 1913

Dr. Lalit of Shyambazar and Probodh Babu arrived. At about four o'clock in the afternoon, they came to the Holy Mother and saluted her. The following conversation took place:

Lalit Babu: Mother, what rules and regulations should one observe regarding food?

Mother: One should not eat the food given at funeral obsequies [sraddha ceremonies]. It does harm to devotional life. Sri Ramakrishna used to forbid it. Besides, first offer to God whatever you eat. One must not eat unoffered food. As your food is, so will be your blood. From pure food you get pure blood, pure mind, and strength. Pure mind begets ecstatic love [prema bhakti].

Lalit Babu: *Mother, we are householders. What shall we do at the* sraddha *ceremony of our relatives?*

Mother: *Supervise the ceremony and give help to your relatives so that they may not be offended; but try somehow to avoid taking meals on that day. If you cannot do that, then on the day of the* sraddha *ceremony, eat what is offered to Vishnu or other gods. The devotees can partake of the food of the* sraddha *ceremony if it is offered to God.*

Lalit Babu: *Many a time there remains an excess of unused foodstuff procured for the* sraddha *ceremony. Can one cook and eat that?*

Mother: *Yes, you can. That will not injure you, my child. A householder cannot help it.*

Probodh Babu: *Mother, the Master loved renunciation, but how little we practice it.*

Mother: *Yes, you will acquire it slowly. You make some progress in this life, a little more in the next, and so on. It is the body alone that changes, the Atman [Self or soul] always remains the same. Renunciation of lust and gold. The Master used to say, "I can change Kamarpukur into gold if I so desire by asking Mathur Babu to do so, but what good will that do? It is all transitory." Regarding some devotees, the Master used to say that it was their last birth. He would remark, referring to some devotee, "You see, he has no desire whatsoever for anything. This is his last birth."*

The devotees prostrated themselves before the Mother and took their leave of her.

Speaking about the objection of certain people that some of Sri Ramakrishna's *sannyasin* disciples, being *sudras*, are not entitled to *sannyasa* according to orthodox rules, the Mother said, "The disciples of Sri Ramakrishna are *jnanis* and therefore *sannyasins*. A *jnani* can be a *sannyasin*. Take the case of Gaurdasi. A woman cannot be initiated into *sannyasa*, but is Gaurdasi a woman? She is more than a man! How many men are there like her? See what she has achieved—built a school, acquired horses, a carriage, and so forth. The Master used to say, 'If a woman embraces *sannyasa*, she is certainly not a woman; she is really a man.' He further used to say to Gaurdasi, 'I am pouring the water; you will make the clay.'"

March 28, 1913

It was morning. The disciple entered the inner apartment of the Holy Mother's house and found her cutting the kalmi green. Seeing her cutting something else along with it, he said, "What is this that you are cutting up with the kalmi green?" "This is grass," the Mother said. "This is also a kind of green. The complexion of Krishna was like this grass."

The disciple was seated for his midday meal. Radhu's mother arranged a leaf plate and a cup of water in the verandah of her house for another guest, perhaps one of her relatives. A cat drank a little water out of the cup, so Radhu's mother changed the water. The cat again drank some of the water, and again she changed it. A third time the cat drank, whereupon Radhu's mother chased it and screamed, "You rogue, you burnt-faced cat, I will kill you!" It was the hot season. The Holy Mother was there. She said, "No, no, you must not prevent a thirsty animal from drinking. Besides, the cat has already touched the water." At this Radhu's mother shouted in anger, "You don't have to become compassionate toward the cat. You have shown enough compassion toward man. Why not reserve your kindness for man?"

The Mother said in a serious voice, "He is unfortunate, indeed, who does not gain my compassion. I do not know anyone, not even an insect, for whom I do not feel compassion."

The disciple was seated for the evening meal. The Mother herself had cooked a curry, potatoes, and other vegetables. She gave some of them to the disciple and said, "Eat, and tell me how you like."

Disciple: This is a patient's diet. Who cooked it?

Mother: I myself.

Disciple: You yourself?

Mother: Yes.

Disciple: Well, it could be done better. It is not exactly to the taste of people of our part of the country.

Mother: You had better taste a little of the liquid portion.

Nalini: Oh Aunt, you never put any red chili in your curry. Can anybody relish it?

Mother (to Nalini): *Don't listen to him.* (addressing the disciple) *When you eat it, you will find it tastes good.*

Disciple: For some days past I have been asking about the curries you prepare, and I have tasted some of them; but they all taste alike.

Mother: Very well. One day I shall cook as they do in your part of the country. You must show me how to cook. I am sure you add a lot of chilies. Is it not so?

Disciple: Not so much. But a curry does not necessarily taste bad because it is not made very hot.

Mother (to Nalini): *Bring some gram tomorrow. I shall make some soup. I used to cook very well; now I am out of practice. At Kamarpukur, Lakshmi's mother and I used to cook. She could cook very well.*

May 12, 1913

Radhu was indisposed, being laid up with pain and fever. Her eccentric mother began to scold the Holy Mother, saying, "You are about to kill my daughter with medicines." As she kept on scolding she lost all control over her tongue. Varada was called in. He chased Radhu's mother out of the house. The Holy Mother, too, could bear it no longer. She spoke some sharp words to Radhu's mother and then said, addressing the disciple, "I was married to a husband who never addressed me as *tui* [denoting an inferior person].... And look at this Radhu's mother. How she abuses me day and night! I do not know what sin I committed to deserve all this. Perhaps I worshiped Siva with a thorny bilva leaf. That thorn has now become this thorn of a Radhu's mother."

Referring to Radhu's illness, the Holy Mother said, "My mind does not dwell upon Radhu even in the slightest degree. I am sick of her illness. I force my mind upon her. I pray to the Master, saying, 'O Lord, please divert my mind a little to Radhu. Otherwise who will look after her?' I have never seen such illness. Perhaps in her former birth she died of an illness for which she had not performed any penance. If a man dies of a particular illness without doing the necessary penance, he gets the same illness in his next birth;[18] but this rule does not apply to a holy man."

> Kedar's mother: *The monk dies repeating the name of God, and therefore he attains to God.*
>
> Mother: *Yes, that's true. The other day a young man died at Koalpara. Will he be reborn? No. This was his last birth.... At the time of his illness at Cossipore, the Master once remarked, "I am ill. The officers of the Kali temple may criticize me for not performing any penance." Then, addressing Ramlal, he said, "Take these ten rupees and go to Dakshineswar. Offer the money to Mother Kali, and distribute it among the brahmins and others." A sadhu is not entitled to perform any ritual; therefore the Master asked Ramlal to offer the money to his Chosen Deity and later on distribute it among the brahmins and others. In ancient times, the hermits and rishis used to live in the forest. Could they perform penances like the Chandrayana? They used to only offer fruits and roots to their*

A view of the Dakshineswar Temple Garden on the Ganges River

Chosen Ideal and later on distribute them among the needy.
That was enough for them.
Radhu's mother: My aunt died of a certain illness. Do you mean
to say she has been born again with that illness?
Mother: Do you think that your aunt has not been reborn?
Certainly she has again taken birth and inherited that illness as
well. Many a time a man born in a particular family takes
birth and dies again and again in the same family as a result of
his karma.

June 8, 1913

Surendranath Bhaumick and Dr. Durga Prasad had been staying at the house of the Holy Mother. They would depart that afternoon. In the morning, after their bath, they came to the Holy Mother and saluted her. She blessed them by placing her hand on their heads and asked them to take their seats. After the exchange of a word or two, Surendra said to the Holy Mother, "Mother, while worshiping the Master I find one difficulty. Suppose a devotee has a general belief that his Ishta Devata and the Master are one and the same. He worships the goddess through the image of the Master. Afterwards he surrenders the fruits of the *japa* to the image of the Master, uttering the words, 'O great goddess, through thy grace,' and so forth. This creates a confusion in my mind."

The Mother said with a smile, "Don't worry, my child. Our Master alone is Mahesvara and Mahesvari as well [the supreme god and supreme goddess]. He alone is the embodiment of all deities. He alone is the embodiment of all mystic syllables. One can worship through him all gods and goddesses. You can address him as Mahesvara as well as Mahesvari."

Surendra: Mother, I cannot concentrate my mind in meditation
at all.

Mother: It does not matter much. It will be enough if you look at the picture of the Master. The Master was ill at Cossipore. The young disciples used to attend him by turn. Gopal also was there. One day, instead of serving the Master, he went for meditation. He meditated for a long time. When Girish Babu heard of it, he remarked, "The one upon whom he is meditating with closed eyes is suffering on a sickbed, and fancy—he is meditating upon him!" Gopal was sent for. The Master asked him to stroke his legs. He said to him, "Do you think I am asking you to stroke my legs because they are aching? Oh, no. In your previous births you did many virtuous acts; therefore I am accepting your service." Look at the picture of Sri Ramakrishna. That will be enough.

Surendra: Mother, I do not succeed in regularly counting the beads three times a day.

Mother: If you don't, think of the Master and perform your japa whenever you can; at least you can salute him mentally, can't you?

Durga Babu: Mother, I do not quite understand what rules one should observe regarding one's food.

Mother: The Master was very particular about one thing in regard to food. He used to forbid all the devotees from eating the food of the sraddha ceremony. He used to say that it injured one's devotion. Apart from this, you may eat what you like, but remember the Master when you do so.

Durga Babu: Mother, while performing my duties in the hospital, many a time I feel thirsty. I feel compelled to drink water irrespective of place and persons. As a matter of fact, I do so. What do you say to that, Mother?

Mother: What else can you do? You do it in connection with the discharge of your duty. Remember the Master while you drink the water. As you do this while on duty, it will not injure you.

Is it ever possible for those who are called upon to perform various odd duties to observe all religious injunctions regarding food?[19]

Surendra: You see, Mother, we householders live in families with many relations. Sometimes it happens that while the food is being cooked, some members of the family partake of it; later on that food is brought to me. I hesitate to offer that food to God.

Mother: That is inevitable in the case of householders. We also have to face similar situations. For instance, there may be a sick person in the family. Part of the food may be kept aside for him. But when food is placed on the plate, remember the Master, think that he himself has given this food, and eat it. Then it will not have any injurious effect on the growth of devotion.

Surendra: Mother, how can I describe to you my mental condition? You are the inner guide. You understand everything. I have been undergoing all these sufferings for the last few years. But for your blessings, I would have perhaps been dead by this time.

Mother: Yes, my child, you do not have to tell me of the sufferings in the life of the world. There is no limit to it. In your case, it is inevitable. Look at me, my child: what sort of life I am leading by the will of the Master, how much I am suffering on account of this girl [referring to Radhu].

Surendra: Yes, Mother, your condition gives us consolation and hope. You yourself know the sufferings of the world; therefore we can expect your compassion.

Mother: Don't be afraid, my child. The Master is there. He alone will protect you both here and hereafter.

Surendra: Mother, we are living so far away. Are dreams real?

Mother: Yes, they are. Dreams regarding the Master are real, but he forbade his disciples to narrate, even to him, dreams regarding himself.

Surendra: Mother, we do not know what the Master was like.
We have not seen him. So for us you are the Master and
everything else.
Mother: Don't fear, my child. The Master will look after you.
He will watch over you here and hereafter. He will protect you
always.

After the meal, the two devotees took leave. Uncle Varada accompanied them. He was going to Calcutta. The Holy Mother walked part of the way with them and looked on until they disappeared.

Surendra was the headmaster of a school at Ballaratanganj. Some butchers of that place used to flay cows alive. One day, the rogues did so in front of the school. Surendra, the other teachers, and the students—Hindus and Muslims alike—made a strong protest. The butchers were beaten. This created some trouble. Surendra was threatened by the butchers. At this time, several students of the school were preparing to leave for Jayrambati for taking initiation. Surendra sent a letter to the Holy Mother through them. The boys also narrated the incident to her. She was extremely shocked and said, "If you do not protest against such an act, who will do so?" According to her instruction, a letter was written to Surendra, giving him assurance and encouragement. Furthermore, he was asked to see that a repetition of such a cruel action did not take place. Later on, the Holy Mother again wrote to Surendra, saying, "If God really exists, then he shall certainly redress the grievance." Some time later, a lawsuit was filed, and, as a result, butchery of that heinous kind was stopped.

July 14, 1913

The disciple and Mukunda were seated in the porch of the Holy Mother's house for their midday meal. The Mother was seated in the porch of the adjoining house. Nalini arrived, dressed in white. She had taken her bath because a crow had dropped filth on her.

Mother: I am an old woman now, but I have never heard of a crow dropping filth like that. Your mind is impure. Can the mind lose its purity without great sins? The sister of Krishna Bose had such obsessions. While bathing in the Ganges she would ask people whether the top of her head was under water. That is an obsession. As a result, the mind never feels pure. An impure mind does not easily become pure. The more you emphasize your obsession, the more obsessed you become. It is true of all things.

Disciple: I have seen Mahapurushji [Swami Shivananda] handle dogs and then go to the shrine room to worship the Master. Perhaps someone would pour a little water in his hand, and he would sprinkle a few drops over his face. At that time, Ganges water was used for everything.

Mother: It is quite different with them. How pure is their mind. It is the mind of the sadhu. They are gods, indeed, who live on the bank of the Ganges. Can anyone but gods live on the bank of the Ganges? Sins committed daily are expiated by ablution in the Ganges.

Nalini: Golap-Ma one day washed the bathroom in the Udbodhan Office and then dressed fruits for offering in the shrine after merely changing her cloth. I said to her, "What is this, Golap-Didi? Go and bathe in the Ganges." Golap-Ma said to me, "Why don't you do it if you so desire?"

Mother: How pure is Golap's mind, how high-souled she is. Therefore, she does not discriminate so much between pure and impure things. She does not at all bother about rules regarding external purity. This is her last birth. In order to acquire a mind like that, you need a different body. Pure air blows for eight miles on both the banks of the Ganges. This air is the embodiment of Narayana. The mind is rendered pure as the result of many austerities. God, who is purity itself, cannot be attained without austerities.... What else does one obtain by

the realization of God? Does one grow two horns? No. The
mind becomes pure, and through a pure mind, one attains
knowledge and spiritual awakening.

Disciple: *There are devotees who surrender themselves to God*
but do not practice austerities. Will they attain to this state?

Mother: *That they surrender themselves to God, that they live*
placing implicit trust in him, is their spiritual discipline. Alas,
my Naren said, "Let me have millions of births; what do I
fear?" It is true. Does a man of knowledge ever fear rebirth? He
does not commit any sin. It is the ignorant person who is always
seized with fear. He alone gets entangled. He becomes polluted
by sin. For millions of births he suffers from endless miseries, he
undergoes infinite pains, and at last he craves for God.

Disciple: *Yes, through experience he gets his lessons and then*
attains knowledge.

Mother: *Yes, the calf makes the sound of "Ham Hai, Ham Hai"*
[I am, I am]. He makes the same sound even after drums and
other instruments are made from his hide and entrails. At last
he goes into the hand of a carder, and then he makes the sound
"Tum Hai, Tum Hai" [it is Thou, it is Thou].[20]

September 18, 1913

In the course of a letter to a devotee, the Holy Mother wrote: "There is no happiness whatever in human birth. The world is verily filled with misery. Happiness here is only a name. He on whom the grace of the Master has fallen alone knows him to be God himself. And remember, that is the only happiness."

A *sannyasin* disciple had gone to Rishikesh, visiting the Holy Mother at Jayrambati on the way. In a few days he wrote to the Mother, saying, "Mother, once you remarked that I would get the vision of the Master in the course of time, but that has not happened as yet." Hearing the contents of the letter, the Mother said to the disciple, "Write to him: 'Sri Ramakrishna has not gone to Rishikesh for your sake or simply because you are there.' He has become a *sannyasin*. What else is he to do but call upon God? He will reveal himself to the devotee when it is his sweet will."

A woman wrote to the Mother, "Mother, I am young in years. My father-in-law and mother-in-law do not allow me to go to you. How can I go against their will? It is my desire to receive your blessing." The Mother asked the disciple to write to her, "Child, you need not come here. Call on the Lord who pervades the entire universe. He will shower his blessings upon you."

September 30, 1918

It was morning. The Holy Mother was dressing fruits for the worship. The disciple was reading to her a letter written by a devotee. He had written in such a strain that it seemed as if he were piqued with God. The Mother dictated the reply: "The Master used to say, 'Sages like Suka and Vyasa were at best big ants.' God has this infinite creation. If you do not pray to God, what does it matter to him? There are many, many people who do not even think of God. If you do not call on him, it is your misfortune. Such is the divine maya that he has thus made people forget him. He feels, 'They are quite all right. Let them be.'"

Disciple: Mother, it is not that people do not want to see God. Otherwise, why should such a question arise in their mind at all? The thing is that they feel greatly hurt that God, whom they like to feel as their very own, moves away from them. Buddha, Chaitanya, Jesus Christ, and others like them did so much for their devotees in order to ensure their welfare.

Mother: That was also the attitude of our Master. It is not possible for me always to recollect all the devotees. I say to the Master, "O Lord, please bless all, wherever they may be. I

cannot remember every one." And see, it is he who is doing
everything. Otherwise why should so many people come?
Disciple: That is true, indeed. It is rather easy for men to believe
Kali, Durga, and other deities to be God, but is it easy to
accept a man as God?
Mother: That depends upon his grace.

A day later, a devotee arrived. The disciple said to the Mother, "Mother, it is this devotee who wrote to you that letter." The Mother said, "Is it so? I see he is a good boy." Then she said to the devotee, "You see, it is the nature of water to flow downwards but the sun's rays lift it up toward the sky; likewise it is the very nature of the mind to go to lower things, to objects of enjoyment, but the grace of God can make the mind go toward higher objects."

It was about half past ten in the morning. A householder devotee arrived and saluted the Mother. "Mother," said he, "why do I not see the Master?" The Mother said, "Continue to pray without losing heart. Everything will happen in time. For how many cycles did the munis and rishis of old practice austerities to realize God, and do you believe you will attain to him in a flash? If not in this life, you will attain to him in the next. If not in the next, it will be after that. Is it so easy to realize God? But this time the Master has shown an easy path; therefore it will be possible for all to realize God."

After the devotee left her, the Mother said, "He is so deeply engrossed in worldliness. He is the father of scores of children, and still he says, 'Why do I not see the Master?' Many women used to come to the Master. They would say to him, 'Why can't we concentrate our mind upon God? Why can't we steady our mind?' and things like that. Sri Ramakrishna used to tell them, 'You still smell of the lying-in room. First get rid of that smell. Why are you so worried about God-realization now? Everything will happen in the course of time. In this life we have met. In the next we shall again meet. Then you will attain to your goal.' It is easy to see a person as long as he lives in the body.

I am now living here, so one can see me by merely coming here. How few have the good fortune to see the Master now with physical eyes. Vijaya Goswami saw the Master at Dacca. He felt his body. At that the Master said, 'That my soul goes out is not good; perhaps this body will not last for many more days.'

"Can you tell me who has seen God? He made Naren attain to God-realization. Suka, Vyasa, and Siva are like big ants at the most; they had glimpses of him. One may see a vision in a dream, but to see God in a physical form is a matter of rare good fortune.

(excitedly) "Why can't one meditate if one has a pure mind? Why should one not be able to see God? When a pure soul performs japa, he feels as if the holy name bubbles up spontaneously from within himself. He does not make an effort to repeat the name. One should practice japa and meditation at regular times, giving up idleness. While living at Dakshineswar, I used to get up at three o'clock in the morning and practice japa and meditation. One day I felt a little indisposed and left the bed rather late. The next day I still woke up late through laziness. Gradually I found that I did not feel inclined to get up early at all. Then I said to myself: Ah, at last I have fallen a victim to idleness. Thereupon I began to force myself to get up early. Gradually I got back my former habit. In such matters, one should keep up the practice with unyielding resolution.

"Austerities, worship, pilgrimage, the earning of money—one should do all these in the days of youth. You see, I visited so many places at Benares and Vrindavan on foot in my early years, but now I need a palanquin to go even a few feet. I lean upon others. In old age, the body deteriorates. It does not possess any strength. The mind loses its vigor. Is it possible to do anything at that time? It is quite right that the young sannyasins of our Math have been directing their mind to God from an early age. This is the right time for them to do so. (to the disciple) My child, austerities or worship—practice all these things right now. Will these things be possible later on? Whatever you want to achieve, achieve now; this is the right time."

Disciple: Lucky indeed are those who receive your blessings now. Those who come later cannot have this rare opportunity.

Mother: What do you mean? Do you mean to say they will not succeed? God exists always everywhere. The Master is always there. They will succeed through his grace. Are not people of other countries making spiritual progress?

Disciple: The mind feels longing when it knows that it is loved, but do you really love us?

Mother: Do I not love you? I love even those who do a little for me, and you are doing so much. Whenever I touch anything at home, I remember you. I often think of those of you who are with me, and as for those who live far away, I say to the Master, "O Lord, please look after them. I cannot always remember them."

October 1918

The Mother was seated on her bedstead. The disciple was reading to her the letters of her devotees. Krishnalal Maharaj was also there. The letters contained such statements as "The mind cannot be concentrated," etc. The Holy Mother listened to these and said in a rather animated voice, "The mind will be steadied if one repeats the name of God fifteen or twenty thousand times a day. It is truly so. O Krishnalal, I myself have experienced it. Let them practice it first; if they fail, let them complain. One should practice *japa* with some devotion, but this is not done. They will not do anything. They will only complain, saying: Why do I not succeed?"

A devotee entered the room and asked the Mother about meditation and *japa*.

Mother: Repeating the name of God a fixed number of times, by telling the rosary or by counting on fingers, is calculated to direct the mind to God. The natural tendency of the mind is to run this way and that way. Through these means, it is attracted to God. While repeating the name of God, if one sees his form and becomes absorbed in him, one's japa stops. One gets everything when one succeeds in meditation.

The mind is by nature restless. Therefore, at the outset, to make the mind steady, one may practice meditation by regulating the breathing a little. That helps to steady the mind. But one must not overdo it. That heats the brain. You may talk of the vision of God or of meditation; but remember, the mind is everything. One gets everything when the mind becomes steady.

It is quite natural that man forgets God. Therefore, whenever the need arises, God himself incarnates on earth and shows the path by himself practicing sadhana. This time, he has also shown the example of renunciation.

4

Conversations from the Diaries of Several Monastic and Lay Disciples

Spiritual Practices in General

The following are the notes of a series of conversations that a monastic disciple had with the Holy Mother on spiritual practices in general:

> Disciple: Mother, is it good to practice asanas and pranayamas [yogic postures and breathing exercises]?
>
> Mother: These practices lead to supernatural powers, which deflect a man from the spiritual path.
>
> Disciple: Is it good to be going about from one place of pilgrimage to another?
>
> Mother: If the mind feels at rest in a particular place, there is no need of pilgrimage.
>
> Disciple: I find it impossible to meditate. Please awaken my kundalini.
>
> Mother: It will awaken in course of time. Do japa and meditation. It does not rise of itself. Continuous meditation will make the mind so steady that you will not feel inclined to give it up. When the mind is not in a mood to meditate, do not force it to do so. In such conditions, get up from the seat of meditation after making prostrations. Real meditation is of a spontaneous nature.

The Holy Mother Temple in Jayrambati,
the birthplace of Holy Mother

Disciple: Mother, why is it that the mind does not become
steady? When I try to think of God, I find that the mind is
drawn toward other objects.

Mother: It is wrong if the mind is drawn toward secular objects.
By "secular objects" is meant money, family, etc. But it is nat-
ural for it to think of the work in which one is engaged. If med-
itation is not possible, do japa. Realization will come through
japa. If the meditative mood comes, well and good, but by no
means do it by force.

Disciple: Is it better to do spiritual practices staying at the Math
or Benares than in a solitary place?

Mother: If you undergo spiritual practices for some time in a
solitary place, such as Rishikesh, you will find that your mind
has become strong, and then you can live in any place or
society without being affected by it in the least. When the
plant is tender, it should be hedged round. But if it is grown
up, cows and goats can do it no harm. Spiritual practices in a
lonely place are very essential. Pray to God with tears in
your eyes whenever you want illumination or find yourself
faced with any doubt or difficulty. The Lord will remove all
your impurities, assuage your mental anguish, and give you
enlightenment.

Disciple: I am too weak to undergo spiritual practices. I have
taken shelter at your feet. Please do whatever is necessary for
my uplift.

With folded hands the Mother began praying to the Master: "May the
Master preserve your spirit of renunciation." Then she added, "He is
taking care of you. You have no room for fear. Do the Master's work,
and along with that practice spiritual disciplines, too. Work helps one
to keep off idle thoughts. If one is without any work, such thoughts
rush into one's mind."

Disciple: I have been practicing asanas for some days to keep my health in good condition. These postures help one in digesting food and in practicing continence.

Mother: Be a little careful about it. If you continue such exercises for a long time, the mind may be diverted to the body. Again, if you give it up, it may affect your health. Therefore, you should exercise your discretion.

Disciple: Mother, I only practice it for five or ten minutes for good digestion.

Mother: That's all right. I warned you, because if you practice any exercise and then give it up, it may ultimately impair your health. I bless you, my child, that you may realize God-consciousness.

Disciple: I am practicing a little pranayama, too. Shall I continue it?

Mother: Yes, you may do a little. But don't go to an excess and heat your brain and nervous system. If the mind becomes quiet of itself, then what is the need of pranayama?

Disciple: Nothing is gained, Mother, without the awakening of the kundalini.

Mother: Quite so, my child. The kundalini will gradually be awakened. You will realize everything by the repetition of God's name. Even if the mind is not quiet, still you can sit at a place and repeat the holy name a million times. Before the awakening of the kundalini, one hears the anahata sound,[1] but nothing can be achieved without the grace of the Divine Mother. In the small hours of the morning, I was thinking that perhaps I might not be able to get a vision of Siva. You know that in the temple of Benares the image of Siva is very small.[2] It is under water, covered with flowers and bilva leaves. One can scarcely see the image. No sooner had this idea flashed in my mind than I clearly saw the stone image of Siva, of very dark hue. I at once discovered that it was Visvanath himself whom we worship in the temple. A devotee was passing her hand over the top of the image. I also quickly put my hand on the image.

Disciple: Mother, the stone image does not satisfy us any longer.

Mother: Why do you say so, my child? How many hopeless sinners come to Benares and attain liberation by touching the image of Siva? And he, the great god, carries on his shoulder the iniquities of all without any murmur.

Disciple: What kind of place is suited for spiritual practices, and how should one engage oneself in them?

Mother: Benares is the place for you. Spiritual practices are meant to keep the mind steady at the feet of God, to keep it immersed in his thought. Repeat his name.

Disciple: What is the aim of life?

Mother: To realize God and to remain immersed in his contemplation. You are sannyasins. You are his own. He takes care of your spiritual welfare both here and hereafter. What then is there for you to worry about? Is it possible to contemplate on God always? Sometimes work; at other times think of God.

Disciple: Mother, please give me your blessings that I may have deep meditation and remain absorbed in the thought of God.

She blessed me by putting her hand on my head and said, "Always discriminate between the real and the unreal."

Disciple: Mother, it is easy to practice discrimination in a theoretical way, but we forget it when the time comes for its actual application. It fails us at such times. Please give me power so that I can keep myself in the right path at those critical moments.

Mother: My child, may Sri Ramakrishna protect you always. May you attain knowledge and wisdom.

Disciple: Mother, so many days have passed away, but I have realized nothing.

Mother: God has been gracious to withdraw your mind from
the noise and turmoil of the world and keep it steady at his
feet. Is it a trifle? Swami Yogananda used to say, "We may
not be able to practice meditation and prayer to our heart's
content, but we are free from the anxieties of the world."
Look at me. I am suffering a great deal on account of this
Radhu.

Disciple: It is my desire to spend some time in spiritual exercises
in the solitude of a garden.

Mother: Quite right. This is the proper time to do so. This is just
the proper age for you to undergo these disciplines. You must
practice them, but always be careful about your food. Swami
Yogananda practiced great austerity, and as a result he suffered
much and passed away early in life.

One day in the course of a conversation, a woman disciple asked the
Mother how she might look upon her. The Mother said, "You may
think of me as Radha or in any other way that appeals to your mind.
It will be enough if you think of me even as your mother."

The disciple said to the Mother, "Many devotees see visions, but
I have not seen any." The Mother said, "These are very trifling things."
This filled the disciple's mind with hope. She asked the Mother
whether she would have her spiritual unfoldment. "Surely," said the
Mother with emphasis. "You will have it in course of time."

In answer to the request of the disciple that she might be allowed
to do *puja* [ritualistic worship] to the Master, the Mother said, "You
have your household duties to attend to. You will not be able to do the
worship. Pray to the Master. He will do everything for you. He is your
own as the moon is the uncle of all children."

A devotee once asked the Mother, "Mother, what should be our mode of life?"

 Mother: Spend your life in the same way as you are doing now.
 Pray to him earnestly. Think of him always.

 Devotee: Mother, I am overtaken by fear on seeing how even
 high spiritual persons meet with a fall.

 Mother: If you are constantly in touch with objects of enjoy-
 ment, you are likely to succumb to their influence.

 Devotee: Man cannot do anything by his individual effort. God
 is doing everything through him.

 Mother: Yes, that is true. But is one conscious of this always?
 Blinded by egotism, people think themselves to be independent
 agents in regard to action. They do not depend on God. He
 protects the one who relies on him.

A monastic disciple asked the Holy Mother, "Mother, does one who has been blessed by you as guru need any spiritual discipline?"

 Mother: That is true. But the real point is this: the room may
 contain different kinds of food, but one must cook them. He
 who cooks earlier gets his meal earlier, too. Some eat in the
 morning, some others in the evening, and there are yet others
 who fast because they are too lazy to cook.

 Disciple: Mother, I do not understand what you have said.

 Mother: The more intensely a person practices spiritual disci-
 plines, the more quickly he attains God. But even if he does
 not practice any spiritual disciplines, he will attain him in the
 end—surely he will. Only, the one who spends his time idly,
 without practicing prayer and meditation, will take a long time
 to attain him. You have renounced the world to practice

spiritual disciplines. As you cannot always do them, it is neces-
sary for you to do work also, looking upon it as having been
entrusted to you by the Master. For you, too austere a life is
not advisable. You suffer from colic. Be careful about your
food. It is not a fatal disease, but it is painful.

One day, a disciple asked the Mother, "Mother, how does one attain
the knowledge of Brahman? Should one practice it step by step, or
does it happen spontaneously?" The Mother said, "The path of
Brahman is very difficult. Pray to the Master, and he will give you the
knowledge of Brahman in proper time."

At Koalpara a disciple said to the Holy Mother, "Mother, the mind is
very restless. I can steady it in no way." In reply, the Mother said, "As
wind removes the cloud, so the name of God destroys the cloud of
worldliness."

That day, when another disciple complained to her about the
weakness of his mind, the Holy Mother said, "Can anyone altogether
destroy lust? A little of it remains as long as one has the body; but it
can be subdued as a snake can be subdued by charmed dust."

Regarding faith in God, the Holy Mother once remarked, "Does one
get faith by the mere study of books? Too much reading creates

confusion. The Master used to say that one should learn from the scriptures: God alone is real, and the world illusory. Suppose I write to you a letter asking you to bring certain things for me. How long do you need the letter? As long as you do not know its contents. But when you have known the contents of the letter, do you need the letter any longer? Then you will procure those things and come to me. On the other hand, what is the good of reading the letter day and night?"

One day in the course of conversation, a disciple asked the Mother, "Is it not possible to achieve anything in the worldly life?"

In reply, the Mother said, "My child, this world is like a deep marshy place. Once a man gets entangled there, it becomes very difficult for him to come out. Even Brahma and Vishnu[3] lose their wits in the world. What to speak of men! Repeat the name of God. If you do so, he will cut away your bondage someday. Can anyone get liberation, my child, unless he himself removes the shackles? Have deep faith in God. Look upon the Master as your refuge, even as children regard their parents."

Once at Jayrambati a disciple said to the Mother, "Mother, everybody says that we must pray for something under a *kalpataru*.[4] But we are your children. What special wish should children express before the Mother? The Mother knows what is good for her children, and she always gives them what is good for them. As Sri Ramakrishna used to say, 'The Mother cooks for children different dishes according to their power of digestion.' Now, Mother, please tell me that which would be most beneficial for me."

> *Mother: How little intelligence does a man possess. He may require one thing, but he asks for another. He starts to mold an image of Siva and often ends by making that of a monkey. It is best therefore to surrender all desires at the feet of God. He will do whatever is best for us. But one may pray for devotion and detachment. These cannot be classed as desires.*

One day, the Holy Mother received many letters from her devotees. The disciple read those letters to her in the evening. After hearing the contents, the Mother said, "Do you notice how many different desires have been expressed by these children? Some write, 'We have been practicing so much of *japa*, meditation, and prayer, but we are not achieving anything.' Again, others write about their sufferings and sorrows, their poverty and worries in the world. I cannot listen to these anymore. I always pray to the Master, saying, 'O Lord, please do protect them always here and hereafter.' What else can I, their mother, pray for? But how many are there who truly want to realize God? Where is that earnestness? No doubt they profess great devotion and longing, but they feel satisfied when they get even a tiny bit of enjoyment. They say, 'Ah, how kind is God!' Some devotees write to me inquiring about Radhu. Before anything else, they ask about Radhu only to humor me. No one will even cast a look at her after I finally close my eyes."

One day, the disciple asked the Holy Mother regarding *mukti* and *bhakti* [liberation and the love of God]. The Mother said, "As regards liberation, it can be given any moment, but God does not want to give *bhakti* so easily." She uttered these words in such a way that it seemed as if the gift of liberation was in the palm of her hand. But she immediately changed the topic of conversation.

Once at Jayrambati, a calf was crying in the compound of the Holy Mother's house in the early hours of the morning. It had been separated from its dam, which was going to be milked. On hearing the cries of the calf, the Mother hurried toward it, saying, "Wait, I shall untie you now." So saying, she untied the calf. The disciple was astonished to notice the very tender look on the Mother's face at that time. He found in her the very embodiment of compassion. Ah, could we but cry to God like that calf! Certainly he would then release us from all worldly bondage.

Work and Meditation

The conversation went on until late at night. A disciple said to the Mother, "Kedarnath⁵ says to us: labor hard to fulfill your duties, and then you will achieve everything as ordained by God." The Holy Mother said in reply, "No doubt, you must do your duties. It keeps one's mind in good condition. But it is also very necessary to practice *japa*, meditation, and prayer. One must practice these disciplines at least in the morning and the evening. Such practice is like the rudder of a boat. When a person sits for prayer in the evening, he can reflect on the good and bad things he did in the course of the day. Then he should compare the mental state of that day with that of the previous day. Next, while performing *japa*, he should meditate on his Chosen Ideal. In meditation, he should first think of the face of his Chosen Deity, but he should meditate on the entire body from the feet upward. Unless you practice meditation in the morning and evening side by side with your work, how can you know whether you are doing the desirable or the undesirable thing?"

The disciple said, "Some say that one achieves nothing through work. One can succeed in spiritual life only through *japa* and meditation." The Mother said in reply, "How have they known what will give success and what will not? Does one achieve everything by practicing *japa* and meditation for a few days? Nothing whatsoever is achieved unless Mahamaya clears the path. Didn't you notice the other day that a person's brain became deranged because he forced himself to excessive prayer and meditation? If one's head becomes deranged, one's life becomes useless. The intelligence of man is very precarious. It is like the thread of a screw. If one thread is loosened, he goes crazy. Or he becomes entangled in the trap of Mahamaya and thinks himself to be very intelligent. He feels he is quite all right. But if the screw is tightened in a different direction, one follows the right path and enjoys peace and happiness. One should always recollect God and pray to him for right understanding. How many are there who can meditate and practice *japa* all the time? At first they earnestly practice these disciplines, but like N——,[6] their brains become heated in the long run by constantly sitting on their prayer rugs. They become very vain. They also suffer from mental worries by reflecting on different things. It is much better to work than to allow the mind to roam at large. For when the mind gets a free scope to wander, it creates much confusion. My Naren [Swami Vivekananda] thought of these things and wisely founded institutions where people would do disinterested work."

Again referring to N——, the Holy Mother said, "You see how he has made his mind impure by constantly sitting in one place? His fads and obsessions are constantly increasing. He always complains of mental worries. Why should there be so much worry? Can't all these experiences make him sensible?"

A disciple who lived with the Holy Mother at her bidding used to be always busy with worship in the chapel and other duties. Hearing that some monks of the Belur Math were going out to practice *tapasya*, he said to the Mother, "I don't think it is good for me to be busy with all these duties. I want to practice austerities. Please give me your permission." The Mother said, "Why so, my child? You are now doing my work. You are devoting yourself to the Master's work. Are these in any way less spiritual than austerities? Why should you then abandon these works? If at any time you feel a strong inclination to practice austerities, you may go away for a month or two."

Japa

A woman devotee once asked the Mother to teach her how to offer *puja* to the Master. The Mother said to her, "You lead a worldly life. You will not be able to do the worship. I have given you his name. Practice *japa*. Through that you will achieve everything."

A devotee asked the Holy Mother, "Is it of any use to be merely repeating his name without intense devotion?"

> Mother: *Whether you jump into water or are pushed into it, your cloth will get drenched. Is it not so? Meditate everyday, as your mind is yet immature. Constant meditation will make the mind one-pointed. Discriminate always between the real and the unreal. Whenever you find the mind drawn to any object, think of its transitoriness, and thus try to withdraw the mind back to the thought of God. A man was angling. A bridal party was going along the road with music. But the angler's eye remained fixed on the float. The mind of a spiritual aspirant should be steadfast like that.*

The Holy Mother Temple at the Belur Math,
the monastery and headquarters of the Ramakrishna Order
near Calcutta, India

A monastic disciple said to the Holy Mother, "Mother, it is my desire to select a place where I can practice spiritual disciplines, but my health is not good."

Mother: *Now for some time engage yourself in a little work, but later on, when you feel a strong inclination to practice austerities, you may give up work.*

Disciple: *I practice* japa, *but I cannot concentrate my mind.*

Mother: *Repeat the name of God whether your mind is concentrated or not. It will be good for you if you can repeat the name of God a fixed number of times everyday.*

Disciple: *Mother, shall I practice the repetition of the holy name having in mind a fixed number of repetitions?*

Mother: *If you repeat with an eye to number, your mind may be concentrated on the number alone; therefore, I would advise you to repeat the name of God without being particular about the number.*

Disciple: *Why is it that our minds are not absorbed in God when we repeat his name?*

Mother: *It will come about in due course. Even if the mind is not concentrated, do not give up the repetition of the holy word. Do your duty. While repeating the name, the mind will get fixed of itself on the ideal like a candle flame in a place protected from the wind. It is the wind alone that makes the flame flicker. In the same way, our fancies and desires make our mind restless. Again, the concentration is delayed if one does*

*not utter the holy word correctly. There was a woman who
was asked by her teacher to repeat the sacred word
Rukmininathaya. The woman could not utter such a big
word, so she would repeat "Ruku, Ruku." For that reason her
progress was stopped for a few days, but later on, through the
grace of God, she found the correct word.*

While the Mother was staying at Jagadamba Ashram, Koalpara, she
had the following conversation with a devotee:

Devotee: *Should one wash one's face ceremonially before repeating the holy name of God?*

Mother: *Yes, one should observe these rules when one happens to
be in one's own house. But while one is in the street, one may
repeat the name mentally.*

Devotee: *Should we, in the latter case, repeat only the name of
God or the sacred word we get from our teacher as well?*

Mother: *Yes, you must repeat the sacred word also. Repeating the
name of God once with the mind controlled is equivalent to a million repetitions with the mind away from God. You may repeat
the name for the whole day, but if the mind is elsewhere, that
does not produce much result. The repetition must be accompanied by concentration. Then alone one gets the grace of God.*

Devotee: *Is it sufficient if I continue the spiritual practices I am
now doing, or should I do something more?*

Mother: *Continue what you are doing now. Sri Ramakrishna
has already accepted you as his own.*

Devotee: *It is said that one realizes God by praying to him sincerely for two or three days. I have been praying for such a
long time, but why do I not get any realization?*

Mother: Everything will come in time, my child. The words of Sri Ramakrishna, which are as true as the words of Siva, can never be otherwise. Be devoted to him, and take shelter at his feet. It is enough to remember that there is someone, call him father or mother, who is always protecting you.
Devotee: I have absolute faith in your words.

Once a disciple said to the Mother, "Mother, I cannot count the *japa* while performing it with the beads. If my fingers move, my tongue remains silent. When my hands and tongue become active, the mind does not remain steady."

Mother: You will find later on that your fingers and tongue will remain inactive, but the mind will continue to think of God.

Once a devotee forgot how to count the repetitions of the mantra on his fingers. He wrote to a disciple of the Mother to ask her about it. At this the Mother said, "What does it matter? It can be done in any way. The purpose of all this is to direct the mind toward God."

Regarding meditation and *japa*, the Holy Mother said to a disciple, "It is very necessary to have a fixed time for these things. For it cannot be said when the auspicious moment will come. It arrives so suddenly. No one gets any hint of it beforehand. Therefore one should observe regularity, however busy one may be with duties."

> *Disciple: There are periods of illness, and there are also moments when one is bothered by work. Therefore it is not always possible to observe regularity of time.*
>
> *Mother: One has no control over illness; but even in the midst of the most intense activity, one should at least remember God and salute him.*
>
> *Disciple: What is the best time?*
>
> *Mother: The conjunction of day and night is the most auspicious time for calling on God. Night disappears and day arrives, or day disappears and night arrives—this is the conjunction of day and night. The mind remains pure at this time.*

Regarding weakness of mind, the Holy Mother said to the disciple, "Child, this is the law of nature. Have you not noticed the full moon and the new moon? Likewise the mind is sometimes dominated by good, and sometimes by bad, tendencies."

A certain disciple asked the Holy Mother at Jayrambati how he should practice *japa* while traveling by train or steamer. At this she said, "Repeat the mantra mentally. Gradually your fingers and tongue will stop functioning. Only the mind will work. The mind itself becomes the teacher in the end."

On a festive occasion an athlete was demonstrating various feats, one of which consisted in breaking a big stone placed on his chest. While it was being broken, the Mother was heard saying, "O Lord, save him! O Lord, save him!" After this performance the Mother asked me, "My child, do they know any mantra, or have they any other secret?"

Disciple: No, Mother. It is nothing of that kind. It is the result of continued practice. I have heard the story of a man in America carrying a calf in his arms everyday to the pasture ground. He went on with this practice everyday until it grew into a big ox. Even after it had grown up, he could carry it with as much ease as in its early days. He used to make a display of this feat before all. These are all the results of practice.

Mother: Yes, it is so. Just see the power of habit. By the law of habit man attains realization by the continuous practice of japa.

Divine Grace

A certain *sannyasin* of the Ramakrishna Order had been practicing hard austerities at the Manikarnika Ghat at Benares. When a disciple of the Mother was going to Calcutta, the monk told him, "Please ask the Mother when the grace of God will descend on me." When the disciple communicated this to the Mother, she said in a serious tone, "Please write to him that there is no such rule that the grace of God will fall on one simply because one is practicing austerities. In olden days, the rishis practiced austerities for thousands of years with their feet up and head down and a lighted fire burning under them. Even then, only some of them received the grace of God."

A disciple said to the Mother, "Mother, I have practiced austerities and *japa* so much but have not achieved anything." In reply, he Mother said, "God is not like fish or vegetables that you can buy him for a price."

One day a disciple said to the Mother with great earnestness, "Mother, I am coming to you so frequently, and I have received your grace. But why have I not achieved anything? I feel that I am as I was before." In reply she said, "My child, suppose you are asleep on a bed and someone removes you with the bed to another place. In that case, will you know immediately on waking that you have come to a new place? Not at all. Only after your drowsiness clears away completely will you know that you have come to a new place."

One day a disciple asked the Mother at Jayrambati, "Mother, how does one realize God? Worship, *japa*, meditation—do these help?"

Mother: None of these can help.

Disciple: Then how does one get the vision of God?

Mother: It is only through God's grace. But one must practice meditation and japa. *This removes the impurities of the mind. One must practice spiritual disciplines, such as worship and so forth. As one gets the fragrance of a flower by handling it, or as one gets the smell of sandalwood by rubbing it against a stone, in the same way one gets spiritual awakening by constantly thinking of God. But you can realize God right now if you become desireless.*

One day in 1901, the Holy Mother said to a monastic disciple, referring to spiritual disciplines, "Sit for meditation in the morning and the evening. Keep your head cool, and practice meditation and prayer. It is very difficult to do so. It is rather easy to dig the earth with a spade." Looking at the picture of the Master, she said, "You will achieve nothing without his grace." The disciple told her that he could not practice meditation and prayer regularly on account of his being busy with the duties of the ashrama. The Mother said in reply, "Whose works are these? They all belong to him." Continuing, the Mother said to him, "You will find later on that the mind will become your guru and give you instruction."

One day the Holy Mother said, "We have practiced so much *japa*, we have observed so many spiritual disciplines, but nothing whatsoever is of any avail. How can anyone get liberation unless Mahamaya leaves the path open? O man, take refuge in God. Take refuge in him! Then alone will Mahamaya be gracious and pave the way for liberation."

Then she narrated the following incident in the Master's life at Kamarpukur: "It was the month of Jaishtha. There came a heavy shower of rain in the evening, and the fields flooded. The Master was going to the woods, wading through water. Many catfish were found there, and people were killing them with stones. One fish moved round and round the feet of the Master. At this he said to the people, 'Please do not kill it. See how it has taken shelter at my feet. If any of you can, please put it in the tank at Haldarpukur.' Then he himself took the fish to the pond and left it there. Coming home, he narrated the incident to us and said, 'It is only if one thus takes shelter in God that one is saved.'"

A *sannyasin* disciple wrote to the Mother a letter full of despair. After hearing the contents of the letter, she said seriously and forcibly, "How is that possible? Is the name of the Master a mere trifle? Those who have come here and who think of the Master will certainly see their Chosen Ideal one day. If they are not able to do so during their lifetime, they will at least have his vision at the moment before their death."

The Life of Purity and Renunciation

A young man named Manasa came to the Holy Mother with the desire to receive initiation and the ocher robe from her. The Holy Mother gladly granted his request. That made him very happy. In the evening he was seated in the house of Uncle Kali, singing songs in glorification of the Divine Mother. The Holy Mother liked those songs very much. Radhu, Maku, Nalini, one or two of her sisters-in-law, and some other devotees were with her. One of her sisters-in-law said, "She has made this young man a sadhu." Maku then commented, "That's true. See what our aunt has done. She makes these good young men embrace the monastic life. Their parents have brought them up with great suffering to themselves. All their expectations are centered in their children. What many hopes would they have entertained about them? All these are now shattered. And what will this young man do now? Either he will go to Rishikesh and beg his food, or he will clean the dirt and filth of the sick in the hospital. Why? To marry and settle down in life is also a form of religion. Well, Aunt, if you thus make these young men sadhus, Mahamaya will be angry with you. If they want to be sadhus, let them be so of themselves. Why should you be instrumental to their embracing the monastic life?"

The Holy Mother said to her in reply, "Look here, Maku, these are all divine children. They will live in the world immaculately like unsmelled flowers. What can be nicer than that? You have seen for yourself what kind of happiness worldly life can give. What have you learned from me all these days? Why so much attraction for worldly life? Why so much animal propensity? What sort of happiness do you derive from it? Can you not even conceive in a dream a pure ideal of life? Can't you live with your husband even now as brother and sister? Why this desire to lead a piggish life? This misery of the world has been gnawing into my bones."

All present there were very much moved by the Holy Mother's appeal. Continuing, she added, "An unmarried person who leads a pure life will advance toward God with rapid strides whether he prays to him or not. The others, being tied hand and foot, find it difficult to extricate themselves from the bondage of worldliness even though they try to think of God."

One day, the mother of a monk requested the Holy Mother to ask her son to go back to worldly life. The Holy Mother replied to her, "It is a rare good fortune to be the mother of a monk. People cannot give up attachment even to a brass pot. Is it an easy thing to renounce the world? You are his mother. Why should you worry? Though he has become a sadhu, he will look after you."

Once a young disciple of the Mother received an unexpected marriage proposal from the house of a very wealthy man. He was offered a large sum of money, which could remove forever his pecuniary wants. The young man, after having passed his M.A. examination, had become the headmaster of a school. His mind was not altogether free from the desire for enjoyments. Therefore, he sounded out the Holy Mother to know her opinion about his marriage. Hearing everything, the Mother said, "My child, you are quite all right. Why do you desire to be burned in the fire of worldliness? You are doing good work. Through your help many boys are receiving an education. These students will benefit by association with you and grow into good men; that will be meritorious for you also." But the young man said, "Mother, my mind becomes restless now and then. It craves enjoyments. That frightens me." The Mother said, "Don't be afraid. I tell you that in this Kali Yuga, mental sin is no sin. Free your mind from all worries on this account. You need not be afraid." After hearing this assurance of the Holy Mother, the devotee never again thought of marriage, nor did he allow his mind to be ruffled by momentary impulses.

A woman devotee said to her, "Mother, all your children must be the same to you. But if one writes asking your opinion about his marriage, you permit him to marry; and again, if another wants to renounce the world, you give him a different type of instruction, glorifying the life of renunciation. Is it not rather your duty to lead everyone along the best path?" The Mother said to her, "Suppose a man has an intense desire for enjoyment. Do you think he will listen to me if I forbid him to enjoy that desire? Again, suppose a man, as a result of his many meritorious actions in past births, has understood all these as freaks of maya and regards God as the only real thing. Should I not help him a little? Is there any end of suffering in this life of the world?"

To a woman disciple whose son was refusing to marry, the Holy Mother said: "Ah, all boys nowadays say that they do not want to marry. But, you see, those who belong to a very high plane of existence alone can take to the monastic life and free themselves from all bondages. Again, there are some who are born to have a little taste of this worldly life. I say that one should see through worldly enjoyments, but it is quite a different thing with the disciples and companions of the Master."

Disciple: *Mother, he [the disciple's son] is your son. His future happiness or suffering rests with you. Do whatever you like with him.*

Mother: *I say let him marry and finish all enjoyments in this life; otherwise there is no knowing when he may fall a victim to some unfulfilled desire. But you may be sure of this: that so long as he remains under the Master's protection, he can never slip. You need not at all worry yourself on this account. I have given him a mantra the Master communicated to me and through which one reaches perfection. Can he ever come to grief?*

A disciple asked the Mother, "The Master said that those who would accept him as their spiritual ideal would not be born again. Again, Swamiji [Swami Vivekananda] said that no liberation is possible without being initiated into *sannyasa*. What, then, will be the way out for the householders?" The Mother said in reply, "Yes, what the Master said is true, and what Swamiji said is also equally true. The householders have no need of external renunciation. They will spontaneously get internal renunciation. But some people need external renunciation. Why should you be afraid? Surrender yourself to the Master, and always remember that he stands behind."

The Ideal of *Sannyasa*

The Mother once said to a sadhu:

"Sri Ramakrishna used to say, 'O sadhu, beware!' Sadhus should always be alert. The path of a sadhu is always slippery. While one is on slippery ground, one should walk tiptoe. Is it a joke to become a *sannyasin?* If one had so desired, one could have married and lived the life of a householder. Now that you have given up such intentions, the mind should not be allowed to think of these things. What has been once spat out is not eaten again. The ocher robe of a sadhu protects him as the collar of a dog protects it from danger. No one molests a dog with a collar, as it belongs to someone or other. All gates are open to a sadhu. He has admission everywhere. The mind naturally tends toward evil deeds. It is lethargic in doing good works. Formerly I used to get up at three in the morning and sit up for meditation. One day, I felt disinclined to do so on account of physical indisposition. That one day's irregularity resulted in the upsetting of my routine for several days. That is why I tell that perseverance and tenacity are necessary for success in all good work. While I was living in the Nahabat at Dakshineswar, I used to pray in the moonlit night, 'O Lord, there are stains even in the moon. Let there be no stain in my mind.'"

Mother: *A monk should be above attachment and jealousy.*
He must be the same under all circumstances. Sri
Ramakrishna used to say to Hriday, "You must bear with me
and I must bear with you; then everything will go on well.
Otherwise we shall have to summon the manager to make up
our differences."

Kedarnath was talking to the Mother. He said, "Mother, all your children are learned, but these beings [referring to the inmates of the Koalpara Ashrama] are your illiterate children. Sarat Maharaj has written books on the Master, and these are spreading the Master's message and teachings everywhere.[7] Your other children are giving lectures. So much is being done to spread Sri Ramakrishna's ideas." At this the Holy Mother said, "What do you mean? Our Master did not know much of reading and writing. The real thing is to have devotion to God. Through you much work will be done in this part of the country. The Master was born on earth this time to liberate all, the rich and the poor, the learned and the illiterate. The Malaya breeze is blowing here. He who will unfurl his sail and take refuge in the Master will be blessed indeed. This time all trees and plants, even those having only a little stamina—excepting perhaps the bamboo and the grass—will be transformed into sandalwood by the touch of this Malaya breeze. Why should you be worried? You are my own people. But remember this: an educated sadhu is like an elephant whose tusks are covered with gold." With these words she went into the shrine room.

Karma

A disciple once asked the Holy Mother, "If God be the father and mother of all, then why does he make us commit sin?"

> *Mother: No doubt, God alone has become all these creatures, animate and inanimate; but in the relative world, all beings act and suffer according to their past karma and innate tendencies. The sun is, no doubt, one, but his manifestation differs according to objects and places.*

> *Disciple: If everything happens according to the will of God, then why does he not annul the law of karma?*

> *Mother: Yes, if he wills, he can shorten the period of evolution. But we do not know his will. Even Sri Ramakrishna himself*

had to suffer from this law of karma. One day his elder brother, being in a state of delirium, was about to drink water, which had been forbidden, when the Master snatched the glass from his hand. That irritated his brother, who cursed him, saying, "As you did not allow me to drink water, you also will be unable to eat anything during your last days." Sri Ramakrishna said to him, "Brother, I did so for your good only, and in return you have cursed me." At that, his brother burst into tears and said, "Well, dear, I do not know why I said so. I do not know why such words should have come out of my mouth." Now you see, my child, during the Master's last illness, he also had to suffer from the result of his past karma. He could not eat anything.

A devotee asked the Mother whether *prarabdha* karma[8] could be counteracted by the repetition of the name of God.

Mother: One must experience the result of prarabdha *karma. No one can escape it. But* japa *or repetition of God's holy name minimizes its intensity. It is like the case of a man who is destined to lose his leg but instead suffers only from the prick of a thorn in his foot.*

The Master

The Mother once observed, "How devoted the Master was to truth. Alas, we can not follow his example. The Master used to say that truth alone is *tapasya* in the Iron Age [Kali Yuga]. One attains God by sticking to the truth."

Referring to the Master, the Mother once told a devotee, "Really and truly he was God himself. He assumed this human body to remove the sorrows and sufferings of others. He moved about in disguise as a king walks through his city. He disappeared the moment he became known."

The Mother lived for some time in a rented house at Bosepara in Baghbazar for the treatment of Radhu. A disciple was also there to render personal service to the Mother. One day the Mother asked her [the disciple] to give the food offering to the Master, but the disciple did not know the proper mantra and other procedures. She said to the Mother, "I do not know how to offer food to the Master." The Mother said to her, "Look here, regard the Master as your own and pray to him, saying, 'Come here, take your seat and eat your food.' Further, think that he has come, has taken his seat, and is eating his meal. Does one really need a mantra for serving one who is one's own? It is like receiving one's relatives as guests. The Master will accept your worship in whatever way you perform it." The Mother, however, taught the disciple a mantra with which to offer food to the Master.

By way of consoling a young mother who had lost her only daughter, the Holy Mother once said: "My daughter, what can I tell you? I do not know anything myself. Keep a picture of the Master before you, and know for certain that he is always with you. Open your grief-stricken heart to him. Shed tears and sincerely pray, 'O Lord, draw me toward you, and give me peace of mind.' By doing so constantly, you will gradually attain peace of mind. Have devotion for the Master, and whenever you are in distress, speak it out to him."

One evening, Sister Sudhira and a young girl disciple were seated near the Mother. The Mother said to them, "He who has really prayed to the Master, even once, has nothing to fear. By praying to him constantly, one gets ecstatic love [*prema bhakti*] through his grace. This *prema*, my child, is the innermost thing of spiritual life. The gopis of Vrindavan attained to it. They were not aware of anything in the world except Sri Krishna. A line in one of Nilakantha's songs says: 'One should cherish with great care this precious jewel of *prema*.'" The Mother sang the song.

Then she added, "Ah, how sweet are Nilakantha's songs. The Master loved them dearly. When he lived at Dakshineswar, Nilakantha used to come there now and then and sing for him. How happy we were there! How many people of different temperaments used to come to him. Dakshineswar at that time appeared to us as the abode of bliss."

A woman devotee once asked the Holy Mother, "Mother, many people regularly worship Siva. Can we also do so?" In reply the Holy Mother said, "The mantra I have given you contains everything. Through that, you can worship Durga, Kali, and all gods and goddesses. But if one likes, one can learn the worship of Siva. You don't need it. It only adds to one's worries."

The Holy Mother was asked about the procedure of offering food to the Master. She said, "There is no need of following rituals in offering food to the Master. The mantra one gets from one's guru is enough for everything."

Exhortations

A young man who was a disciple of the Holy Mother had gone to see her during her last illness. The Mother made inquiries about his mother and other relatives, and she told him that she [Holy Mother] might not live long. The young man was much dejected at this and expressed his fear that he would be helpless in life without her. At this, she exhorted him as follows:

"Always remember that Sri Ramakrishna alone is our protector. If you forget this, you will find yourself in a maze. Do you know why I asked you today about your mother and other members of the family? Some time back, I heard about the death of your father. Then I asked if your mother had any other relatives and also about her means of livelihood. I further inquired if she were dependent on you. Coming to learn that she could manage without you, I thought, 'That is good. This boy has pious intentions. Now, through the grace of Sri Ramakrishna, there will be no serious obstacle to prevent him from leading a spiritual life.' Everyone should serve his mother. It is all the more incumbent upon you, because you have all come to me with the purpose of dedicating your life to the service of others. Had your father not left any money for your mother, I would have asked you to earn money and look after her comfort. Through the grace of Sri Ramakrishna, that obstacle has been removed. Just see that the money left at her disposal is not wasted. Make some arrangement about it, and look after her as much as you can. Is it a small advantage for you? One cannot earn money in strictly honest ways. Money always taints the mind. For this reason, I ask you to settle the pecuniary affairs of your mother as soon as possible. Such is the fascination of money that if you involve yourself too much in it, you will feel attracted to it. You may think you are above money and that you will never feel any attraction for it, because you have once renounced it. You may further think that at any moment you may leave it behind. No, my child, never harbor this thought in your mind. Through a tiny little loophole, it will enter into your mind and then strangle you gradually, quite undetected. You will never know it. Especially as you belong to Calcutta, you know how money can draw people into reckless ways of living. Settle your mother's affairs as soon as possible, and run away from Calcutta. Furthermore, if you can persuade your mother to go to a holy place, you both can lead a spiritual life, forgetting your worldly relationship. Just now, your mother is stricken with grief. I think this is the best arrangement. Your mother also is now quite advanced in years. Always talk to her about God. You will really fulfill the duty of a son if you can help her to gather the means for her ultimate journey. You have grown by sucking her milk. How much suffering she underwent to raise you to manhood! Know that service to her is your highest duty. But it is quite a different matter if she stands in the way of your spiritual life. Why don't you bring her to me? I shall see what she is like. I may give her a few words of instruction if it is useful. But beware! Don't involve yourself in worldliness on the pretext of serving your mother. After all, it is only the maintenance of a widow. It means only a very trifling sum. Try to settle her affairs as quickly as possible, be it even at a loss. Sri Ramakrishna could never bear the touch of money. You are all out in the world, taking his name on your lips. Always remember his words. Money is at the root of all the disasters you see in the world. Money may lure one's mind into other temptations. Beware!"

A young householder devotee once spoke somewhat disrespectfully to a *sannyasin*. In the course of a talk with the devotee, Mother said: "The Master is very compassionate toward you. Therefore you have felt such a spontaneous attraction for him even from childhood. You must, however, remember these few things and try to carry them out in your life. Be careful about these three things: First, a house situated on the bank of a river; at any time the river may destroy that house and sweep it away in its current. Second, a snake; you must be very careful when you see one, for there is no knowing when it will come and bite you. Third, a sadhu; you don't know that one word or one thought of his may injure a householder. Whenever you see a sadhu, you should show him respect. You should not show him disrespect by retorts or slighting remarks." All through his life the disciple cherished these words of the Mother.

The Holy Mother said to a woman disciple after her initiation, "Look here, my daughter, I do not usually initiate a woman who has just lost her husband, but I have made an exception in your case, as you have a spiritual temperament. See that I do not have to repent of it. The teacher suffers from the sin committed by the disciple. Always repeat the sacred word with regularity."

Once, the disciple was going to her father-in-law's house when the Holy Mother gave her the following advice:

"Don't be familiar with anybody. Don't take much part in the social functions of the family. Say, 'O mind, always keep to yourself. Don't be inquisitive about others.' Gradually increase the period of meditation and prayer, and read the teachings of Sri Ramakrishna."

Another day the disciple was alone with the Holy Mother. The Mother said to her, "Never be intimate with any man—not even with your own father or brother—and not to speak of others, then! Let me again repeat, don't be intimate with a man, even if God comes to you in that form."

The Mother forbade the disciple to frequent the monastery and other places where the monks lived. She would say, "You may have no bad intention in your mind. You visit them with pure thoughts. But if your presence brings any impure ideas into their minds, then you will also be partly responsible for it." She forbade her to make pilgrimages without discrimination of time or company. She asked her to feed a few holy men if she had the material resources to do so. Pointing to a woman devotee who was present, she said, "Look at her. She has learned a great lesson while visiting a holy place." Quoting from a song, she said, "'Pilgrimage and excursion are causes of misery. O my mind, don't be restless about them.' You can attain more in your house if you are really earnest."

One day, some women devotees were criticizing a particular person. The Mother said to the disciple, "Do not lose your respect for her. It was she who first brought you here."

The disciple wanted to adopt a child. The Holy Mother then told her about her own difficulty by taking such a step in regard to Radhu. "Never take such a step," she said. "Always do your duty to others. But love you must give to God alone. Worldly love always brings in its wake untold misery."

The Mother was feeling better under the treatment of Syamdas Kaviraj. One afternoon, several women devotees came to see her. One of them was particularly bedecked with ornaments and nice clothes. She was a little restless. Addressing them, the Holy Mother said, "You see, the only ornament of a woman is her modesty. The flower feels itself most blessed when it is offered at the feet of the divine image. Otherwise it is better for it to wither away on the tree. It pains me very much to see a dandy making a bouquet of such flowers and putting it to his nose, saying, 'Ah, what a nice smell!' Perhaps the next moment he drops it on the floor. He may even trample it under his shoes. He does not even look at it."

Further Teachings

Once, on hearing from the Holy Mother that she would pass away soon, a devotee felt much dejected, thinking that he would be helpless after her time. To encourage him, she said, "Do you think that even if this body passes away, I can have any release unless every one of those whose responsibility I have taken on myself is out of bondage? I must constantly live with them. I have taken complete charge of everything, good or bad, regarding them. Is it a trifle to give initiation? What a tremendous responsibility have we to accept. How much anxiety have we to suffer for them. Just see, your father has died, and that at once made me feel worried about you. I thought, 'How is it that the Master is again putting him to the test?' That you may come out of this ordeal is my constant prayer. For this reason I gave you all this advice. Can you understand everything I say? If you could do so, that would lighten my worries to a great extent. Sri Ramakrishna is playing with his different children in diverse ways, but I have to bear the brunt of it. I cannot simply set aside those whom I have accepted as my own."

Speaking of the transgressions of the attendants serving great souls, the Holy Mother said, "You see, one may commit a fault while serving a great soul. It happens in this way: While he enjoys the privilege of such service, his egotism increases. He then wants to control, like a doll, the person he serves. He wants to boss the latter in everything—eating, sitting, or rising. He loses the spirit of service. But why should it be so with those who serve their superiors, forgetting their own comforts and looking upon the latter's pleasure and pain as their own? And you are talking of the downfall of the attendants! Many great souls surround themselves with riches and splendor. This attracts many to come to them as attendants. Such attendants become intoxicated with the enjoyment of their position, and so they pave the way to their own ruin. Tell me how many there are who can render service in a proper spirit."

Then the Mother explained this with a parable. She said, "You see, the reflection of the moon falls on the water of the lake. At this, the small minnows jump about in ecstatic joy, thinking that the moon reflected in the water is really one of them. But when the moon sets, they remain as before. After exhausting themselves in glee, they fall into a state of depression. They cannot understand what it is all about."

Once, a disciple wanted to take his mother to Benares on a pilgrimage, but she did not agree to it because the time was not auspicious. He spoke about it to the Holy Mother. In reply, she said, "My child, they say that pilgrimage to holy places at an improper time destroys the merit of previous pious acts. But this also is true: one should carry out all pious intentions as early as possible."

The disciple could not grasp the meaning of these statements, which apparently had a twofold significance. Seeing his confusion, she said, "In the opinion of worldly men, it is not proper to visit a holy place at an inauspicious time. It is true that one may put off such a pious intention, considering the impropriety of the time, but death does not make any distinction of time. As none knows when death may come, one should carry out pious intentions whenever the opportunity presents itself, without waiting for a particular time."

One day, a disciple said to the Mother, "Mother, no bad ideas come to my mind." With a start she stopped him and said, "Don't say that. One must not say such a thing."

Speaking to Nalini and some other girls, Holy Mother asked, "Can you tell me what one should desire of God?" "Why, Aunt," said Nalini, "one should desire for divine knowledge, devotion, and such other things that make one happy in the world." The Mother said, "In one word, one should desire of God desirelessness. For desire alone is at the root of all suffering. It is the cause of repeated births and deaths. It is the obstacle in the way of liberation."

A woman devotee told the Mother about her misunderstanding with a friend. At this, the Mother replied, "If you love any human being, you will have to suffer for it. He is blessed indeed who can love God alone. There is no suffering in loving God."

An orthodox woman disciple once said to the Holy Mother, "Mother, I was surprised to see the young widows at your place partaking of dishes prohibited to them in our part of the country. Society objects to it."

Mother: You see, the fact is these are social matters, and they vary in different parts of the country. In our part, young widows are allowed greater latitude in the matter of food and wearing of jewelry. They naturally desire these things. If they are not allowed to eat delicacies publicly, they will eat them stealthily. But in case they are first shown some leniency and gradually allowed to know that they are doing something against the social injunction, they may give it up of their own accord…. But don't let your mind be disturbed over these trivial details. That will make you forget the Master. Whatever people may say, remember the Master and do what you consider to be right.

The last time the Holy Mother was at Jayrambati, the brahmin woman cook came to her at about nine o'clock in the evening and said, "Mother, I have touched a dog. I must bathe." The Mother said, "It is now late in the evening. Don't bathe. It is enough to wash your hands and feet and change your cloth." The cook said, "Oh, that won't do!" The Mother said, "Then sprinkle some Ganges water on your body." That also did not satisfy the cook. At last the Mother said to her, "Then touch me."

The Mother once said, "You see, whenever you go from one place to another, observe the things around you, and also keep yourself well informed about what happens in the place where you live. But keep your lips shut."

One day, the Mother said to a disciple, "You see, my son, it is not a fact that you will never face dangers. Difficulties always come but they do not last forever. You will see that they pass away like water under a bridge."

One day at Jayrambati, someone used harsh words when speaking to Radhu's insane mother. At this, the Holy Mother remarked, "One should not hurt others even by one's words. One must not speak even an unpleasant truth unnecessarily. By indulging in rude words, one's nature becomes rude. One's sensitivity is lost if one has no control over one's speech. The Master used to say: One should not ask a lame person how he became lame."

One morning, while the Holy Mother was rubbing her body with oil, someone was sweeping the courtyard. After the work was all done, that person threw the broomstick aside. At this the Mother said, "What is this? You have thrown away the broomstick with such disrespect when the work is done. It takes only the same length of time to put it gently in a corner as it does to throw it aside. One should not trifle with a thing, though it may be very insignificant. If you respect a thing, the thing also respects you. Will you not again need that broomstick? Besides, it is also a part of this family. From that standpoint also, it deserves to be treated with respect. Even a broomstick should be treated with respect. One should perform even an insignificant work with respect."

One day, Mini, the pet cat of Radhu, was lying on one side of the courtyard. A woman devotee was caressing it with her foot.

Gradually she placed her foot on its head. At this the Mother said to her, "O my child, what are you doing? The head is the place of the guru. One should not touch the head with the foot. Salute the cat." The woman devotee said, "I never knew that, Mother. Today I have learned a lesson."

Notes

Chapter 1

1. Girish Chandra Ghosh was the greatest of Bengali dramatists and an ardent householder disciple of Sri Ramakrishna.
2. Also known by the premonastic name of Rashbehari, whose diary constitutes the third chapter in this book.
3. Food offered to the deity or partaken of by the guru or a holy man is called *prasad*. It is believed to be spiritually potent.
4. The expression "I am going" denotes a kind of final parting, like "farewell" or "goodbye" in English. But the parting words "Let me come again," like the German *auf Wiedersehen*, denote the possibility of meeting again. A few days before the Master's death, as Yogin-Ma was leaving for Vrindavan, Sri Ramakrishna said to her absentmindedly, "Go." After she departed, he was sorry for having used such an unlucky word. They never met again in the physical body.
5. A name of Kali.
6. Lit., that which holds together. As such, it means the inmost constitution of a thing, the law of its inner being.
7. A name of Sita, the consort of Rama.
8. The head of the Criminal Investigation Department of the Government of Bengal, who was in charge of the political prisoners and *détenus*, once visited the present writer in his internment camp. The officer saw a set of *The Gospel of Sri Ramakrishna* in the original Bengali on his desk and said: "I find that almost every *détenu* keeps these books. I learned the Bengali language to read them in the original, but I did not find a single statement against the British rule." The writer told the police officer that the patriotism of the revolutionaries was inspired by religion.

   A commission appointed by the Government of India to investigate the activities of the Indian revolutionaries remarked in the course of its report that the revolutionaries carried in one pocket the Bhagavad Gita and in the other a bomb. To the fighters for Indian freedom, India was a spiritual entity, the birthplace of the eternal truths of the Hindu religion and philosophy. During the thousand years of foreign domination, the spiritual ideals declined. To revive those ideals, the country had to be politically free. Therefore, one found a strong spiritual element in the struggle for India's political freedom.

9. This is how Indians were lured to buy British cloth.

10. Worship of Durga, an aspect of the Divine Mother.

11. Swami Saradananda once explained the meaning of the term "last birth" to the present writer. He said that Holy Mother did not say to all her disciples that after this present birth they would not be born again. If she gave this assurance to a particular disciple, the latter would of course be liberated at the hour of death. But in this very life he would practice God-consciousness intensely to get a foretaste of the bliss of which he was assured hereafter. The swami said further that the term "last birth" need not be taken literally. What she perhaps meant was that in the case of her disciples a limit had been put to the apparently endless chain of births and deaths. They might have to be born a few times more. As for worldly-minded people, there was no knowing when they would attain liberation.

12. Referring to Sri Ramakrishna.

13. It is said that the female cuckoo lays her eggs in a crow's nest, where they are hatched. The mother crow regards the young cuckoos as her own offspring and brings them up. But when the cuckoos grow up they return to their own mother.

14. The premonastic name of Swami Shivananda.

Chapter 2

1. In Bengal, women put on this mark as indicative of the married state as distinguished from maidenhood and widowhood.

2. According to the Hindu custom, the water that has been touched by a revered person cannot be used for washing the feet.

3. A nephew of the Holy Mother.

4. Girish Chandra Ghosh.

5. This is the crazy sister-in-law who figures so often in these conversations. She was the mother of Radhu.

6. Durgacharan Nag, also known by the familiar name Nag Mahashay, was an exceptional householder devotee of Sri Ramakrishna.

7. A sacred Hindu festival when the Lord Vishnu at Jagannath is taken in procession in a car.

8. The popular Hindu belief is that by seeing the image of Vishnu in the car at Puri, one realizes God.

9. The Absolute; the Supreme Reality.

10. The general custom is that initiation is given before the teacher takes his or her meal.

11. A form of worship in which the most important item is the waving of light and incense before the image.

12. The spiritual power lying dormant at the base of the spinal column.

13. A book on Sri Ramakrishna's teachings in Bengali. Its English translation is known as *The Gospel of Sri Ramakrishna*.

14. That is, undergo suffering and death incidental to the embodied state.

15. The Indian custom is that anyone taking leave should be told, "Come again." It is very inauspicious to say "Go" to anybody.

16. She passed away that very night.

17. The reference is to the story contained in the *Devimahatmya*, a great devotional text of those who worship the Divine Mother, in which a king named Suratha and a merchant named Samadhi, both exiles from home and country, worship the Divine Mother and receive her grace.

18. It is sacrilegious to offer to a man the gifts that are meant for the deity, and hence this fear that it may bring about some misfortune. Sri Ramakrishna also seems to show this feeling at first in his mood as a humble devotee, but the subsequent part of the conversation would show that worship of him is not improper if one understands his divine aspect. It is indicative of the alternating moods of a devotee and of the divinity that used to be on him.

19. Tradition has it that the birth of Sri Ramakrishna was heralded by the vision his father had at Gaya of the deity who announced that he would be born as his son. Hence the spiritual association he had with Gaya was likely to overwhelm him if he went to that place.

20. The day previous to the commencement of the Hindu festival of Durga Puja.

Chapter 3

1. There are three words in Bengali by which one can address another. *Apani* is used when a person addresses a superior entitled to respect. *Tumi* is used to address an equal and is a term of intimacy and endearment. *Tui* is used to address inferiors.

2. Hindu widows, according to traditional custom, are required to put on a white sari without any border and to give up all ornaments. The Mother at first wanted to follow this custom of Hindu widows, but Sri Ramakrishna appeared in a vision and told her not to do so, as he was not really dead.

3. The tutelary deity of Sri Ramakrishna's family at Kamarpukur.

4. The white cloth is the symbol of the householder; whereas the monks put on ocher clothes.

5. He was an outstanding holy man of the Vaishnava sect. He visited the Holy Mother in Vrindavan.

6. In this connection I [Swami Arupananda, also known as Rashbehari] am reminded of another incident. The Holy Mother was in Benares. I had left a day or two before for Gaya to perform the *sraddha* ceremony for my dead ancestors. I had said to the Holy Mother before my departure, "Mother, please give your blessings that my ancestors may attain heaven." On the very night of the day I offered food and drink in Gaya for the gratification of my departed ancestors, Bhudev, the Mother's nephew, who had accompanied her to Benares, saw the Holy Mother in a dream engaged in *japa* with a crowd of people around her saying, "Please give me salvation! Please give me salvation!" The Mother sprinkled over them the holy water kept in a jar and said, "Go away, you are saved!" Then they departed in great happiness. Then another man appeared. The Mother said to him, "I cannot continue like this any longer." He begged of her a long time and at last received her grace. The next day Bhudev narrated this dream to the Holy Mother, and she said in reply, "Rashbehari has gone to Gaya to perform the *sraddha* ceremony of his ancestors. Therefore all these people have obtained salvation." In fact, while offering oblations for my departed ancestors with great sincerity, I also offered food and drink for the salvation of all persons whose names I could not remember at that time. I prayed for the salvation of all of them.

7. It is for this reason that one does not walk over the shadow of an elder. One day, while living at Jayrambati, I [Swami Arupananda] was returning home after my bath. The Mother was also coming back from the tank. I was walking by her side, and now and then I stepped over her shadow. The Mother asked me to walk on her other side. At first I did not know that I had been walking over her shadow.

8. A devotee had once accepted from the Holy Mother the ocher robe of the monastic life. He suffered from illness for some years and had been

to several places for a change of air. Later he spent some time at his home instead of living at the monastery. One day he came to Jayrambati and returned the ocher robe to the Holy Mother. Referring to the incident, the Holy Mother said, "Alas, his mind has become impure on account of his eating the food of worldly minded people."

9. See note 13 chapter 1.

10. *Paramahamsa:* lit., great swan; one belonging to the highest order of *sannyasins. Hamsa:* a swan.

11. Girish Babu had the intense desire to be taken to the Ganges at the time of death. Therefore he made these remarks. His brother said, "Does my brother need the Ganges for the welfare of his soul?"

12. Dwaraka is a great place of pilgrimage in western India, Gujarat. It is reputed to be the place where the palace of Sri Krishna, the greatest of divine incarnations, stood. Dattatreya was a great sage of the Puranas, considered to be a divine incarnation. Shrines dedicated to him are, however, rare.

13. *Jada* means "inert," "idiotic." He is called so for the following reason: On account of his attachment to his pet deer, he had to be born as a deer. Afterwards, he again attained human birth. Though his spiritual evolution was arrested during these births, he had not lost the memory of his glorious attainments in his birth as King Bharata. So when he was again born as a man, he was endowed with divine knowledge immediately at birth; but to avoid complications from attachments as he had gotten into before, he shunned all associations by pretending to be dumb and senseless. So he was called Jada Bharata. Eventually he gave proof of his spiritual attainments.

14. A *sannyasin* devotee once asked the Holy Mother, "I have been practicing religious disciplines. I do not relax my efforts in that direction. But it appears that the impurities of the mind are not growing less." The Mother said, "You have rolled different threads on a reel—red, black, and white. While unrolling you will see them all exactly in the same way." There are two kinds of desire: one that stimulates enjoyment and the other that quickens dispassion. Though externally they appear the same, their effects are different.

15. Karma, or the result of past actions, is divided into three categories: *prarabdha, agami,* and *sanchita. Prarabdha* is that which has already begun to fructify; *agami* is that which is ready to fructify; and *sanchita* is that which is stored up or held in reserve. It is illustrated by the familiar example from archery. *Prarabdha* is like an arrow that has left

the bow; it must strike the target. *Agami* is like an arrow that is attached to the bowstring; it is ready to be released but can be withheld. And *sanchita* is like the arrows in the quiver; it is held in reserve.

16. A name of God.

17. A canto of the *Skanda Purana,* a Hindu religious scripture, relating especially to Benares.

18. The idea is that an illness is brought about by one's bad karma. In the case of the last illness, it may be that one dies before the karma is fully exhausted, and in that case, one may have to suffer for that residuary karma in the next birth, the suffering taking the shape of the same old disease. Hence one should perform penance, charity, worship, and the like as atonement for one's sinful karma during one's last illness, and thus one gets over the effects of that karma.

19. This part of the conversation is to be understood in light of the injunctions of the Hindu scriptures on the purity of the food consumed by spiritual aspirants. Insofar as the vital energies of the body are renovated by the food consumed and insofar as the vital energies condition the functioning of the mind, the food taken in has an effect on the state of one's mind. Food is contaminated or made impure not only by hygienic causes but also by its qualities and contacts. Certain foods are condemned because they are obtained by injuring other creatures or are found from experience to lead to mental excitement. The motive and character of the giver and the person preparing the food are said to make food impure. In later times, these ethical and spiritual injunctions became petrified into rigid caste rules in the matter of dining. The Holy Mother does not seem to favor these caste rules very much but accepts the validity of the original spiritual principles behind them. The *sraddha* food is condemned because the sins of the dead are supposed to contaminate it.

20. The reference is to the following parable of Sri Ramakrishna: So long as egotism is not eradicated, there is no salvation. Look at the young calf and the troubles that come upon it through egotism. As soon as it is born, it cries "Ham Hai, Ham Hai"—I am, I am. And look at the bitter experiences it has to pass through. For when it grows up, if it is an ox, it is yoked to the plough or made to drag heavily loaded carts; if a cow, it is kept tied to a post and is sometimes killed or eaten. In spite of all this suffering and even after its death, the animal does not lose its egotism, for the drums that are made out of its hide continue to give the same egotistic note "Ham." At last it learns humility when the cot-

ton carder makes bowstrings out of its entrails, for then it sings through the bowstrings "Tu Hai, Tu Hai"—Thou Art, Thou Art. The "I" must go and give place to "Thou." This does not happen until one becomes spiritually awakened.

Chapter 4

1. A sound that may be heard in meditation at a certain stage of spiritual unfoldment; the *anahata* sound is also applied to Om.
2. This conversation took place at Benares.
3. The creator god and preserver god, two persons of the Hindu Trinity.
4. The mythological wish-fulfilling tree.
5. Kedarnath Datta, later known as Swami Keshavananda.
6. Name not given.
7. *Sri Sri Ramakrishna Lilaprasanga* by Swami Saradananda. Its English translation is known as *Sri Ramakrishna, The Great Master.*
8. See note 15 in chapter 3.

Glossary

anahata A sound that may be heard in meditation at a certain stage of spiritual unfoldment; the word is also applied to Om.

Arupananda, Swami A *sannyasin* disciple of Holy Mother, also known by the premonastic name of Rashbehari, whose diary constitutes the third chapter of this book.

asana Yogic posture for meditation.

ashrama Hermitage.

Atman Self or soul. It also denotes the Supreme Soul, which, according to Advaita Vedanta, is one with the individual soul.

Baburam See Premananda.

bel A tree whose leaves are sacred to Siva.

Belur Math The head monastery of the Ramakrishna Order near Calcutta.

Benares The holiest of all places of pilgrimage for Hindus noted for the temple of Visvanath; modern-day Varanasi.

Bhagavad Gita An important Hindu scripture, part of the *Mahabharata* epic, containing the teachings of Sri Krishna.

Bhagavati A name of the Divine Mother.

bhakti Devotion; love of God.

Bhudev A nephew of the Holy Mother.

bilva Same as bel.

Bose, Balaram A householder disciple of Sri Ramakrishna.

Brahma The creator god; the first person of the Hindu Trinity, the other two being Vishnu and Siva.

brahmacharya The state of a *brahmachari*.

brahmachari(n) A celibate student undergoing mental and moral training under a preceptor in the old Hindu style; a novice in a Hindu monastery preparing for the life of a monk.

Brahman The Absolute; the Supreme Reality.

Brahmananda, Swami A *sannyasin* disciple of Sri Ramakrishna, also known by the premonastic name of Rakhal.

brahmin The highest caste in Hindu society.

Chaitanya, Sri A prophet born in 1485, who lived at Navadip, Bengal, and emphasized the path of divine love for the realization of God; he is also known as Gauranga.

Chandra Devi Sri Ramakrishna's mother.

Cossipore A suburb of Calcutta where Sri Ramakrishna stayed for treatment and passed away.

Dakshineswar The suburb of Calcutta wherein is situated the Kali temple of Rani Rasmani, in which Sri Ramakrishna stayed for the greater part of his life.

Durga A name of the Divine Mother.

Durgacharan Nag An exceptional householder disciple of Sri Ramakrishna.

Durga Puja The great autumnal worship of the Divine Mother.

fakir A Muslim ascetic.

Ganges An important river of North India, having its source in the Himalayas. The Hindus consider it very sacred and look upon it as a goddess. Sri Ramakrishna and the Holy Mother held it in great reverence, and while in Calcutta they generally stayed close to its banks.

Gauranga See Chaitanya.

Gaurdasi Same as Gauri-Ma, this being the term by which the Holy Mother addressed her.

Gauri-Ma A woman disciple of Sri Ramakrishna and a companion of the Holy Mother.

Gaya An important place of pilgrimage where Hindus from all parts of India go to perform the obsequies of their ancestors, the belief being that rites performed at Gaya release the souls of the dead from all obstructions to higher evolution.

ghat Bathing place on a lake or river.

Ghosh, Girish Chandra The greatest of Bengali dramatists and an ardent householder disciple of Sri Ramakrishna.

Golap-Ma A woman disciple of Sri Ramakrishna and a companion of the Holy Mother.

Gopala The baby Krishna.

gopis The milkmaids of Vrindavan, companions and devotees of Sri Krishna.

hamsa Swan; a symbol of the spiritual nature.

Ishta, Ishtam, Ishta Devata The form or an aspect of the deity one specially selects for devotional purposes; Chosen Ideal.

Isvarakoti A soul perfect at the very birth and born only for the good of humanity, unlike others who are born to work out their own salvation.

Jagaddhatri Puja A special worship of the Divine Mother in one of her aspects known as Jagaddhatri.

Jagannath Literally, Lord of the universe, but the word is especially used to denote the deity of the great temple at Puri.

japa Silent repetition of a divine name or mystic syllable, keeping count either with a rosary or the fingers. This kind of repetition occupies an important place in the Hindu system of spiritual practice.

Jayrambati The Holy Mother's native village.

jnana Knowledge of God arrived at through reasoning and discrimination; also denotes the process of reasoning by which the ultimate Truth is attained. The word is generally used to denote knowledge by which one is aware of one's identity with Brahman.

jnani One who follows the path of knowledge, consisting of discrimination, to realize God; generally used to denote a nondualist.

Jogin See Yogananda.

Kali The Mother of the universe.

Kali The premonastic name of Swami Abhedananda, a *sannyasin* disciple of Sri Ramakrishna.

Kali Yuga The last of the four long ages of Hindu mythology, namely, Krita, Treta, Dvapara, and Kali. Their order of succession is according to the degree of degeneration of spirituality and righteousness in them. The present age is Kali, the most degenerate, and owing to the general lowering of standards in it, even a little spiritual practice is supposed to lead to great results.

kalpataru The celestial tree of Hindu mythology, which gives all that one happens to desire while under the tree.

karma Actions in general, especially applied to the accumulated results of the actions of previous births.

Kathamrita A book on Sri Ramakrishna's teachings in Bengali by Mahendranath Gupta, or "M." Its English translation is known as *The Gospel of Sri Ramakrishna*.

khichuri A preparation of rice, pulses, vegetables, and spices all boiled together.

Krishna, Sri A divine incarnation, described in the *Mahabharata* and *Bhagavatam*.

kundalini The spiritual power of a person, lying dormant at the base of the spinal column.

Lakshmi A niece of Sri Ramakrishna, also know as Lakshmi-Didi

Lakshmi A name of the Divine Mother in her aspect as the consort or female counterpart of Vishnu or Narayana.

Lalit Babu A householder disciple of the Holy Mother.

luchi Flour flattened into disks and fried in clarified butter.

M. Mahendranath Gupta, the author of *The Gospel of Sri Ramakrishna* and a prominent householder disciple of Sri Ramakrishna.

Mahabharata A celebrated Hindu epic.

Mahamaya One of the names of the Divine Mother.

Mahapurushji A familiar name of Swami Shivananda.

mahasamadhi The great *samadhi*.

Maku A niece of the Holy Mother.

mantra A divine name or mystic syllable used for continuous repetition by spiritual aspirants; also sacred texts chanted at the time of rites and worship.

Master, The An honorific name for Sri Ramakrishna.

Math See Belur Math.

maya Ignorance obscuring the vision of God; the cosmic illusion on account of which the one appears as many, the Absolute as the relative; it is also used to denote attachment.

mukti Liberation from the bondage of the world, which is the goal of spiritual practice.

muni A holy man given to solitude and contemplation.

Nag Mahashay A familiar name of Durgacharan Nag.

Nahabat The small building to the north of Dakshineswar Kali temple, where the temple orchestra used to play at stated hours. The Holy Mother was accommodated in this building while living at Dakshineswar.

Nalini A niece of the Holy Mother.

Narayana A name of Vishnu.

Naren, Narendra The premonastic name of Swami Vivekananda.

Niranjan The premonastic name of Swami Niranjanananda, a *sannyasin* disciple of Sri Ramakrishna.

Nivedita, Sister The monastic name of Miss Margaret Noble, an English disciple of Swami Vivekananda.

Panchavati A grove of five sacred trees planted by Sri Ramakrishna in the temple garden at Dakshineswar for his practice of spiritual discipline.

paramahamsa Literally, great swan; one belonging to the highest order of *sannyasins*.

Prakriti Primordial Nature, which, in association with Purusha, creates the universe.

pranayama Control of breath; one of the disciplines of yoga.

prasad Food or anything else that has been offered to the deity. Devotees consider it sanctifying to partake of it.

prema Ecstatic love, divine love of the most intense kind.

Premananda, Swami A *sannyasin* disciple of Sri Ramakrishna, also known by the premonastic name of Baburam.

puja Ritualistic worship.

Puri A famous place of pilgrimage for the Hindus, where the temple of Jagannath is situated.

Purusha The eternal Conscious Principle; the universe evolves from the union of Prakriti and Purusha. The word also denotes the soul and the Absolute.

Radha The great woman contemporary and devotee of Sri Krishna.

Radhu A niece of the Holy Mother. Her full name was Radharani, but she used to be called either Radhu or Radhi. The posthumous daughter of the Holy Mother's fourth brother, she was her ward in a special sense.

Radhu's mother See Surabala.

Rakhal See Brahmananda.

Rama, Sri The hero of the *Ramayana*, regarded as a divine incarnation.

Ramakrishna, Sri A great saint of Bengal, regarded as a divine incarnation, whose life inspired the modern renaissance of Vedanta.

Rashbehari See Arupananda.

rishi A seer of Truth; the name is also applied to the pure souls to whom were revealed the words of the Vedas.

rudraksha Beads made from *rudraksha* seeds used in making rosaries.

sadhana Spiritual discipline.

sadhu Holy man; a term generally used with reference to a monk.

samadhi Ecstasy, trance, communion with God.

sannyasa Monastic life.

sannyasin A monk.

Sarada The given name of the Holy Mother.

Saradananda, Swami A *sannyasin* disciple of Sri Ramakrishna, also known by his premonastic name of Sarat.

Sarat See Saradananda.

Shakti Power, generally the Creative Power of Brahman; a name of the Divine Mother.

Shivananda, Swami A *sannyasin* disciple of Sri Ramakrishna, also known by his premonastic name of Tarak.

Sita The wife of Rama.

Siva The destroyer god; the third person of the Hindu Trinity, the other two being Brahma and Vishnu.

sraddha A religious ceremony in which food and drink are offered to deceased relatives.

Subodhananda, Swami A *sannyasin* disciple of Sri Ramakrishna, also known by his premonastic name of Subodh.

sudra The fourth caste of Hindu society.

Surabala An insane sister-in-law of the Holy Mother, referred to also as Pagli, mad woman, crazy sister-in-law, etc. She was the wife of Holy Mother's youngest brother, Abhay Charan, and the mother of Radhu.

tapasya Austerity.

Tarak See Shivananda.

Udbodhan Office The Holy Mother's Calcutta residence.

Upanishads Scriptures that contain the inner or mystic teachings of the Vedas, dealing with the ultimate truth and its realization.

Vedanta One of the six systems of orthodox Hindu philosophy.

Vedas, The most sacred scriptures of the Hindus.

Vishnu The preserver god; the second person of the Hindu

Trinity, the other two being Brahma and Siva; the personal God of the Vaishnavas.

Visvanath God of the universe, especially denoting the deity of Siva at Benares.

Vivekananda, Swami The foremost of Sri Ramakrishna's *sannyasin* disciples, known also by the premonastic name of Narendra, or by the still shorter term, Naren.

Vrindavan A place of pilgrimage, considered the holiest by the Vaishnava devotees of Radha and Krishna.

Yogananda, Swami A *sannyasin* disciple of Sri Ramakrishna, also known by his premonastic name of Jogin or Yogen.

Yogin-Ma A woman disciple of Sri Ramakrishna and a lifelong companion of the Holy Mother.

Yogin See Yogin-Ma.

Credits

Grateful acknowledgment is given for permission to use material from the following sources:

"The Embodiment of Divine Grace" by Swami Adiswarananda, from *Prabuddha Bharata*, 2004, used by permission of the publisher, Advaita Ashrama, Calcutta, West Bengal, India.

From *Holy Mother, Being the Life of Sri Sarada Devi, Wife of Sri Ramakrishna and Helpmate in His Mission* by Swami Nikhilananda, © 1962, used by permission of the publisher, Ramakrishna-Vivekananda Center of New York, New York, New York.

From *Sri Sarada Devi, The Holy Mother, Book 2: Her Conversations* translated by Swami Nikhilananda, 1980, used by permission of the publisher, Sri Ramakrishna Math, Madras, India.

About the Translator

Swami Nikhilananda (1895–1973), a direct disciple of Holy Mother Sri Sarada Devi, was a distinguished monk of the Ramakrishna Order of India and a major figure in introducing the teachings of Yoga and Vedanta to America and the West. A gifted writer, he is noted for his beautiful and scholarly translations of the spiritual literature of India. Among his books is his translation into English from the original Bengali of *The Gospel of Sri Ramakrishna*, a work that has made the immortal words of this great prophet of the nineteenth century available to countless readers throughout the world. He founded the Ramakrishna-Vivekananda Center of New York in 1933 and was its spiritual leader until his passing away in 1973.

About the Editor

Swami Adiswarananda, a senior monk of the Ramakrishna Order of India, is the Minister and Spiritual Leader of the Ramakrishna-Vivekananda Center of New York. Born in 1925 in West Bengal, India, Swami received his undergraduate and Master's degrees from the University of Calcutta. He joined the monastic order of Sri Ramakrishna in 1954 and was ordained a monk in 1963. Before being sent by the Ramakrishna Order to its New York center in 1968, he taught religious subjects in one of the premier colleges of the Order and was later editor of *Prabuddha Bharata: Awakened India*, the English-language monthly journal on religion and philosophy published by the Order. Swami is a frequent lecturer at colleges, universities, and other religious, educational, and cultural institutions, and his writings appear regularly in many scholarly journals on religion and philosophy. He is also the author of *The Vedanta Way to Peace and Happiness* and *Meditation and Its Practices: A Definitive Guide to Techniques and Traditions of Meditation in Yoga and Vedanta* (both SkyLight Paths).

Other Interesting Books—Spirituality

Lighting the Lamp of Wisdom: *A Week Inside a Yoga Ashram*
by *John Ittner;* Foreword by *Dr. David Frawley*

This insider's guide to Hindu spiritual life takes you into a typical week of retreat inside a yoga ashram to demystify the experience and show you what to expect from your own visit. Includes a discussion of worship services, meditation and yoga classes, chanting and music, work practice, and more.

6 x 9, 192 pp, b/w photographs, Quality PB, ISBN 1-893361-52-7 **$15.95**;
HC, ISBN 1-893361-37-3 **$24.95**

Waking Up: *A Week Inside a Zen Monastery*
by *Jack Maguire;* Foreword by *John Daido Loori, Roshi*

An essential guide to what it's like to spend a week inside a Zen Buddhist monastery.
6 x 9, 224 pp, b/w photographs, Quality PB, ISBN 1-893361-55-1 **$16.95**;
HC, ISBN 1-893361-13-6 **$21.95**

Making a Heart for God: *A Week Inside a Catholic Monastery*
by *Dianne Aprile;* Foreword by *Brother Patrick Hart,* OCSO

This essential guide to experiencing life in a Catholic monastery takes you to the Abbey of Gethsemani—the Trappist monastery in Kentucky that was home to author Thomas Merton—to explore the details. "More balanced and informative than the popular *The Cloister Walk* by Kathleen Norris." —*Choice: Current Reviews for Academic Libraries*

6 x 9, 224 pp, b/w photographs, Quality PB, ISBN 1-893361-49-7 **$16.95**;
HC, ISBN 1-893361-14-4 **$21.95**

Come and Sit: *A Week Inside Meditation Centers*
by *Marcia Z. Nelson;* Foreword by *Wayne Teasdale*

The insider's guide to meditation in a variety of different spiritual traditions. Traveling through Buddhist, Hindu, Christian, Jewish, and Sufi traditions, this essential guide takes you to different meditation centers to meet the teachers and students and learn about the practices, demystifying the meditation experience.

6 x 9, 224 pp, b/w photographs, Quality PB, ISBN 1-893361-35-7 **$16.95**

Spiritual Biography

The Life of Evelyn Underhill
An Intimate Portrait of the Groundbreaking Author of Mysticism
by *Margaret Cropper*; Foreword by *Dana Greene*

Evelyn Underhill was a passionate writer and teacher who wrote elegantly on mysticism, worship, and devotional life. This is the story of how she made her way toward spiritual maturity, from her early days of agnosticism to the years when her influence was felt throughout the world. 6 x 9, 288 pp, 5 b/w photos, Quality PB, ISBN 1-893361-70-5 **$18.95**

Zen Effects: *The Life of Alan Watts*
by *Monica Furlong*

The first and only full-length biography of one of the most charismatic spiritual leaders of the twentieth century—now back in print!

Through his widely popular books and lectures, Alan Watts (1915–1973) did more to introduce Eastern philosophy and religion to Western minds than any figure before or since. Here is the only biography of this charismatic figure, who served as Zen teacher, Anglican priest, lecturer, academic, entertainer, a leader of the San Francisco renaissance, and author of more than 30 books, including *The Way of Zen, Psychotherapy East and West* and *The Spirit of Zen.*
6 x 9, 264 pp, Quality PB, ISBN 1-893361-32-2 **$16.95**

   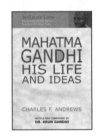

Simone Weil: *A Modern Pilgrimage*
by *Robert Coles*

The extraordinary life of the spiritual philosopher who's been called both saint and madwoman.

The French writer and philosopher Simone Weil (1906–1943) devoted her life to a search for God—while avoiding membership in organized religion. Robert Coles' intriguing study of Weil details her short, eventful life, and is an insightful portrait of the beloved and controversial thinker whose life and writings influenced many (from T. S. Eliot to Adrienne Rich to Albert Camus), and continue to inspire seekers everywhere. 6 x 9, 208 pp, Quality PB, ISBN 1-893361-34-9 **$16.95**

Mahatma Gandhi: *His Life and Ideas*
by *Charles F. Andrews*; Foreword by *Dr. Arun Gandhi*

An intimate biography of one of the greatest social and religious reformers of the modern world.

Examines from a contemporary Christian activist's point of view the religious ideas and political dynamics that influenced the birth of the peaceful resistance movement, the primary tool that Gandhi and the people of his homeland would use to gain India its freedom from British rule. An ideal introduction to the life and life's work of this great spiritual leader.
6 x 9, 336 pp, 5 b/w photos, Quality PB, ISBN 1-893361-89-6 **$18.95**

Spiritual Practice

The Sacred Art of Bowing
Preparing to Practice
by *Andi Young*

This informative and inspiring introduction to bowing—and related spiritual practices—shows you how to do it, why it's done, and what spiritual benefits it has to offer. Incorporates interviews, personal stories, illustrations of bowing in practice, advice on how you can incorporate bowing into your daily life, and how bowing can deepen spiritual understanding.
5½ x 8½, 128 pp, b/w illus., Quality PB, ISBN 1-893361-82-9 **$14.95**

Praying with Our Hands: *Twenty-One Practices of Embodied Prayer from the World's Spiritual Traditions*
by *Jon M. Sweeney*; Photographs by *Jennifer J. Wilson*;
Foreword by *Mother Tessa Bielecki*; Afterword by *Taitetsu Unno, PhD*

A spiritual guidebook for bringing prayer into our bodies.

This inspiring book of reflections and accompanying photographs shows us twenty-one simple ways of using our hands to speak to God, to enrich our devotion and ritual. All express the various approaches of the world's religious traditions to bringing the body into worship. Spiritual traditions represented include Anglican, Sufi, Zen, Roman Catholic, Yoga, Shaker, Hindu, Jewish, Pentecostal, Eastern Orthodox, and many others.
8 x 8, 96 pp, 22 duotone photographs, Quality PB, ISBN 1-893361-16-0 **$16.95**

   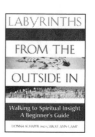

The Sacred Art of Listening
Forty Reflections for Cultivating a Spiritual Practice
by *Kay Lindahl*; Illustrations by *Amy Schnapper*

More than ever before, we need to embrace the skills and practice of listening. You will learn to: Speak clearly from your heart • Communicate with courage and compassion • Heighten your awareness for deep listening • Enhance your ability to listen to people with different belief systems. 8 x 8, 160 pp, Illus., Quality PB, ISBN 1-893361-44-6 **$16.99**

Labyrinths from the Outside In
Walking to Spiritual Insight—A Beginner's Guide
by *Donna Schaper* and *Carole Ann Camp*

The user-friendly, interfaith guide to making and using labyrinths—for meditation, prayer, and celebration.

Labyrinth walking is a spiritual exercise *anyone* can do. This accessible guide unlocks the mysteries of the labyrinth for all of us, providing ideas for using the labyrinth walk for prayer, meditation, and celebrations to mark the most important moments in life. Includes instructions for making a labyrinth of your own and finding one in your area.
6 x 9, 208 pp, b/w illus. and photographs, Quality PB, ISBN 1-893361-18-7 **$16.95**

SkyLight Illuminations Series
Andrew Harvey, series editor

Offers today's spiritual seeker an enjoyable entry into the great classic texts of the world's spiritual traditions. Each classic is presented in an accessible translation, with facing pages of guided commentary from experts, giving you the keys you need to understand the history, context, and meaning of the text. This series enables readers of all backgrounds to experience and understand classic spiritual texts directly, and to make them a part of their lives. Andrew Harvey writes the foreword to each volume, an insightful, personal introduction to each classic.

Bhagavad Gita: *Annotated & Explained*
Translation by *Shri Purohit Swami*; Annotation by *Kendra Crossen Burroughs*

"The very best Gita for first-time readers." —Ken Wilber

Millions of people turn daily to India's most beloved holy book, whose universal appeal has made it popular with non-Hindus and Hindus alike. This edition introduces you to the characters, explains references and philosophical terms, shares the interpretations of famous spiritual leaders and scholars, and more. 5½ x 8½, 192 pp, Quality PB, ISBN 1-893361-28-4 **$16.95**

  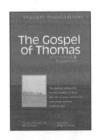 

The Way of a Pilgrim: *Annotated & Explained*
Translation and annotation by *Gleb Pokrovsky*

This classic of Russian spirituality is the delightful account of one man who sets out to learn the prayer of the heart—also known as the "Jesus prayer"—and how the practice transforms his life. 5½ x 8½, 160 pp, Illus., Quality PB, ISBN 1-893361-31-4 **$14.95**

The Gospel of Thomas: *Annotated & Explained*
Translation and annotation by *Stevan Davies*

Discovered in 1945, this collection of aphoristic sayings sheds new light on the origins of Christianity and the intriguing figure of Jesus, portraying the Kingdom of God as a present fact about the world, rather than a future promise or future threat. This edition guides you through the text with annotations that focus on the meaning of the sayings. 5½ x 8½, 192 pp, Quality PB, ISBN 1-893361-45-4 **$16.95**

Rumi and Islam: *Selections from His Stories, Poems, and Discourses— Annotated & Explained*
Translation and annotation by *Ibrahim Gamard*

Offers a new way of thinking about Rumi's poetry. Ibrahim Gamard focuses on Rumi's place within the Sufi tradition of Islam, providing you with insight into the mystical side of the religion—one that has love of God at its core and sublime wisdom teachings as its pathways. 5½ x 8½, 240 pp, Quality PB, ISBN 1-59473-002-4 **$15.99**

SkyLight Illuminations Series
Andrew Harvey, series editor

Zohar: *Annotated & Explained*
Translation and annotation by *Daniel C. Matt*

The cornerstone text of Kabbalah.

The best-selling author of *The Essential Kabbalah* brings together in one place the most important teachings of the *Zohar*, the canonical text of Jewish mystical tradition. Guides you step by step through the midrash, mystical fantasy, and Hebrew scripture that make up the *Zohar*, explaining the inner meanings in facing-page commentary. Ideal for readers without any prior knowledge of Jewish mysticism.
5½ x 8½, 176 pp, Quality PB, ISBN 1-893361-51-9 **$15.99**

Selections from the Gospel of Sri Ramakrishna
Annotated & Explained
Translation by *Swami Nikhilananda*; Annotation by *Kendra Crossen Burroughs*

The words of India's greatest example of God-consciousness and mystical ecstasy in recent history.

Introduces the fascinating world of the Indian mystic and the universal appeal of his message that has inspired millions of devotees for more than a century. Selections from the original text and insightful yet unobtrusive commentary highlight the most important and inspirational teachings. Ideal for readers without any prior knowledge of Hinduism.
5½ x 8½, 240 pp, b/w photographs, Quality PB, ISBN 1-893361-46-2 **$16.95**

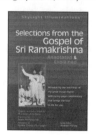

Dhammapada: *Annotated & Explained*
Translation by *Max Müller* and revised by *Jack Maguire*; Annotation by *Jack Maguire*

The classic of Buddhist spiritual practice.

The Dhammapada—words spoken by the Buddha himself over 2,500 years ago—is notoriously difficult to understand for the first-time reader. Now you can experience it with understanding even if you have no previous knowledge of Buddhism. Enlightening facing-page commentary explains all the names, terms, and references, giving you deeper insight into the text.
5½ x 8½, 160 pp, b/w photographs, Quality PB, ISBN 1-893361-42-X **$14.95**

Hasidic Tales: *Annotated & Explained*
Translation and annotation by *Rabbi Rami Shapiro*

The legendary tales of the impassioned Hasidic rabbis.

The allegorical quality of Hasidic tales can be perplexing. Here, they are presented as stories rather than parables, making them accessible and meaningful. Each demonstrates the spiritual power of unabashed joy, offers lessons for leading a holy life, and reminds us that the Divine can be found in the everyday. Annotations explain theological concepts, introduce major characters, and clarify references unfamiliar to most readers.
5½ x 8½, 240 pp, Quality PB, ISBN 1-893361-86-1 **$16.95**

Global Spiritual Perspectives

Spiritual Perspectives on America's Role as Superpower
by *the Editors at SkyLight Paths*

Are we the world's good neighbor or a global bully?

Explores broader issues surrounding the use of American power around the world, including in Iraq and the Middle East. From a spiritual perspective, what are America's responsibilities as the only remaining superpower?

Contributors:
Dr. Beatrice Bruteau • Rev. Dr. Joan Brown Campbell • Tony Campolo • Rev. Forrest Church • Lama Surya Das • Matthew Fox • Kabir Helminski • Thich Nhat Hanh • Eboo Patel • Abbot M. Basil Pennington, ocso • Dennis Prager • Rosemary Radford Ruether • Wayne Teasdale • Rev. William McD. Tully • Rabbi Arthur Waskow • John Wilson
5½ x 8½, 256 pp, Quality PB, ISBN 1-893361-81-0 **$16.95**

 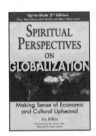 

Spiritual Perspectives on Globalization, 2nd Edition
Making Sense of Economic and Cultural Upheaval
by *Ira Rifkin*; Foreword by *Dr. David Little, Harvard Divinity School*

What is globalization? What are spiritually minded people saying and doing about it?

This lucid introduction surveys the religious landscape, explaining in clear and nonjudgmental language the beliefs that motivate spiritual leaders, activists, theologians, academics, and others involved on all sides of the issue. This edition includes a new Afterword and Discussion Guide designed for group use.
5½ x 8½, 256 pp, Quality PB, ISBN 1-59473-045-8 **$16.99**

Spiritual Innovators: *Seventy-Five Extraordinary People Who Changed the World in the Past Century*
Edited by *Ira Rifkin* and *the Editors at SkyLight Paths*; Foreword by *Robert Coles*

Black Elk, Bede Griffiths, H. H. the Dalai Lama, Abraham Joshua Heschel, Martin Luther King, Jr., Krishnamurti, C. S. Lewis, Aimee Semple McPherson, Thomas Merton, Simone Weil, and many more.

Profiles of the most important spiritual leaders of the past one hundred years. An invaluable reference of twentieth-century religion and an inspiring resource for spiritual challenge today. Authoritative list of seventy-five includes mystics and martyrs, intellectuals and charismatics from the East and West. For each, includes a brief biography, inspiring quotes, and resources for more in-depth study.
6 x 9, 304 pp, b/w photographs, Quality PB, ISBN 1-893361-50-0 **$16.95**;
HC, ISBN 1-893361-43-8 **$24.95**

Meditation/Prayer

Finding Grace at the Center: *The Beginning of Centering Prayer*
by *M. Basil Pennington, OCSO, Thomas Keating, OCSO, and Thomas E. Clarke, SJ*
The book that helped launch the Centering Prayer "movement." Explains the prayer of *The Cloud of Unknowing*, posture and relaxation, the three simple rules of centering prayer, and how to cultivate centering prayer throughout all aspects of your life.
5 x 7¼,112 pp, HC, ISBN 1-893361-69-1 **$14.95**

Prayers to an Evolutionary God
by *William Cleary*; Afterword by *Diarmuid O'Murchu*
How is it possible to pray when God is dislocated from heaven, dispersed all around us, and more of a creative force than an all-knowing father? In this unique collection of eighty prose prayers and related commentary, William Cleary considers new ways of thinking about God and the world around us. Inspired by the spiritual and scientific teachings of Diarmuid O'Murchu and Teilhard de Chardin, Cleary reveals that religion and science can be combined to create an expanding view of the universe—an evolutionary faith.
6 x 9, 208 pp, HC, ISBN 1-59473-006-7 **$21.99**

 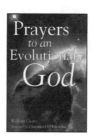  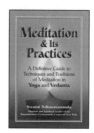

Meditation without Gurus
A Guide to the Heart of Practice
by *Clark Strand*
Short, compelling reflections show you how to make meditation a part of your daily life, without the complication of gurus, mantras, retreats, or treks to distant mountains. This enlightening book strips the practice down to its essential heart—simplicity, lightness, and peace—showing you that the most important part of practice is not whether you can get in the full lotus position, but rather your ability to become fully present in the moment.
5½ x 8½, 192 pp, Quality PB, ISBN 1-893361-93-4 **$16.95**

Meditation & Its Practices
A Definitive Guide to Techniques and Traditions of Meditation in Yoga and Vedanta
by *Swami Adiswarananda*

The complete sourcebook for exploring Hinduism's two most time-honored traditions of meditation.
Drawing on both classic and contemporary sources, this comprehensive sourcebook outlines the scientific, psychological, and spiritual elements of Yoga and Vedanta meditation.
6 x 9, 504 pp, HC, ISBN 1-893361-83-7 **$34.95**

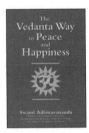